ARTIFICIAL INTELLIGENCE AND PROBLEM SOLVING

ARTIFICIAL INTELLIGENCE AND PROBLEM SOLVING

Dr. Danny Kopec
Christopher Pileggi
David Ungar
Shweta Shetty

MERCURY LEARNING AND INFORMATION
Dulles, Virginia
Boston, Massachusetts
New Delhi

Publisher: David Pallai
MERCURY LEARNING AND INFORMATION
22841 Quicksilver Drive
Dulles, VA 20166
info@merclearning.com
www.merclearning.com
1-800-232-0223

D. Kopec, C. Pileggi, D. Ungar, & S. Shetty. *Artificial Intelligence and Problem Solving.*
ISBN: 978-1-944534-58-5

Library of Congress Control Number: 2016940534

161718321 Printed in the United States of America

This book is printed on acid-free paper.

Our titles are available for adoption, license, or bulk purchase by institutions, corporations,
etc. For additional information, please contact the Customer Service Dept. at
800-232-0223(toll free).

*The companion files for this title are also available for downloading via FTP by writing to
the publisher at info@merclearning.com.* All of our titles are available in digital format at
authorcloudware.com and other digital vendors.

CONTENTS

PREFACE

We live in times that are transitional and fast-paced. Just about everyone seems to own at least one electronic device, such as iPhones, smart phones, notebooks, and so on, that they consider vital to their existence. Patience is short, and everyone wants quick results (i.e., Google) without having to do a lot of difficult research. Students come to classes unabashedly deploying these devices, and instructors don't know if they're text messaging/social networking or addressing the topic at hand. Attention spans seem to be very short. We are consistently distracted by the small things that need to, or can, be done. In the end, our lives seem to be made up of small, choppy episodes as we go about conducting our daily tasks. The notion that one sits still at a desk uninterrupted for many hours seems foreign to our society today. Persistence, trial and error, search, inquisitiveness, and simply "thinking" appear to be activities of the past. And it is clear that there will be no turning back from this technological age and our dependency on technology. Yet, over and over again, we hear that our children's test scores are declining.

One perspective on intelligence measures the ability to solve problems. Another considers how an individual or a society is able to survive under adverse conditions. So the natural question is: what will happen to our society and our children if someone "turns off the power"?

Therefore, a book about solving problems that uses nontrivial and sometimes difficult problems is especially timely, since it addresses the needs of a number of possible constituent audiences. This book assembles in one place a set of interesting and challenging Artificial Intelligence (AI)–type problems that students regularly encounter in computer science, mathematics, and AI courses. These problems are not new, and students from all backgrounds can benefit from the kind of deductive thinking that goes into solving them. Another constituent audience is the computer science, mathematics, or AI instructor who is looking for answers to these problems. This addresses not only solutions, but explores the kinds of thinking, methods, and applications used in computer science and AI techniques to solve these problems. Furthermore, a solid understanding of how amenable a solution is to humans (hence the notion of the "Human Window") adds more depth to how the problems and their solutions can and should be presented. This book is also helpful to anyone who would like to improve his or her problem-solving skills. No doubt today's young people will soon discover that they are lacking in these basic skills, and this book will be one resource they can turn to for help practicing and enhancing their problem-solving skills. Furthermore, there will be benefits from developing and maintaining life-long learning skills.

Another element of the book which is unique is the discussion of problems which essentially have proven intractable for humans, and have demonstrated that they require the use of a computer to solve. These problems are presented, analyzed along with their solutions in Chapters 13 through 16 – namely, Chapter 13 *Sudoku*, Chapter 14 *Map Coloring and the Chromatic Number*, Chapter 15 *Cryptography*, and Chapter 16 *Random Walks on Graphs and Monte Carlo Methods*. We are very pleased that Dr. James Cox, my colleague and friend at Brooklyn College was willing to completely rework a paper which is to appear in a Special Issue of "Mathematics and Computer Simulation" (2016) co-authored with our colleague Dr. Paula Whitlock and Wen-ju Cheng.

The companion files for this title are also available for downloading via FTP by writing to the publisher at info@merclearning.com. This book is available in digital format at authorcloudware.com and other digital vendors.

It must be emphasized that this book is not about solving problems quickly. Skillful problem solving—whether learning to play chess, becoming a competent violinist, or reading this book—requires *time*. So get ready to enjoy, learn, benefit, and grow!

Danny Kopec
Merrick, NY
June, 2016

LIST OF FIGURES AND TABLES

List of Figures

List of Tables

CHAPTER 1

INTRODUCTION

These days, students have an abundance of technologies available to help them solve problems —be it in school or in life. Unfortunately, most students use technology primarily for entertainment and social networking. As far as using technology for educational purposes is concerned, applications, for the most part, are limited to finding quick answers or solutions to assignments. In fact, information about almost every subject is so readily available and accessible that during the past two decades, evidence of students' efforts to solve problems that require critical thinking has become somewhat rare.

Problem solving, issue analysis, and decision making (once considered standard for college graduates) are increasingly becoming the most sought-after skills in the employment market [1]. Thus, developing these skills will be helpful not only in education but in employment and other areas of life as well. However, people are often overwhelmed by complex problems and tend to get lost in them [2]. A systematic way to teach students how to understand a problem, using the appropriate techniques according to the specific problem types, is clearly needed.

1.1 GOALS AND PURPOSE OF THIS BOOK

The goal of this book is to collect, classify, and study human and machine solutions to some classic problems that have frequently been posed in mathematics, computer science, and Artificial Intelligence (AI). Overall, we classify and view these problems as AI problems because of their particular characteristics: they are non-trivial, at least for humans; they involve logic; they may involve search and memory; solutions to these problems involve certain techniques, such as deduction, inference, solving subproblems, and pattern recognition, which are applicable and extendable to other problems; they are by and large well-known and have survived the test of time; some of these problems have been used as a testbed for AI problem-solving techniques—for example, The 15 Puzzle, Mastermind, The Knight's Tour Problem, The Red Donkey Puzzle, and Cryptarithms; and they are amenable for studying human problem-solving activity. The long-term, higher goal of our work is the development of a theory for problem solving. The problems we have chosen for investigation include the following:

1. **The Missionaries and Cannibals Problem:** In this problem, a group of three missionaries and three cannibals are to be transported safely from the East bank of a river to the West bank, using a boat that can carry only two passengers at a time. The condition is that in any state the cannibals can never outnumber the missionaries. The goal is to get everyone to the other side of the river in the fewest number of boat trips.

2. **The 12 Coins Problem:** In this problem, there are 12 coins, and we must determine the 1 coin that weighs differently from the other 11 with only three weighings, using a balance scale.

3. **Cryptarithms:** Some examples are SEND + MORE = MONEY or DONALD + GERALD = ROBERT. The goal of these problems is to find the unique numbers (from 0 to 9) representing the letters of the alphabet that satisfy the equations.

4. **The Red Donkey Puzzle:** This is a sliding block puzzle in which a 2" × 2" square block must be moved from the top of a 4" × 5" board to the bottom center. The other pieces in the puzzle include four 1" × 2" vertical blocks, four 1" × 1" square blocks, and one 2" × 1" horizontal block.

5. **The 15 Puzzle:** This is another sliding block puzzle in which 15 unit square blocks (numbered 1 to 15) must be rearranged in ascending order in a clockwise direction on a 4" × 4" grid.

6. **The Knight's Tour Problem:** This puzzle involves finding a path on a chessboard such that a chess knight visits every square on the board exactly once. A more strict variation of the problem requires the knight to return to the square of origin on its last move. It is common for the knight to start on the square in the lower left corner of the board (known as A1).

7. **Mastermind:** This is a two-player code-breaking board game where one of the players (called the code-breaker) has to decode or guess the code created by the other player (called the code-maker) in at most 10 guesses. This code is represented by a sequence of colored pegs arranged in a particular order.

8. **The Monty Hall Problem:** This problem involves guessing which door out of three has a prize (e.g., a car) behind it. The dilemma lies in whether to stick with your first choice or switch doors after the game host tells you which of the three doors does not have the prize behind it.

9. **Rubik's Cube:** This popular sliding block puzzle is a three-dimensional cube composed of small cubes with different colors on each surface. The goal is to arrange these small cubes so the cube overall has only one color on each surface.

10. **The Prisoner's Dilemma:** Here we consider a set of problems arising from classical game theory that involves an optimal scheme for how prisoners can get a minimal sentence, depending on whether they cooperate or defect in their private confessions.

11. **Miscellaneous Problems:** We have also chosen five smaller problems which are in the same genre as the ten problems presented in this book, but on a smaller scale. The five problems primarily involve developing a strong graphical abstraction and understanding of the problem, devising schema, using probability, and logic.

This book focuses on solutions to these classic problems using specific problem-solving strategies such as searches, problem reduction, deduction, and mathematical formulas. It also examines how people typically try to solve problems and presents ideas for how to analyze problems and break them down to make them more manageable and easier to solve.

1.2 BACKGROUND AND PREVIOUS WORK

Human problem solving is an important topic that has been widely studied and is the basis for both Artificial Intelligence and its "cousin" from psychology: cognitive science. From our perspective, before we develop and use machines to solve problems for us, we must first have a thorough understanding of how humans think and solve problems.

Much of the inspiration for our work comes from George Polya's book *How to Solve It*. This little book proved groundbreaking and survived the test of time in helping problem solvers to become more cognizant of their activities and how they can be more successful. (See Chapter 2 for more about Polya's work.)

Allen Newell and Herbert Simon have contributed significantly to the topic of problem solving and their research is summarized in the book *Human Problem Solving*. According to Newell, Shaw, and Simon, a problem has a set of paths, only one (or some) of which leads to a desired goal. Finding that correct path(s) is solving the problem. A problem is also defined as the difference between an existing state and a desired state [3]. Newell and Simon give several examples of problem solving, such as solving a maze or crossword puzzle, finding the combination of a safe, and translating one language into another [4]. Their research includes topics such as representation of external environment in an internal form, strategies such as the creation of subgoals and subproblems to reach a solution, working backward from a goal, and using heuristics to find the best path to a solution. They also stress the process of relying on simple abstractions of a problem space as a way to approach more complex problems.

Cerveny, Garrity, and Sanders discuss two types of problem solving. One is linear problem solving, which involves performing a sequence of steps to reach a goal, and the other is concurrent problem solving, which is iterative in nature and involves comparing the current state with an ideal state and performing the steps required to reach that ideal state [5].

Gunzelmann and Anderson state that the two important initial steps to solving a problem are understanding the problem and representing the problem in an internal form. They also stress the importance of planning in problem solving. Humans tend to increase the degree of planning if it is rewarded with faster solutions [6].

Finding the path leading to a goal is sometimes not enough. Due to constraints such as time, computing power, and other resources, solving a problem efficiently with optimum resource utilization is necessary. According to Anzai and Simon, several strategies are available for solving a problem, some more efficient than others. The efficiency of a strategy depends on various factors such as speed, load on memory, and ease of retention of information in memory, among others [7].

1.3 CONTRIBUTIONS OF THIS BOOK

1. Classification of the problems under consideration.

2. Discussion of general problem-solving techniques as applicable to the problems under consideration.

3. Application of appropriate problem-solving strategies to the selected problems as required by the respective problem domains.

4. Study of people's problem-solving behaviors in a problem-solving setting.

5. Recommendations of appropriate strategies and approaches in proper order according to problem type.

6. Exposition of Donald Michie's concept of the "Human Window" for solving AI-type problems [8].

1.4 REFERENCES

1. Ruggiero, V.R. (1998). *The Art of Thinking*. Boston, MA: Addison-Wesley.

2. Coleman, P.T. (2011). *The Five Percent: Finding Solutions to Seemingly Impossible Conflicts*. New York: Public Affairs, Perseus.

3. Newell, A., Shaw, J.C., and Simon, H.A. (1958). *The Process of Creative Thinking.* Pittsburgh, PA: Carnegie-Mellon University, The Rand Corporation.

4. Newell, A., and Simon, H.A. (1972). *Human Problem Solving.* Englewood Cliffs, NJ: Prentice-Hall.

5. Cerveny R.P., Garrity, E.J., and Sanders, G.L. (1990). "A Problem-Solving Perspective on Systems Development." *Journal of Management Information Systems* (Vol. 6, No. 4)(6) 4: 103–122. Published by: M.E. Sharpe, Inc. Stable. Available at *http://www.jstor.org/stable/40398777.* Accessed on December 23. Source: *For the Learning of Mathematics* (1) 2: 35–42. Published by: FLM Publishing Association. Stable Available at *http://www.jstor.org/stable/40247714.* Accessed on December 23, 2012.

6. Gunzelmann, G., and Anderson, J.R. (2003). Problem Solving: Increased Planning with Practice. *Cognitive Systems Research* 4(1): 57-76.

7. Anzai, Y., and Simon, H.A. (1979). The Theory of Learning by Doing. *Psychological Review*, 86 (2): 124-140.

8. Michie, D. (1982). Experiments on the Mechanization of Game-Learning: 2—Rule-Based Learning and the Human Window. *The Computer Journal* 25 (1): 105–113.

PROBLEM SOLVING AND TRADITIONAL ARTIFICIAL INTELLIGENCE PROBLEMS

2

PROBLEM SOLVING

Problem solving is an important skill that helps us in all aspects of life. Therefore, it is essential that we follow a systematic approach in solving problems. Polya's work [1] was groundbreaking because it led to the development of a five-step sequence for problem solving, which essentially can be universally applied, independent of domain.

2.1 POLYA'S FIVE STEPS FOR PROBLEM SOLVING

1. Understand the problem.

2. Develop an algorithm (plan).

3. Implement the algorithm (coding in computer science).

4. Test the algorithm (debugging).

5. Revise the algorithm (possibly returning to steps 1 to 4) .

The wonderful thing about Polya's five steps [1] is that they can be applied with only slight revision to mathematical problems, computer programming, engineering, management science, business, and more!

1. Understand the Problem

What Polya means by this is don't even bother trying to solve a problem before you have spent some time acclimating yourself to it. Learn the essence of the problem. Try to classify the problem.

What kind of problem is it? Can the problem be broken down into parts? What is a good representation for the problem? Is the problem related to other problems that you have encountered or solved?

Even as we write this section we have run into a PROB-LEM. The laptop keeps dying. Certain computers have been known to have problems with their power supply. So we wonder, what could it be? The power supply (one of the two power supplies available is not the right one for the machine)? So we try both power supplies. Nothing changes. It became fairly clear that the power supply was not the problem. Every few minutes the laptop dies, and that does not portend well for successfully completing this book by our deadline. One solution we tried was to simply stop work early and let the machine "cool off" overnight. It seemed to be better in the morning, but after about an hour of operation, it died again.

What other unique symptoms are there to the problem?

We have noted that in the past few weeks the laptop seems to feel pretty hot (on the top left, above the keyboard) where there is a fan vent.

Postmortem to the Problem: A week or so later, the computer's motherboard and fan were replaced under warranty. The machine is now working fine.

2. Develop an Algorithm

Clearly, problem solving without thinking is not very effective. For example, in chess, we say it is better to play with a plan, even a bad plan, than no plan at all. We work by the following definition for an algorithm:

"A well-defined, possibly repeating, finite series of steps to solve a problem."

Having noted the problem described in the box above, and coupled with a previous experience (also described above), and recalling that we had seen a youngster once solve a problem with his computer by simply opening it up and replacing a fan, an idea emerges:

There is a very small (5-inch fan) available that is sometimes used during hot summer days for quick local cooling. Perhaps that fan could be used to cool the laptop.

3. Implement the Algorithm

This is when you must take action. In our head we have dozens of ideas and plans all the time. Plans without implementation become something like "little bad memories" or reminders that we should keep lists, notes, and so on, and not just leave everything in our head. Still, you cannot do everything at once, and people are not machines. We need some kind of order in our lives and in our activities—some directive—and thus a PLAN that enables us to assess the effectiveness of a proposed problem solution.

The little 5-inch fan has been blowing for about 45 minutes, and the laptop is still working fine. The area on the top left is still hot, but not as hot as it was before (just using the sense of touch). Does this mean that the problem is solved?

4. Test the Algorithm

Testing is a very important step in problem solving. All of us want to be able to say, "The problem has been solved!" How much of that decision is based on desire, emotion, ego, or just the desire to move on? For people who are goal oriented, ambitious, conscientious, obsessive, or just plain determined, making the decision whether or not to accept a solution can be overwhelming. Hence we have to answer the following questions:

Does the solution work? Does it work fully? Does it work partially? Now how confident are you that you have solved the problem? How much more work is necessary to be certain that the problem has been solved? More than an hour and a half later, the fan solution seems to be working.

5. Revise the Algorithm

Based on the outcomes above, can we make a decision as to how to proceed? Do we return to Stage 1, in which we reconsider our understanding of the problem? Or do we consider alternative solutions/plans/algorithms (Stage 2)? Did we correctly implement the planned solution or algorithm?

Alongside the "fan" solution, alternate solutions have been considered, such as using another laptop or backing up all the key files in question. One may resort to these alternative plans, depending on the result of the current algorithm/testing.

A problem has provided some given data, some unknowns, some conditions, an initial state, and a goal state. The aim is to use the given data to find the unknowns while moving from the initial to the goal state. During the initial stages of problem solving, the solver's goals are to understand the problem and represent it in an internal form [2].

One of the key steps in facilitating problem **understanding** is to represent the problem in a format that clearly presents the various problem states (stages) of a proposed solution and the transitions between them. This often reduces the complexity of the problem. Some problems may best be expressed in a graphical way, like a diagram or a graphical sketch, whereas others may be better represented in a search tree format.

An important aspect of **knowledge representation** is the level of detail. A knowledge representation can be extensional or intensional. *Extensional representations* show every step, case, or example, whereas *intensional representations* are short and implicit—for example, a formula [3]. We need to choose the representation that best represents the problem and helps us understand and solve it easily.

According to Polya, an important step in understanding a problem is **isolation of the principal parts**—that is, the data, the conditions, and the unknowns in a problem. These are examined individually, in relation to one another and in relation to the whole problem [1]. Each of these approaches helps us understand the problem better.

Once we understand the problem, we go on to **planning** to solve it. It is a way to manage the complexity of the problem. It is observed that if planning leads to faster solutions, the degree of planning increases [4].

One of the ways to deal with a complex problem is to *solve a simpler version of the problem*. The solutions and methods used for the simpler problem can then be used to plan for the harder problems [5].

Solving a problem involves searching through a large number of possibilities consisting of a set of paths leading to a goal state. We may also create subgoals and solve them to reach the final goal [6]. Algorithms and heuristics are two of the basic ways to solve a problem.

Algorithms in computer science will typically be computationally intensive and involve an exhaustive search in the state space. Therefore, they will always lead to the goal state and are 100% correct [7]. The heuristic approach to problem solving is more suitable for humans with their limitations in terms of memory capacity and processing speed.

A heuristic is a rule of thumb that allows one to select one or a few of the possible paths through the state space that are more likely to lead to the goal state. Though heuristics usually lead to solutions with relatively less processing [4], this does not always guarantee a solution and sometimes may even lead us in the wrong direction [7].

2.2 PROBLEM-SOLVING TECHNIQUES

We will now examine some problem-solving techniques. Whole books can be written about many of these techniques, but our purpose here is simply to introduce and distinguish these techniques from one another in the hope that the problem solver will find them useful.

■ Induction

In mathematics, induction is often used as a soundproof technique. Unfortunately, when used in the real world, it is not necessarily sound.

Example 1: I find a black raven. I find 100 black ravens. Every raven I find is black. Therefore, the next raven I find will be black. (This is not necessarily true.)

Example 2: Every time a team gets a 3 to 0 lead in a playoff series in baseball, it wins. This has happened 39 times in history, but in 2004, the Yankees had a 3 to 0 lead against the Boston Red Sox—and they lost!

■ Deduction

Deduction involves the attempt to reach a conclusion from some facts that logically follow one another. Often it may involve general information from which we try to reach a specific conclusion [8.][°]

Example 1: The famous *modus ponens* is a common example:

All men are mortal. Socrates was a man. Therefore, Socrates was mortal.

Example 2: There was a burglary at 365 85th Street, Apt. 4B, between 4:00 and 6:00 pm. John Stealer was the only person seen

---

[°] An excellent book on deduction is Human Reasoning: The Psychology of Deduction, by. Ruth M.J. Byrne, Jonathan B.T. St. Evans, Stephen E. Newstead,. For example, they point out that in the case of modus ponens, the inference about Socrates being mortal is relatively easy, but if people are told the number is not a 5, b but they saw the odd numbered series "1, 3,..." they would likely conclude that the next number should be "5." A is an inference (know as modus tollens), which is much more difficult for people to comprehend.

(by security camera) to enter and leave that apartment between those hours. Thus, it is logical to assume (by deduction) that John Stealer was the burglar.

Example 3: In medicine we use deductions to determine what disease is afflicting a patient. For example, if a patient has a fever, headache, and sore throat, it would probably be determined that she has the flu because she has "flulike" symptoms.

■ Abduction

Abduction is an attempt to make a deduction that is not sound. This is discussed in John Sowa's book *Conceptual Structures*. He gives this example:

Example 1: All Quakers are pacifists. Richard Nixon was a Quaker. *Modus ponens* would suggest that Nixon was a pacifist. (This is not necessarily true.)

Example 2: Chocolate is the food of love. I am in love. Hence, the chocolate I ate made me fall in love.

Example 3: Smoking causes cancer. Tom has cancer. Hence, Tom was a smoker.

■ Empirical

The term *empirical* is often used with the terms *data* and *evidence*—for example, "empirical data suggest" or "empirical evidence shows." This refers to the data or evidence that is available or has been observed.

Example 1: Empirical evidence suggests that smoking causes cancer.

Example 2: Empirical data suggest that distracted drivers cause a large proportion of motor vehicle accidents. This would suggest that text messaging while driving—something that distracts drivers—should be illegal (*modus ponens*).

■ Exhaustive Enumeration

This is an attempt to solve a problem by considering every possibility in a search space. It is certainly not efficient.

Example 1: In a class, you could find out who an unsigned exam paper belonged to by exhaustive enumeration—for example, by checking all the exam papers that *did* have signatures.

Example 2: The possibilities for "win," "draw," and "loss" in tic-tac-toe can fairly easily be determined by exhaustive enumeration.

Example 3: All the possibilities for playing chess could theoretically be identified by exhaustive enumeration, but since there are 10^{42} estimated reasonable games, it is not possible in practice.

■ Contradiction

Contradiction is a problem-solving technique often used to prove something is true or is impossible. It is based on trying to demonstrate that the opposite of an argument, cannot coexist with the argument itself.

Example 1: Given some premise like A > B, then A = B cannot be true at the same time.

Example 2: If a person is suspected of committing a crime but has an alibi (e.g., proof that she was out of the country at the time of the crime), then that would be proof by contradiction.

■ Recursive

Recursive problems or solutions involve describing a problem (or function) in terms of itself. Recursive problem-solving techniques are subtle and elegant. They involve applying the same steps over and over but to different "arguments." For these reasons, recursive programs are much shorter than their iterative counterparts.

Example 1: Fact(N) = N * Fact(N – 1); Fact(1) = 1

Here, the function Factorial is defined in terms of itself but applied to a different argument.

Example 2: To solve the Towers of Hanoi problem with seven discs, one need only solve the problem for six discs. To solve the Towers of Hanoi, all that needs to be done is to solve the problem for five discs. The process repeats itself until the exit condition is met. This is recursion at work. It is a kind of divide-and-conquer technique. Remember, however, that there must be an "exit" condition—for example, when there is only one disc left (the biggest disc), it must be moved to the goal peg.

■ **Divide and Conquer**

Divide and conquer is a problem-solving technique based on the notion of breaking up a problem into smaller parts. Few problems can be solved "at once," so it is better if they are broken up into logical components.

Example 1: One cannot just sit down and write an entire book, but one can begin with an outline, a few words, a phrase, a complete sentence, and finally a paragraph. Almost all problem solving involves some form of divide and conquer.

Example 2: Driving 20 hours straight to Miami is virtually impossible. But breaking the trip up into four segments of 5 hours each is much more manageable.

■ **Solving a Subproblem**

Similar to divide and conquer, this involves identifying specific components of a problem and solving them. The components may be independent of one another (hence no dependency), but each component is a part of the same whole problem.

Example 1: If we need to identify all the factors of a number, finding first the odd factors and then the even factors is a way of finding the independent subproblems of the problem.

Example 2: If a solution can lie in any of four quadrants, solving one quadrant is solving a subproblem.

■ **Solving a Subgoal**

This is distinct from solving a subproblem because to solve the main problem, you must be able to solve smaller problems that are parts of the larger problem.

Example 1: A building cannot be constructed without preparing its foundation.

Example 2: In the case of The 12 Coins Problem, you cannot solve 12 coins until you can solve 4 coins.

Example 3: In the case of The Red Donkey Puzzle, you cannot get the donkey piece to its goal until it can pass the horizontal, which obstructs it.

- **Problem Reduction**

This involves turning a problem into a simpler problem or simpler form.

Example 1: We use algebra to simplify an equation.

Example 2: In a cryptarithm, if we solve for the leftmost characters, we will have fewer possibilities for the other characters.

- **Solving a Related Problem**

When we are "in tune" with a problem, we are able to identify and solve related problems.

- **Using Prior Knowledge**

When we guessed that the problem with the laptop was that it was getting too hot (it continues to work "cooled down"), that guess was based on prior knowledge and experience. As it is said, "experience counts." Experience should not be underrated. The more you can employ your knowledge and experience to support your problem solving, the shorter and more effective the process is likely to be.

Example 1: While making a decision as to what route to take to a certain destination, a certain road is avoided because it is known there is often heavy traffic or roadwork.

Example 2: Knowing the hypotenuse of a triangle helps solve the problem of finding the area of a parallelogram.

Example 3: Having taken a professor's course before, you are more familiar with his or her teaching and examination question styles.

- **Generate and Test**

This problem-solving method literally entails how it is named. Solutions are produced according to the constraints on a problem. A common example is The Eight Queens Problem (see Lucci and Kopec, 2013, p. 72), where queens are "placed" on a chessboard (the "generation" component) and then "tested" as to whether they meet the problem constraints.

Example 1: In The Eight Queens Problem, a new queen is placed in a new row and column at each "generation."

Example 2: A man notes that he left his car near the elevator on the fifth floor of the parking garage. This information helps him generate potential solutions to the problem of finding his car in the parking garage when he returns.

■ Imposing a Structure: Hierarchy

Being able to structure a problem is always better than having to tackle the problem cold without any prior knowledge. Structure can be conducive to identifying subgoals and subproblems that can and should be solved.

Example 1: By having a corporate structure, it is clear who is responsible for what.

Example 2: By developing a problem tree, it is clear how to proceed from one component of a problem to another.

Example 3: A map helps to identify the points on a trip with the goal of reaching a destination.

■ Solving an Analogous Problem (Analogy)

Problem solving is thinking. Thinking should involve looking for patterns and relationships among problems. For example, if we realize that taking a certain approach to a situation has worked before, we are likely to use the same (or a similar) approach again in the future.

In his biography, the great Chess World Champion Mikhail Botvinnik (1948–1963) related the story of how the Russian government would only support his computer chess research (with powerful computers) when he could solve some power station problems (he was an electrical engineer), using more powerful computers.

Example 1: Outsourcing for help. If outsourcing has worked before in a problem situation (e.g., you need a book cover designed), you will likely outsource again.

Example 2: Eating pizza before going to bed causes acid reflux. Hence, you should avoid eating anything with tomato sauce before going to bed (i.e., tomato sauce contributes to acid reflux).

■ Come Up With a "Bright Idea"

This is akin to the expression "Think outside the box." Do not think in a conventional way. Sometimes this can be aided by getting away from the problem—akin to "incubation" below. Bright ideas are not cheap, and it is hard to figure out how an individual comes up with a bright idea. For some people, their brightest ideas occur in the shower. The key is being relaxed so you can think freely without pressure. The idea you come up with must in some way support your problem-solving goal.

Example 1: Your car is getting old, and you would like to buy a new one. It makes more sense to buy a used car that is about two to five years old and has low mileage. Doing this saves money but still produces a viable solution.

Example 2: Often in life, we find that we make snap judgments that do not work out. While in certain situations (see below—intuition), it is good to go with your instincts, it is sometimes better to hold off making any decision at all (i.e., "incubation" or "sleep on it"). Or as we sometimes say in chess instructions, sometimes the best move is not to make any move at all. This may aid in "coming up with a bright idea."

■ Intuition

Intuition can be a very powerful problem-solving method. It is not accidental, and it is certainly formed with the aid of prior experience. Intuition may come from instincts, which may come from having confronted analogous problems or situations. Intuition must be distinguished from unfounded guessing. There is usually a basis for intuition that may be hard to identify or express.

Example 1: "My intuition is that it would be a good idea for you not to deal with. . . ." This suggestion is usually based on facts, wisdom, and prior experience.

Example 2: "Try substituting 1 for L in the right side of the equation. . . ." Advice like this does not come from lack of knowledge but more often from prior knowledge or experience.

- **Consider Boundary Conditions**

In computer science, it is important to solve problems for all values of X. Therefore, testing for cases when X is either very large or very small is important for the purpose of having a general and complete solution.

Example 1: Consider when X = 0.

Example 2: Consider when X is very large.

- **Working Backward (Retrograde Analysis): Backtracking**

Sometimes it is important to be able to reconstruct the steps that led to a problem situation (e.g., in the case of having lost something or in accident analysis). Lucci and Kopec (2013, p. 235) discuss this topic.

Example 1: What chess piece fell off that square?

Example 2: What were the causes of a car accident?

- **Incubation**

This is a highly recommended approach to problem solving. It essentially suggests "sleeping on a problem." Sometimes getting away from a problem is the best thing you can do. Recognize when you have worked long enough on a problem, and then just get away from it—for a while. While you are mentally "away" from the problem, your subconscious may still be working on it.

Example 1: If you have worked a few hours on a problem and are still stuck, it may be most effective to give the problem a rest, have a cup of coffee (maybe even take a few hours off), and come back to it later or even the next day.

- **Decomposition (Equivalence Classes): Cases**

Occasionally, it is possible to solve a problem by breaking it down into distinct cases. If this can be done, a large problem is broken into smaller problems that are more manageable. This is akin to solving subproblems.

Example 1: A large manufacturing problem is broken down into stages that are ordered and can be achieved.

2.2.1 Heuristics

One of the most important ideas that has come out of Polya's work is the notion of heuristics or "rules of thumb." In effect, heuristics are a very powerful problem-solving technique that are used universally. That's why we think it deserves its own section. Judea Pearl considered this topic so important that he wrote an entire book about it [10]. When one considers how we go through our daily lives, it is apparent that we are indeed a heuristically controlled species. Heuristics also play an important role in the decision-making process and in the lives of other species.

Heuristics may be viewed as "attributes," "features," "factors," "characteristics," or even "hunches" that contribute to the decision-making process in problem solving, but they are not simply idiosyncrasies or superstitions. Let us consider some examples:

Example 1: In baseball, when a player at bat is physically small and light in stature, the outfield will tend to play in, although he may have considerable power. The outfielders are applying a natural heuristic that *usually* works—but sometimes it simply doesn't apply.

Example 2: The heuristic for driving on highways says if traffic is heavy and things are moving very slowly, you should stay in the right lane. This usually helps. Also, if you are talking on the phone while driving (hands-free), you should stay in the right lane.

Example 3: Before teaching a class, it is a good idea to get to your office at least two hours in advance to check for any materials you may need and review them.

Example 4: Avoid rush hour! Try to avoid driving into New York City between 7:30 am and 9:00 am, and avoid driving out of New York City between 4:00 pm and 6:00 pm.

Example 5: Brook's Rule: Whatever the amount of time a programmer tells you is necessary to complete a job, multiply it by three. This is because people are not good estimators of the time and effort needed to complete a job—what Brooks calls "gutless estimating."

Example 6: When developing a computer program, consider the general case data as well as the boundary cases—for example, when N = 0 and N is a very large number.

Example 7: For The Knight's Tour Problem, when given a choice of moves, always move to the edge. This heuristic will work most of the time.

Example 8: In baseball, it is easier for the outfielder coming in to catch a fly ball than for the infielder going out. Hence, the infielder should usually defer to the outfielder.

Example 9: There is the heuristic "Be aggressive but not stupid." Those five words represent a heuristic that means a lot and can cover many domains. For example, in football, it would mean aggression without committing penalties. In chess, it means playing actively with your pieces but not giving your pieces away. In baseball, it could mean trying to steal bases without getting thrown out.

The same concept could be generalized to many situations in life. There are times when you must be firm or "aggressive," but not so aggressive that your action becomes "stupid." That would apply to social situations or even academic ones. Let us say you are listening to a lecture in class and disagree strongly with the professor. If you can make your point in a strong, articulate, intellectual manner, without being abusive or overly loud, and you have valid supporting evidence for your view, then you are more likely to be taken seriously than someone who is just very aggressive, outspoken, and impolite.

Example 10: If you have something troubling you and it is late at night, it is often better to "sleep on it" than try to resolve it when you are tired. This is a "common sense" heuristic. It is a fact that when you are tired, you are apt to make bad decisions. Sometimes you may have done or said things when tired that you have regretted for a long time. After a good night's sleep, your frame of mind is usually more organized, optimistic, and ready to take on the challenges of a new day.

Example 11: "Don't do today what you can put off to tomorrow." What a bad heuristic! It's pretty much saying, "Put off until tomorrow what you need to do today." That, however, is obviously a bad idea and a familiar one to all of those who are certified procrastinators.

The concept could easily be an extension of Example 10, but we do not advocate it, nor is it what we are trying to say here. Do not confuse work with "a problem." If there is work that you are already doing, it is not a bad idea to do as much of that work as you can while your mind is working well and you are not overly tired. In other words, get done what you can in one sitting. There is always some overhead involved in leaving a project. The longer you leave a project, the more time you have to spend trying to regain your final status, ideas, and plan. Yes, if you can accomplish small parts of a project in some systematic, regular work schedule, that is excellent (incubation may even be occurring), but it is not better than actually getting something done. Nonetheless, it is always a good idea to review work that you have done—whether under time pressure or when you were tired. The Institute of Medicine's landmark report *To Err Is Human* attributes many human errors to sheer tiredness. One must be able to recognize tiredness and the need to stop working when necessary.

2.2.2 Additional Heuristics for Problem Solving

In this section, we present some additional heuristics that have been effectively employed by problem solvers.

1. **Look for a simpler, related problem.** This will no doubt lead to a better understanding of the problem itself.

2. **Work backward from specific to general.** That is, take the facts to try to deduce what the nature of the problem is. In AI, this is called *backward chaining*.

3. **Word forward from general to specific.** In essence, we are trying to use generalizations to reach a specific conclusion. For example, say we encounter one bad student in a school. Then we encounter several bad students in the school. Hence, all the students we have encountered are bad. So when we encounter

a new student in that school, we will probably assume that he or she is a bad student. Of course, this reasoning is unsound, and it can lead to uncalled-for prejudices.

4. **Narrow the condition.** See if the problem can be understood better and solved if the conditions are more restrictive.

5. **Widen the conditions to see if that will make the problem easier to understand and solve.** Methods #4 and # 5 may help in problem comprehension.

6. **See if there is a counterexample that will disprove your hypothesis for a solution.**

7. **Change the conceptual mode.** This is like incubation. See if you can look at the problem from a different perspective. This may include restating the problem, drawing diagrams, or choosing alternative representations.

8. **Try to approximate a proposed answer.** It is always a good idea to determine if you are in the "right ballpark."

9. **Consider if all the data have been used.** It is usually a good idea to see how different data affect a solution.

10. **Look for patterns.** Patterns can lend insight to problem solutions.

2.3 THE HUMAN WINDOW

The solutions to problems must fall inside the Human Window (Figure 1). The *Human Window* is a region constrained by human memory capabilities and computational limitations [3]. Thus, solutions must be executable within the limitations of human memory and must be comprehensible. Furthermore, the solutions should be 100% correct and be of manageable grain size (i.e., the solutions must be neither too memory intensive nor too computation intensive) [3].

The Human Window illustrates the limitations of the human brain's ability to process information and the need for Artificial

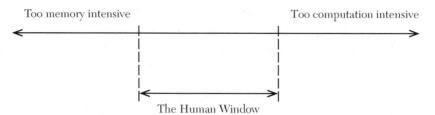

FIGURE 1 Human Window Solutions.

Intelligence solutions to fall within its boundaries. The late Donald Michie is credited with this idea. For a solution to fall within the boundaries of the Human Window, that solution must be ideal in terms of, *correctness, grain size, executability*, and *comprehensibility* [8].

The **correctness** of a solution is determining whether or not it is 100% correct. A solution to a complex problem that is incorrect will not fit well within the Human Window.

The **grain size** of a solution refers to the computational and memory constraints of humans and the Human Window. The key idea is that the solutions to problems of sufficient complexity (i.e., AI-type problems) are limited in terms of the amount of detail with respect to computation and memory needed by people to execute the solutions and comprehend them. The solutions to complex problems should have a manageable grain size—that is, not too computationally intensive (large grain size) or memory intensive (i.e., a database, small grain size).

The **executability** of a solution is measured by how easily one can find the solution, and the **comprehensibility** of a solution is measured by how well one can understand it. Although these criteria assess how well a solution fits within the Human Window, executability and comprehensibility are not necessarily dependent on each other. For example, some solutions to problems can be executed but not necessarily understood. Other types of solutions may be easy for people to understand, but they may be unable to execute them.

Along with the above criteria, it is also important to take into consideration the level of detail of a solution to a complex problem in terms of its knowledge representation and determine whether or not it is **extensional** (explicit, detailed, and long) or **intensional** (implicit, short, and compact). Extensional representations will usually show every case, every example, of some information, while intensional representations will often be short (e.g., a formula or an expression that represents some information).

This book presents solutions to the chosen problems that include sections on the Human Window for each. In this section, various human solutions will be compared based on a set of Human Window criteria.

Kopec has addressed several of the selected problems in his courses and has accumulated a number of solutions and resources for their study and solution. For each of the above complex problems, we have found and analyzed solutions that have already been developed. Among those solutions, we have ranked each of them based on our assessment of how they meet the above criteria (see Section 2). Using these justifications and our opinion, we have evaluated solutions that may be considered the "Most Human Window Compatible (MHWC)" and the "Least Human Window Compatible (LHWC)" for each complex problem. We have also attempted to find the solutions to the problems that can be deemed the "best" for a machine by evaluating the runtime and space efficiency of specific algorithms. Finally, Christopher Pileggi has also attempted to determine the best way to *represent* these solutions.

We look at the *problem solutions* from these points of view:

1. Intensional versus extensional solutions

2. Choice of knowledge representation

3. Suitability in terms of meeting the constraints of the Human Window (i.e., correctness, grain size, executability, and comprehensibility)

4. Problem-solving method

5. Flexibility

6. Mode of conveyance

7. Possible optimality

Finding the most and least Human Window–compatible solutions for complex problems based on these factors can be beneficial in a number of ways. For example, finding the best and most suitable solution for humans can be very beneficial to the study and understanding of problem solving. The same can be said for finding the optimal solution for a machine problem. Not only will these solutions apply to the problems they are meant for, but they may also provide a gateway to solving other human and computational problems. They can also be used as effective teaching tools.

2.4 HUMAN WINDOW CRITERIA AND RANKING OF SOLUTIONS

For each complex problem in the book, we ranked the solutions under consideration based on the following criteria:

Intensional versus Extensional: The solution to a problem will fall under the category of being either intensional or extensional. An *extensional* solution is one that can be explicit, detailed, and usually very long, while an *intensional* solution is one that is usually implicit, short, and compact. We indicate whether a solution is extensional or intensional.

Intensionality/Extensionality: Although determining whether a solution is intensional or extensional is imperative, that doesn't make the category black and white. An intensional solution can be measured on how intensional it is, and an extensional solution can be measured on how extensional it is. For example, consider two extensional solutions to The Missionaries and Cannibals Problem: a graph with images and a table with directions. The graph with images can be considered as more extensional than the table. As a matter of fact, we can say a solution is even more extensional if it were, for example, to involve watching the missionaries and cannibals crossing the riverbank in person. We will give each solution a rank between 1 and 10 to rate how intensional or extensional a solution is, with 10 being the highest level of intensionality or extensionality.

Choice of Knowledge Representation: When analyzing and ranking solutions to identify which is considered "most suitable," it is important to take note of how each solution is represented. By analyzing the rankings and taking note of how a problem is represented, a conclusion can be drawn as to which representation (e.g., table, tree, pseudocode, etc.) may be considered ideal for humans. For each solution, we will indicate what choice of representation was used and analyze its affects and attributes.

Meeting the Constraints of the Human Window: This is important as to whether or not a solution falls within the Human Window. That is, does it meet each of the following constraints? For each solution, we will answer this question with a "yes" or "no." However, to fully answer this question, we must first analyze each of the following criteria:

- **Correctness:** To understand a solution, the solution must be correct. Otherwise, the solution is essentially meaningless. For each solution, we indicate if it is correct, incorrect, or correct but with cycles. That is, the solution provides the correct answer but with some extra steps involved (i.e., backtracking).

- **Grain Size:** The tradeoff between the amount of memory and computation needed to carry out a solution is essential for a solution to fall within the constraints of the Human Window. Too much or too little of either may make a solution so unclear that it is either not comprehensible (too small a grain size) or not executable (too large a grain size). For each solution, we rank this aspect of it in terms of its grain size. *Very Small* means the level of memory needed to carry out the solution is too high, while *Very Large* means the level of computation needed to carry out the solution is too high. *Ideal* means there is a balance between how much a person needs to memorize and calculate to be able to understand (comprehend) and carry out (execute) a solution.

- **Executability:** The executability of a solution is the measurement of how well a person can actually carry it out. The number of steps needed, the resources required (i.e., tables), and the background required (i.e., mathematics) are only some of the factors that determine whether or not a person can execute a particular solution. Each solution is ranked on its executability from 1 to 10, 10 meaning it is very executable.

- **Comprehensibility:** Although a solution may be executable, that does not necessary mean a person can comprehend it. One's comprehensibility of a solution is how well he or she can understand it. This can be determined by factors such as images, colors, the size of the solution, the organization of data, and so on. Since we are not experimenting with human subjects for the Human Window analysis, the ratings are based on our experience with people and their attitudes toward complex problems. Our basis will range between adept problem solvers and non–problem solvers, and we will determine a possible average between the two. Each solution is ranked from 1 to 10, 10 meaning it is very comprehensible.

Problem-Solving Method: Just as we must take note of a solution's choice of representation, it is also important to note the problem-solving method(s) used. Although there are a wide variety of methods to choose from, the average person may prefer one method over another. For example, one may find it significantly easier to solve a problem by breaking it up into subgoals instead of using a top-down approach. With that, comparing a solution's ratings to the method(s) used to solve it may determine which method or methods a person prefers. For each solution, the method(s) used to carry it out is indicated.

Flexibility of Solutions: It is possible that a particular solution can be represented differently. The flexibility of a solution is how easily it can be represented in some other way, without changing the problem-solving method used or detracting from its suitability in terms of meeting the constraints of the Human Window. Solutions can be changed, however, to make them more suitable, especially in terms of their comprehensibility. For example, a black-and-white image may be easier to comprehend if it were in color. Each solution is ranked on its flexibility from 1 to 10, with 10 meaning it is very flexible.

Mode of Conveyance: Another important attribute of a solution is how "portable" it is. For example, consider two fully comprehensible solutions—one that can be presented by hand and one that can only be carried out through an image maker on a computer. The one that can be hand drawn is more portable because it can be used anywhere to solve a problem. On the other hand, this may affect a solution's ability to meet the constraints of the Human Window. Each solution is rated on the possible ways it can be conveyed.

Possible Optimality: A property that makes a solution commendable overall is its optimality. That is, the solution is carried out in the least number of possible steps. Not only does this reduce the problem size, but it also tells us what the best possible solution may entail. We indicate whether or not a solution is optimal.

Along with these rankings, each of these 10 problems is ranked on two additional factors:

Difficulty Level: This measures how difficult we perceive each problem to be based on our study of its solutions. The rating is based on how difficult we find the problems after attempting to solve them and how difficult we feel others would find them. Each solution is ranked from 1 to 10, with 10 meaning it is very difficult.

Complexity: Not only is it important to measure how easy or hard it is for a person to understand a solution, but it also important to measure how easy or hard it is for a machine. Each problem's complexity of the best machine solution is specified in terms of Big-Oh notation.

2.5 CLASSIFICATION

Table 1 classifies the problems according to the type of problem-solving method used. Each of the problems is discussed in terms of background historically, choice of suitable representation, problem-solving techniques used, its solution(s), human

No.	Problem	Problem Type
1	The Missionaries and Cannibals Problem	Logic, constraint satisfaction, search
2	The 12 Coins Problem	Logic, optimizing information
3	Cryptarithmetic	Combinatorics, constraint satisfaction, solving subproblems
4	The Red Donkey Puzzle	Sliding block puzzle, search, constraint satisfaction, solving subproblems
5	The 15 Puzzle	Sliding block puzzle, search, heuristics, constraint satisfaction
6	The Knight's Tour Problem	Search, heuristics
7	Mastermind	Logic, optimizing information
8	The Monty Hall Problem	Logic, probability
9	Rubik's Cube	Subgoals, patterns, subproblems
10	The Prisoner's Dilemma	Game theory, Nash Equilibrium, Pareto Optimality, schema
11	a. Cards/Coins in the Dark b. Ten Pirates and Their Gold c. Halmos's Handshake Problem d. Airline Seats Problem e. The Birthday Problem	Probability, logic Schema, logic Permutations, logic Probability, logic Probability, logic

TABLE 1 Classification of Problems.

problem-solving approaches, Human Window analysis, and the best machine solutions.

2.6 REFERENCES

1. Polya, G. (1945). *How to Solve It*, 2nd ed. Princeton, NJ: Princeton University Press.

2. Burton, L., and Burton, M. (1980). "Problems and Puzzles." For the Learning of Mathematics (1) 2: 20–23. Published by: FLM Publishing Association. Stable *http://www.jstor.org/stable/40247710*. Accessed on December 23, 2012.

3. Lucci, S., and Kopec, D. (2013). *Artificial Intelligence in the 21st Century*. Dulles, Virginia: Mercury Learning, Inc.

4. Gunzelmann, G., and Anderson, J.R. (2002). Problem Solving: Increased Planning with Practice. *Cognitive Systems Research* **4** (2003) 57–76.

5. Minsky, M. (1960). Steps Toward Artificial Intelligence. In Computers and Thought, (Eds. E. Feigenbaum and J. Feldman), McGraw-Hill, New York, pp. 406-450.

6. Newell, A., and Simon, H.A. (1972). *Human Problem Solving*. Englewood Cliffs, NJ: Prentice-Hall.

7. Unterrainer, J.M., and Owen, A.M. (2006). "Planning and Problem Solving: From Neuropsychology to Functional Neuroimaging." *Journal of Physiology—Paris* 99: 308–317.

8. Jonathan St. Evans, B.T., Newstead, S.E., and Byrne, Ruth M.J. (1993). *Human Reasoning: The Psychology of Deduction*, Hove, England: Lawrence Erlbaum Associates.

9. Kopec, D. (1983). *Human and Machine Representations of Knowledge*. Edinburgh, Scotland: University of Edinburgh.

10. Pearl, J. (1984). *Heuristics: Intelligent Search Strategies for Computer Problem Solving*. Reading, MA: Addison-Wesley.

3

THE MISSIONARIES AND CANNIBALS PROBLEM

FIGURE 2 The Missionaries and Cannibals Problem

3.1 BACKGROUND

The Missionaries and Cannibals Problem (Figure 2) is a river-crossing puzzle and is a variant of the Jealous Husbands Problem (another variant is The Brothers and Sisters Problem), which first appeared in the ninth-century manuscript originally entitled *Propositiones ad Acuendos Juvenes* (Problems to Sharpen the Young) [1]. River-crossing problems usually involve transporting objects from one riverbank to the other, using a boat that can carry a certain number of objects. The goal is to transport the objects optimally (in the least number of trips) while satisfying some *constraints*.

Around the thirteenth century, The Jealous Husbands Problem became popular throughout northern Europe. The problem involved husbands and wives as the entities, with the restriction being that the husbands were not allowed to outnumber the wives on either bank [2]. By the end of the nineteenth century, the problem had a revival and became known as The Missionaries and Cannibals Problem. The rules were exactly the same as The Jealous Husbands Problem, but wives were replaced with missionaries and the husbands were replaced with cannibals [3].

Today, The Missionaries and Cannibals Problem is widely used in the field of Artificial Intelligence. It is considered an important problem for several reasons. One is because it is an example of a toy problem, which is a problem that seems insufficient and not worth studying or solving but helps explain a more general problem-solving technique. Another is because of its use in the study of problem representation. It is, as computer scientist Saul Amarel pointed out, a prime example of the fact that "the choice of appropriate representations is capable of having spectacular effects on problem-solving efficiency" [4].

On the whole, The Missionaries and Cannibals Problem is a relatively simple problem. Any solution is optimal if it can move all six missionaries and cannibals to the opposite bank in 11 steps while adhering to the constraints of the problem. From analyzing the problem, it can be concluded that there are four ways to achieve the goal state in 11 steps.

The problem is stated as follows: Given three missionaries and three cannibals on the west bank of a river, find a way to safely transport everyone to the other side of the river. The constraints on the problem are:

1. The boat can only carry two persons at a time.

2. At any point in time (state), the cannibals cannot outnumber the missionaries.

3.2 CHOOSING AN APPROPRIATE REPRESENTATION

This problem is quite easy to understand and can be tackled by adults as well as children. However, choosing the correct sequence of transformations from the starting state to the goal state, while adhering to the constraints of the problem, can be challenging. Experience has demonstrated that the choice of representation is very closely related to successfully solving the problem. The representation not only has to clearly depict the various states in the problem but the moves and transitions from one state to another as well. The following figure shows one way to represent the initial state:

MMM CCC		

In this figure, the three boxes represent the west bank, the river, and the east bank, respectively. M stands for missionary, and C stands for cannibal.

Since the boat is initially stationary, it is not shown. When the boat is in motion, it can be represented by an arrow that shows in which direction the boat is moving. Thus, the following figure represents two cannibals being transported from the west bank of the river to the east bank:

MMM C	CC $\longrightarrow$	

The transition can be shown as follows:

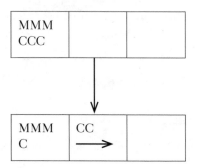

The problem state can be represented in other ways. For example, the initial state can be represented as a set of three numbers, with the first number representing the number of missionaries, the second number the number of cannibals, and the third number the presence or absence of a boat. However, this would only represent the state on one side of the river.

For example, 331 represents the initial state on the west bank with three missionaries, three cannibals, and a boat. Similarly, the state at the west bank after transporting two cannibals to the other side can be represented as 310.

The transition can be shown as:

331 310

It is clear that the first representation is more extensional when compared to the second one. One could use a verbal description or use a formal notation [6] to describe the states, the moves, and the transition between the moves, but it is quite apparent that the graphical notation is more transparent and facilitates visualization of states of the problem.

From the initial state, it may seem there are many possible moves. However, when one delves deeper and considers the constraints of the problem, it can be seen that two entities must be in the boat to get the boat back to the west bank. In addition, to avoid the constraint of cannibals outnumbering the missionaries, either two cannibals or one missionary and one cannibal can be transported on the first move. Further moves that lead to safe states are shown in Figure 3.

FIGURE 3 Search Tree Diagram.

3.3 SOLUTION

One of the ways to represent this problem and its various moves is in the search tree format, as shown in Figure 3. A minimum of eleven moves are required to reach the goal state.

Yet another way of representing the solution is a *state transition diagram* (Figure 4). The boxes on the left side depict all the safe states on the west bank, and the boxes on the right side depict the corresponding states on the east bank. Only states that are safe for both sides of the river are shown. The arrows represent the transition from one state to another as well as the direction of the boat.

The moves represented in Figure 4 can also be translated to a *problem state space matrix*, as shown in Figure 5. The two matrices depict the set of problem states on the two banks of the river. The darker-shaded cells correspond to the unsafe states where the cannibals outnumber the missionaries, and the lighter-shaded cells depict the safe states. The striped cells depict the states corresponding to the unsafe states on the other side of the river. For example, having two missionaries and one cannibal on the east bank is a safe state per se. However, when you consider the corresponding state on the west bank, (i.e., one missionary and two

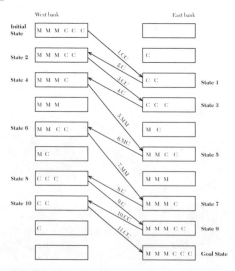

FIGURE 4 State Transition Diagram.

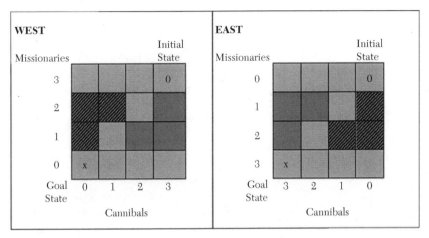

FIGURE 5 Problem State Space Matrix.

cannibals), you know it is an unsafe state for the west bank, and thus this state is invalid and should be avoided. Therefore, the solution involves transitioning from the initial state (cell marked 0) to the goal state (cell marked X).

The moves are numbered and are mentioned in the cell representing the state after the move is made. The moves made on the west bank (i.e., the departing of the boat) are represented by odd numbers in the matrix labeled WEST, and the moves made on the east bank are represented by even numbers in the matrix labeled EAST. The solution in matrix form is shown in Figure 6.

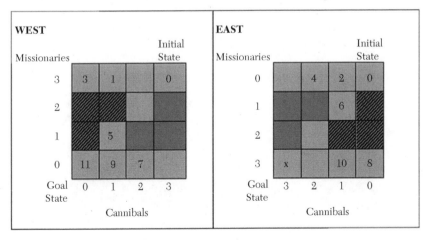

FIGURE 6 Solution Using Problem State Space Matrix.

Another way of representing the matrix is portrayed in Figure 7 [4]. This figure represents the problem state space of the west bank at all times. The odd-numbered moves (from the west bank) are represented with the arrows with black arrowheads, and the even-numbered moves (from the east bank) are represented with the arrows with white arrowheads.

Figure 7 helps us understand a very important aspect of the problem: *symmetry under time reversal* [4]. This means that the moves from the start and end of the solution are similar and opposite. That is, if we work backward from the solution, we are moving the cannibals and missionaries from the east bank to the west bank. This property can help us perform a *bidirectional search* of the problem and thus reduce the search by a factor of two.

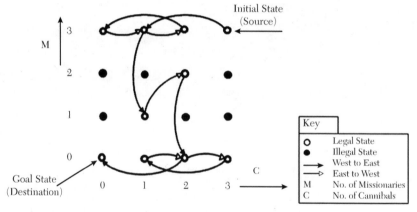

FIGURE 7 State Transitions in Problem State Space.

3.4 HUMAN PROBLEM SOLVING

As part of our research, we observed students trying to solve The Missionaries and Cannibals Problem. They spent about 20 minutes on it, and some were able to come up with the solution. Most of them used the diagram the instructor used while introducing the problem. Some tried other representations, but the pictorial representation seemed to be the easiest for them to understand.

Most students recognized that a key subgoal of the problem was to first isolate the missionaries and cannibals. Second, due to the nature of the initial state, it was natural to first transport all the cannibals to the other side of the river. But that is just a temporary solution. The next step is to get all the missionaries to the other side of the river. However, this involves moving the cannibals back to the original state to fetch the missionaries.

Figure 8 shows the diagram the instructor used when he presented the problem.

FIGURE 8 Instructor's Diagram for The Missionaries and Cannibals Problem.

Here is how three students tackled the problem. (The complete solutions are available in Appendix A.)

Student 1:

The student uses a diagram similar to the instructor's (Figure 9).

The diagram represents the states after every move.

A written explanation of each move accompanies the diagram.

The student starts with two entities on the boat but realizes that one has to stay back and the other has to return to fetch other people.

The student starts with an M and a C but abandons the solution after two steps.

FIGURE 9 Student 1's Partial Solution.

The next attempt is made by moving two Cs first but again abandoning the attempt after three steps.

In the third attempt, two Ms are moved first, but this fails to satisfy the constraint imposed by the problem in the second move.

The student goes back to the first attempt and tries again, this time reaching the sixth step and successfully moving one C and one M to the other side of the river.

The time allotted is over (Figure 10).

	W	E	
0	MMM CCC		
1	MM CC	MC	M and C leave
2	MMM CC	C	M leaves
3	MMM	CCC	CC leaves
4	MMM C	CC	C leaves
5	MC	MM CC	MM leave
6	MM CC		MC leave

FIGURE 10 Student 1's Solution.

Conclusion

The student tries the three possible first moves, and, after reaching dead ends, he learns about good and bad moves. By the third attempt, the student has evaluated the best of the three possible first moves. In the fourth attempt, the student makes this move and proceeds further, carefully avoiding the moves that violate the problem constraint. The student has gathered this knowledge from the previous three trial-and-error attempts.

The student first tries to understand the problem by using the trial-and-error technique and plans for the next attempt.

Student 2:

The student uses characters M and C to represent individual missionaries and cannibals respectively, and uses arrows to depict the direction of the boat.

No other explicit representation of the moves is shown.

First, all the cannibals are transferred to the east bank of the river.

Then all the cannibals are returned to the west bank, and all the missionaries are brought to the east bank, carefully avoiding violating the problem constraint.

Finally, after all the missionaries are moved to the east bank, the cannibals are transferred one by one to the east bank (Figure 11).

Conclusion

The student solves the problem in time. It seems she recognizes that one of the subgoals is to separate the Cs from the Ms by moving all the Ms or all the Cs first. However, while transferring the Ms, some Ms and some Cs sometimes have to be transferred together to maintain balance to avoid having Cs outnumber Ms. The student realizes that moving the Cs back to the west bank again is necessary to get all the Ms on the east bank.

FIGURE 11 Student 2's Solution.

Student 3:

Student 3 uses a tabular format with three columns to represent the problem and the solution. The first column depicts the state on the west bank, the second column represents the state on the east bank, and the third column represents the move.

The student starts by moving a missionary and a cannibal in the first move and proceeds to move all the cannibals to the east bank.

After this, the student skips some steps, reaches the second to last step, and then the last step, and does not show the moves in the table.

The last two steps are the exact opposite of the first two steps (Figure 12).

3M 3C		MC →
2M 2C	M C	M ←
3M 2C	C	2C →
3M	3C	
M C	2M 2C	
	3M 3C	

FIGURE 12 Student 3's Solution.

Conclusion

It may be possible that the student was able to identify that this solution has time reversal symmetry and thus jumped to the last few steps and was either trying to figure out or gave up figuring out the steps in between. It seems there was an attempt to use bidirectional search, as the end states were mentioned with some steps in the middle missing. It may be possible that apart from searching from the initial state toward the goal state, the student was working backward toward the goal.

Analysis of the Solution

We realize it will be easier to solve the problem if we separate the missionaries and cannibals. This can be done by either moving all the missionaries or all the cannibals to the other side of the river first. Trying to move all the missionaries first is impossible because after moving two of them, we get into an unsafe state. Moving all the cannibals to the other side is possible. This is accomplished after the first four moves. However, at least one cannibal has to return back to fetch the missionaries. Now we can start moving the missionaries to the other side. The sixth move is extremely important. It maintains the equilibrium by moving a missionary and a cannibal to the west bank to get the last of the missionaries from that side in the seventh move, while also ensuring a safe state on the east bank.

Note that this step seems like it is leading away from the solution (i.e., this move causes the distance between the current state and the goal state to increase) [5]. The next four steps get the remaining cannibals back on the east bank.

By analysis, it was found that people divide the problem into three or four major subproblems [5]. It is evident from the solution in Figure 15 that the first four steps involve moving all the cannibals to the east bank. The next three steps involve carefully moving back the cannibals to retrieve all the missionaries, while carefully balancing the number of missionaries and cannibals on either side of the river. Finally, the last four steps again move all the cannibals to the east bank.

3.5 HUMAN WINDOW ANALYSIS OF SOLUTIONS

After doing some research, we have collected a number of solutions for The Missionaries and Cannibals Problem for use in our analysis of the Human Window. In this section, we present our findings and an analysis of those findings. We also present the solution we have determined to be the most and the least Human Window compatible and an explanation as to why it is considered as such.

When analyzing the solutions (Table 2), we can see there are a wide variety of possible representations that can be used to describe and solve this problem. One important detail to note is that every one of them is extensional. This may be due to the problem's relatively small state space, which makes it possible to show the solution in a reasonably sized image, graph, table, and so on. There are only 16 legal states in total, and only the legal states are required to describe the solution. Another reason is because the problem is not part of an even larger problem. That is, there will always be three missionaries and three cannibals in the problem, and these numbers do not vary.

We can see that the majority of solutions were either table or graphical representations. This is most likely because this is a problem that involves visualization, as there is an environment with two kinds of entities interacting with it. Also, graphs and tables help provide visualization that minimizes the need for descriptions.

Overall, the solutions had mixed rankings for each of their categories. Some were more executable than comprehensible and some more comprehensible than executable. However, those that contained images or graphics generally fit more within the Human Window. It can also be seen that they have a higher ranking of extensionality as well, while those represented by text or tables were ranked relatively low. Finally, these solutions used a graphical/visual representation as their primary problem-solving technique, while others, especially those represented by tables, used more of a top-down approach.

Difficulty
2/10

Complexity
O(n)

Name	Int or Ext?	Intly/ Extly	Repr	HW?	Corr?	Grn Sz	Exec	Compr	Prob Solv Mthd	Flex	Mode of Conv	Opt?	Tot
Constraint Rules	Ext.	1/10	Table	Y	Y	Small	6/10	2/10	Const. Satisf.	5/10	Table Generator; Hand	Y	14/40
Copin Diagram	Ext.	5/10	Graphic Diagrm	Y	Y	Small	9/10	6/10	Tp-Dwn; Graphic Rep.	8/10	Graphic Img Maker; Hand	Y	28/40
Game	Ext.	9/10	Imgs	Y	Y	Ideal	10/10	9/10	Tp-Dwn;Vis. Rep.	10/10	Img Maker; Hand	Y	38/40
Logic Diagram	Ext.	3/10	State Diagrm	Y	Y	Small	7/10	5/10	Graphic Rep.	7/10	Graphic Img Maker; Hand	Y	22/40
Ma's Table	Ext.	1/10	Table	Y	Y	Ideal	9/10	4/10	Tp-Dwn; Table Repr.	8/10	Table Generator; Hand	Y	22/40
O+G	Ext.	6/10	Descr. w/ Img	Y	Y	Ideal	10/10	7/10	Tp-Dwn; Vis. Rep.	9/10	Text Doc.; Img Maker; Hand	Y	32/40
Prolog Table	Ext.	2/10	Table	Y	Y	Ideal	10/10	7/10	Tp-Dwn; Table Rep.	8/10	Table Generator; Hand	Y	27/40
Symmetric	Ext.	7/10	Graphic Img	Y	Y	Ideal	10/10	8/10	Graphic Rep.	10/10	Graphic Img Maker	Y	35/40
Text Symbol	Ext.	1/10	Text Imgs	Y	Y	Ideal	10/10	7/10	Tp-Dwn; Vis. Rep.	9/10	Text Doc.; Hand	Y	27/40
Z	Ext.	2/10	Graph/ Grid	Y	Y	Ideal	7/10	3/10	Graphic Rep.	7/10	Graphic Img Maker; Hand	Y	29/40

Key

Int or Ext?: Intensional or Extensional—Is the solution intensional or extensional?

Intly/Extly: Intensionality/Extensionality—How intensional or extensional is the solution?

Rep.: Representation—How is the solution represented?

HW?: Human Window—Does the solution exist in the Human Window?

Corr?: Correctness—Is the solution correct?

Grn Sz: Grain Size—How much computation (large) or memory (small) does one need to solve the solution?

Exec: Executability—How executable is this solution?

Compr: Comprehensibility—How comprehensible is this solution?

Prob. Solv. Mthd: Problem-Solving Method—What method is used in the solution to solve the problem?

Flex: Flexibility—How flexible is this solution (i.e., can this solution be represented in other ways)?

Mode of Conv: Mode of Conveyance—In what ways can this solution be reproduced/replicated?

Opt?: Optimal—Is the solution optimal?

TABLE 2 Ranking The Missionaries and Cannibals Problem Solutions According to the Human Window.

3.5.1 The Most Human Window–Compatible Solution

The Most Human Window–Compatible (MHWC) solution is the "Symmetric Solution" (Figure 13). (A good example of this solution can be found at [6].) This solution is a depiction of the state space of the problem as a graphical image. The vertices of

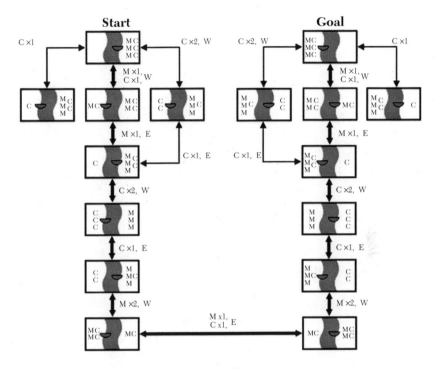

Key:

M = Missionary   W = West Bank
C = Cannibal   E = East Bank

For example, M ×1, W
One missionary travels to the west bank

FIGURE 13 The "Symmetric Solution."

this graph are the problem's state representations. These representations show a visual of the environment, indicating the river, the boat, the bank that the boat is closest to, and letters that represent the missionaries and cannibals. Each of these components is separate from the others, and the environment is completely redrawn in each state. Finally, a key is provided to indicate the meaning of the initials. Each of these details makes the overall representation highly comprehensible.

The edges of the graph indicate which states are adjacent to each other. They also are given a weight that indicates how many missionaries and/or cannibals are to be placed in the boat to move between each state. This is done with the use of numbers and initials. This makes the solution very executable.

This solution shows all of the legal states and how they are reached, including the states that do not lead to a solution. This provides a depiction of the entire state space, revealing every possible solution to the problem, and allows a person to solve the problem in any way he or she sees fit. One of the most intriguing details about the solution is that it reveals another method of problem solving: the use of subgoals. When you examine this solution further, you will notice that the first half of the solution is an exact mirror image of the second half. This shows that when the first half of the problem is solved, the second half can be solved by replicating the steps for the first half in reverse and placing the missionaries and cannibals on reverse banks. The solution depicts this symmetry by presenting the graph as a symmetrical image. Finally, this symmetry once again reveals the benefits of using a bidirectional search to solve this problem. That's why this is the MHWC solution, despite the fact that it did not receive the highest overall ranking on the table.

3.5.2 The Least Human Window–Compatible Solution

The solution that is the Least Human Window–Compatible (LHWC) in our assessment is the "Constraint Rules Solution" (Figure 14). It is called this because it uses constraint satisfaction as its problem-solving method. For this solution, to find the goal state, one must follow a set of constraints, or "Production Rules" (see Section 3.6). These rules correspond to the constraints one must adhere to when attempting to solve The Missionaries and Cannibals Problem.

The main idea behind using this method to find the solution is (1) for each step, look at the current state; (2) look at the rules provided to see which can be followed; (3) implement this rule; and (4) indicate the new state as well as the rule used. This process is to be continued until a goal state is reached.

Although these rules efficiently achieve the goal state in the least number of moves possible (an ideal approach for a computer program), a solution such as this may be too complicated for people, especially with regard to a relatively small problem such as The Missionaries and Cannibals Problem. Humans prefer visual and intuitive representations, especially when constraints are involved. Further analyzing Figure 14, we can see that the solution is divided into two parts: a table of these Production Rules and a table that depicts an example solution when following these rules. We will analyze both.

The example solution table shows a possible transition of states if one were to apply the Production Rules to The Missionaries and Cannibals Problem. Each step is represented by a row, and it shows the current state and the rule applied to get to that state. When analyzing the table, a possible issue that arises with this method is tracing the solution in general. To fully understand how the solution is carried out, one must either memorize each rule, which is simply too difficult, or continuously refer back to the table to find a corresponding rule, which can be very tedious.

Aside from the example table provided in the figure, comprehending the Production Rules may be hard in and of itself. (An example of these rules can be found in [7].) This is because they appear similar to "if statements" commonly used by computer scientists. The average person may very well not be able to understand the real implications behind a series of "if" statements. However, an implementation of the Production Rules is a better solution for a machine rather than a human being (see Section 3.6).

Additionally, for the solution in general, the missionaries and cannibals can be seen to be represented by variables, and the banks and the boat are represented by functions that take those variables as parameters. Again, a computer scientist or mathematician can probably understand this better than the average person.

Key

x = Missionaries (x = 0, 1, 2, or 3)

y = Cannibals (y = 0, 1, 2, or 3)

$W(x, y)$ = Number of missionaries and/or cannibals on the west bank

$E(x, y)$ = Number of missionaries and/or cannibals on the east bank

$B(x, y)$ = Number of missionaries and/or cannibals on the boat and crossing the river to get to the opposite bank

Constraint Rules

Rule No.	Constraint
1	$B(2, 0)$ iff : $(x - 2 \geq y \; \| \; x - 2 = 0$ in one bank$)$ && $(x + 2 \geq y$ in the other$)$
2	$B(1, 0)$ iff : $(x - 1 \geq y \; \| \; x = 0$ in one bank$)$ && $(x + 1 \geq y$ in the other$)$
3	$B(1, 1)$ iff : $(x - 1 \geq y - 1 \; \| \; x = 0$ in one bank$)$ && $(x + 1 \geq y + 1 \; \| \; x = 0$ in the other$)$
4	$B(0, 1)$ iff : $(y - 1 < x \; \| \; x = 0$ in one bank$)$ && $(y + 1 \leq x \; \| \; y = 0$ in the other$)$
5	$B(0, 2)$ iff : $(y - 2 \leq x \; \| \; x = 0$ in one bank$)$ && $(y + 2 \leq x \; \| \; x = 0$ in the other$)$

Initial State: W(0, 0)   E(3, 3)
Goal State: W(3, 3)   E(0, 0)

Example

Step	State			Rule Applied
0	W(0, 0);	E(3, 3)		(Init)
1	W(1, 1);	E(2, 2);	B(1, 1)	3
2	W(0, 1);	E(3, 2);	B(1, 0)	2
	....			
10	W(2, 2);	E(1, 1);	B(1, 0)	2
11	W(3, 3);	E(0, 0);	B(1, 1)	3

FIGURE 14 The "Constraint Rules Solution."

3.6 BEST MACHINE SOLUTION

For a computer, The Missionaries and Cannibals Problem is generally easy to solve. The best solutions for the problem are those that find a solution quickly and take very little space, usually representing a problem state space with a search tree, whereby the initial state is the root of the tree. Along with the bidirectional search [8], search algorithms such as the **breadth-first search, depth-first search,** and **iterative-deepening** have proved to be very effective in solving this problem. This is because the state space for the problem is so small, especially when the constraints are met, thereby reducing the depth and the branching factor of the tree.

Additionally, a set of Production Rules are used to help guide these searches to the goal state. The Production Rules are the constraints that must be followed to solve the problem correctly (i.e., without breaking the rules). These rules are essentially "if-then" statements. According to Robertson, "Some researchers claim to be able to predict the extent to which the rules that apply in one area can transfer [domain-specific knowledge] to another" [9]. An example of these rules can be seen in Figure 14 (see Section 3.5.2) [7]. With the rules implemented and the constraints put into place, the worst-case scenario for any search algorithm is a tree with only 16 nodes (the legal states). Therefore, the overall complexity of The Missionaries and Cannibals Problem is only in the order of **O(n)**.

3.7 RELATED PROBLEMS

Since the Missionaries and Cannibals is a problem from the category of river crossing problems, other problems in the same category are very closely related to it. One of these problems is known as "The Midnight Train Problem," also known as the "Dangerous Crossing Problem" [10]. It belongs in the category of river crossing puzzles. The basic constraints are the same in that the bridge could only hold two people at one time, and one person has to carry something back after crossing the bridge, but the other constraint is that they must all cross the bridge during an allocated time period. The problem involves four people trying to cross a bridge late at night with only a single torch. The torch must be used for crossing the bridge and it has to be brought back from the other side. Each person has a different walking speed and the people crossing the bridge will have to walk at the slowest person's speed. And they must all cross in under a certain time.

Another related problem is the "Jealous Husbands Problem" mentioned briefly by name early in this chapter. It is almost the same premise as the Missionaries and Cannibals Problem, in which three pairs of husbands and wives are trying to cross the river with a boat only capable of carrying two persons at any time. The constraint is that a wife cannot be in the presence of another husband without her own husband also by her side. Otherwise, it would make that wife's husband jealous. This constraint is the name of the problem. It has the same solution as that of the Missionaries and Cannibals Problem.

3.8 PLAYABLE PROGRAM

Some websites have games developed in Flash for The Missionaries and Cannibals Problem where one can try and use different problem-solving techniques. These games are highly extensional representations; the problem solver can actually manipulate the objects and use the trial-and-error technique to find the solution. Furthermore, one would have to draw the representations multiple times before arriving at the solution if one tries to solve this problem manually. Thus, such games get students interested in problems such as this. One such game is available at *http://www.smartestgames.com/game/missionaries-and-cannibals/*.

Thus, choice of representation, the trial-and-error method, planning, solving subgoals, and symmetry are some of the techniques that are helpful in solving a problem like The Missionaries and Cannibals Problem.

3.9 REFERENCES

1. O'Connor, J.J., and Robertson, E.F. (2012). *Propositiones ad acuendos iuvenes by Alcuin*. Accessed on December 4, 2013.

2. Dold-Samplonius, Y., Dauben, J.W., Folkerts, M., and Van Dalen, B. (2002). "Jealous Husbands Crossing the River: A Problem from Alcuin to Tartaglia, Raffaella Franci," *From China to Paris: 2000 Years Transmission of Mathematical Ideas*. Stuttgart: Franz Steiner Verlag.

3. Pressman, I., and Singmaster, D. (1989). "'The Jealous Husbands' and 'The Missionaries and Cannibals.'" *The Mathematical Gazette* (73) 464: 73–81.

4. Amarel, S. (1968). "On Representations of Problems of Reasoning about Actions," *Machine Intelligence* (3): 131–171. *http://aitopics.org/sites/default/files/classic/Machine%20Intelligence%203/MI3-Ch.10-Amarel.pdf*. Accessed on January 8, 2014.

5. Eysenck, M.W. (2002). *Simply Psychology*, 2nd ed. New York: Psychology Press.

6. Wickler, G. (2013). "The Missionaries and Cannibals Problem." *Gerhard Wickler's Home Page*. Edinburgh, Scotland: Artificial Intelligence Applications Institute School of Informatics. Available at *http://www.aiai.ed.ac.uk/~gwickler/missionaries.html*. Accessed on January 8, 2014.

7. Mousavi, F. (2012). "Missionaries and Cannibals Problem in AI." *Programming Notebook*. Available at *http://blog.mousavi.net/2013/07/29/missionaries-and-cannibals-problem-in-ai-2/*. Accessed on January 8, 2014.

8. Lucci, S., and Kopec, D. (2013). *Artificial Intelligence in the 21st Century*. Dulles, Virginia: Mercury Learning Inc.

9. Robertson, S.I. (2001). *Problem Solving*. New York: Psychology Press.

10. *"Murderous Maths Brainbenders"* Available at *http://www.murderousmaths.co.uk/books/BKMMPxbb.htm* Accessed on February 20, 2016.

CHAPTER 4

THE 12 COINS PROBLEM

Image published with permission from Novel Games Limited.
http://www.novelgames.com/en/spgames/coins/
FIGURE 15 The 12 Coins Problem

4.1 BACKGROUND

The 12 Coins Problem (Figure 15) belongs to a class of counterfeit coin problems that involve finding a counterfeit coin among a group of coins. The earliest known appearance of this kind of problem was in E. D. Schell's article in the January 1945 issue of *American Mathematical Monthly,* which required finding an underweight coin among a group of eight coins using a beam balance only twice [1]. There are many variations of the counterfeit coin problems, with some of them providing an extra standard coin for comparison and others revealing whether the odd coin is heavier or lighter than the rest of the coins.

For The 12 Coins Problem in this chapter, given that 1 of the 12 coins has a different weight, the challenge is to find the odd coin in just three weighings and also to determine if the coin is heavier or lighter than the others.

The data given for this problem is:

There is only one odd coin.

The odd coin has a weight different from the others.

The unknowns are:

Which coin is the odd one?

Is the odd coin heavier or lighter than the others?

The constraint is:

Only three weighings are allowed.

4.2 SOLVING A SMALLER PROBLEM

We can convert this problem to a simpler one by reducing the number of coins and the number of weighings. Heeding Polya's advice, "If you can't solve a problem, then if there is an easier problem that you can solve, find it," we look for a problem with fewer coins.

Let us start using the *problem reduction technique.* If we start with only 2 coins, it is impossible to find which of the 2 coins is odd unless we know if the odd coin is heavier or lighter than the other or if we have a standard coin to compare with. Thus, the 2 coins problem is not the minimal problem (without an extra standard coin or the knowledge of the relative weight of the odd coin with respect to the good one). Hence, we can check if the 3 coins problem is an easier version of The 12 Coins Problem. If we reduce the number of coins to 3, we may get an idea that can be applied for solving The 12 Coins Problem.

In the 3 coins problem, if we know that the odd coin weighs less or more, only one weighing is required to identify the odd coin. Otherwise, we must first compare the first and second coins. If they are equal, we know that the third coin is odd. One more weighing of the third coin with any of the first two coins will tell us if the odd one is heavier or lighter than the other two. However, if the scales are not equal in the first weighing, it means one of the first two coins is odd and the third coin is not odd. In any case, after the results of first weighing, the 3 coins problem becomes similar to the "2 coins problem with the standard coin," and thus the odd coin and its relative weight can be found in a total of two weighings. A solution to the 3 coins problem with the coins named A, B, and C is shown in Table 3.

Thus, we can deduce the following:

Coins with equal weights are good coins and can be separated from the coins that have not been weighed yet, and this group of remaining coin(s) contains the odd coin.

Weighing 1 A ? B	Weighing 2 A ? C	Result
A = B (Thus, C is odd)	A = C	Not possible because one of them is odd
	A > C	C is odd and light
	A < C	C is odd and heavy
A > B (Thus, A or B is odd)	A = C	B is odd and light
	A > C	A is odd and heavy
	A < C	Not possible because ONLY one of them is odd
A < B (Thus, A or B is odd)	A = C	B is odd and heavy
	A > C	Not possible because ONLY one of them is odd
	A < C	A is odd and light

TABLE 3 Solution to the 3 Coins Problem

When the scales are unequal, one side of the scale contains the odd coin.

Once the odd coin is detected, we need to know its weight relative to a good coin to determine if it is heavier or lighter than the rest.

Moving to the slightly more complex 4 coins problem, if we divide the coins into two groups of 2 coins and compare the weights of these groups, we know which of the two groups is heavier (or lighter). However, we do not know which group has the odd coin, nor do we know if the odd coin is heavy or light. Thus, very little information is gained from the first weighing. Furthermore, two more weighings are needed to compare the coins in each group individually to identify the odd coin.

Alternatively, we could take the first 3 coins and solve them in two weighings like we did for the 3 coins problem. If both groups weigh the same, we know the fourth coin is odd, and one more weighing with one of the known good coins can tell us if the fourth coin is overweight or underweight. Thus, the 4 coins problem can be solved in three weighings.

This problem helps us conclude that *dividing coins into groups of three gives us more information in the first weighing, as compared to dividing into groups of two*—the information about the group that has good coins only. This is because after the first weighing, we know that either the first two groups or the third one have all good coins, thus separating the good coins from the groups containing the odd coin, and thereby reducing the problem into one with fewer coins.

If we try to solve the 6 coins problem with the knowledge gained from the previous two problems, we can proceed as follows: Divide the coins to three groups of 2 coins. After comparing the first two groups, we know the odd coin is in one of first two groups if they do not weigh the same or that the odd coin is in the third group if the first two groups weigh the same in the first weighing.

In either case, one more weighing of the odd (or possibly odd) group with one of the good group(s) will tell if the odd coin is heavy or light, and the third weighing will help identify the odd coin in the odd group (Table 4).

Weighing 1 AB ? CD	Weighing 2 AB ? EF	Weighing 3	Result
AB = CD (E or F is odd)	AB = EF	Not possible because ONLY one of them is odd	
	AB > EF	E = F	Not possible because ONLY one of them is odd
		E > F	F is odd and light
		E < F	E is odd and light
	AB < EF	E = F	Not possible because ONLY one of them is odd
		E > F	E is odd and heavy
		E < F	F is odd and heavy
AB > CD	AB = EF	C = D	Not possible because ONLY one of them is odd
		C > D	D is odd and light
		C < D	C is odd and light
	AB > EF	A = B	Not possible because ONLY one of them is odd
		A > B	A is odd and heavy
		A < B	B is odd and heavy
	AB < EF	Not possible because ONLY one of them is odd	
AB < CD	AB = EF	C = D	Not possible because ONLY one of them is odd
		C > D	C is odd and heavy
		C < D	D is odd and heavy
	AB > EF	Not possible because ONLY one of them is odd	
	AB < EF	A = B	Not possible because ONLY one of them is odd
		A > B	B is odd and light
		A < B	A is odd and light

TABLE 4 Solution to the 6 Coins Problem

From the 6 coins problem, we can conclude the following:

When we divide coins into groups of 3 coins, we know by the second weighing if the odd coin is heavy or light and which group contains the odd coin.

This is because by the end of two weighings, we know the relative weight of each group with respect to the other two groups, which separates out the odd group and tells us if the odd coin is heavy or light.

The 9 coins problem is a special case, because we divide the coins into three groups of 3 coins. Thus, after comparing one of the three groups with the other two groups in two weighings, we know the odd group and the relative weight of the odd coin. Therefore, the problem is reduced to a 3 coins problem when the relative weight of the odd coin is known. Hence, one more weighing gives us the odd coin.

Alternatively, we could consider the 3 coins in each of the three groups as one big coin. The problem could then be reduced to a 3 coins problem, and after two weighings, we know if the three groups or the big coin is odd and if it is heavy or light. Thus, now we know the group of 3 coins containing the actual odd coin. This problem is thus reduced to a 3 coins problem where we know that the odd coin is heavy or light, and thus one weighing is enough to find the odd coin. This technique is known as *recursion*, where a problem is continuously broken down to a subproblem that, when it reaches the elementary or base case, can be solved directly.

We can conclude that as the number of coins increases, we need to compare as many coins as possible in the first two weighings to reduce the problem to one that is as small as possible. We have just seen how a 9 coins problem was reduced to a 3 coins problem after two weighings.

4.3 SOLUTION

In an observation conducted in an AI class, one of the students came up with the solution to The 12 Coins Problem shown in Table 5.

Weighing 1 ABCD ? EFGH	Weighing 2	Weighing 3	Result
ABCD = EFGH	ABC = IJK	A = L	Not possible because one of them is odd
		A > L	L is odd and light
		A < L	L is odd and heavy
	ABC > IJK	I = J	K is odd and light
		I > J	J is odd and light
		I < J	I is odd and light
	ABC < IJK	I = J	K is odd and heavy
		I > J	I is odd and heavy
		I < J	J is odd and heavy
ABCD > EFGH	**AB**E = **CD**F	G = H	Not possible because one of them is odd
		G > H	H is odd and light
		G < H	G is odd and light
	ABE > **CD**F	A = B	F is odd and light
		A > B	A is odd and heavy
		A < B	B is odd and heavy
	ABE < **CD**F	C = D	E is odd and light
		C > D	C is odd and heavy
		C < D	D is odd and heavy
ABCD < EFGH	**AB**E = CD**F**	G = H	Not possible because one of them is odd
		G > H	G is odd and heavy
		G < H	H is odd and heavy
	AB**E** > CDF	C = D	E is odd and heavy
		C > D	D is odd and light
		C < D	C is odd and light
	AB**E** < CD**F**	A = B	F is odd and heavy
		A > B	B is odd and light
		A < B	A is odd and light

TABLE 5 Solution to The 12 Coins Problem

In this solution, the 12 coins are divided into three groups of 4 coins each. In the first weighing, we know either that the third group of coins, which has not yet been weighed, has the odd coin or that one of the first two groups has the odd coin. In the first case, the problem is reduced to a 4 coins problem. By removing one coin from this group, the problem can be solved as a 3 coins problem in two more weighings. If that fourth coin that was omitted is found to be odd (by the second weighing), it can be weighed against a known good coin to check if it is heavy or light in the fourth weighing.

In the second case, we know the relative weights between the first two groups and can use this knowledge for the next weighing. We then divide the heavier group into 2 coins each and place it on either side of the scale. We then take 2 coins from the lighter group and place one on either side of the scale and conduct the second weighing. This would reduce the number suspect odd coins to 3 possible coins if the scales do not balance or 2 possible coins (the remaining 2 from the lighter group) if the scales do balance. In any case, one more weighing will suffice to detect the odd coin. This solution, though correct, cannot be extended to any number of coins.

We can generalize The 12 Coins Problem to an n coins problem. It was found that the number of weighings required to find an odd coin among n coins can be deduced from the following formulas developed by Bennet Manvel in his article "Counterfeit Coin Problems" in *Mathematics Magazine*:

An underweight coin in a set of k coins can be found in ?$\log_3 k$? weighings.

If we know only that the counterfeit coin is a different weight, then $[\log_3 (2k + 3)]$ weighings are required.

$[\log_3 (2k + 1)]$ weighings are required if a standard coin is provided.

°Please note that $[x]$ means the "ceiling" of x, or the smallest integer greater than or equal to x, where x is a real number [1].

In Table 6, we tabulated the number of weighings for several n coin problems using the formulas for the three cases mentioned above.

No. of Coins $= k$	Case 1: Finding an **underweight** coin in a set of k coins No. of weighings = $[\log_3(k)]$	Case 2: Finding an **odd** coin with a different weight when a standard coin is provided No. of weighings = $[\log_3(2k + 1)]$	Case 3: Finding an **odd** coin with a different weight No. of weighings = $[\log_3(2k + 3)]$
3	1	2	2
4	2	2	3
6	2	3	3
9	2	3	3
11	3	3	3
12	3	3	3
13	3	3	4
39	4	4	4
40	4	4	5
120	5	5	5

TABLE 6 Number of Weighings Required to Find an Odd Coin Among n Coins in Different Cases

The graph in Figure 16 illustrates the application of the formulas in Table 6.

Noteworthy is how the $\log_3$ growth rates seem to define a stepwise function.

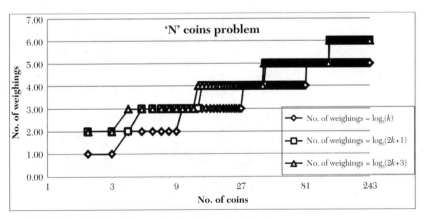

FIGURE 16 Graphical Depiction of Some of the *n* Coins Problems

Another solution that Jack Wert created is available at *http://www.cut-the-knot.org/blue/OddCoinProblems.shtml* and *http://www.cut-the-knot.org/blue/OddCoinProblemsShort.shtml*. This is a solution for The 12 Coins Problem that can be extended to any $(3^n - 3)/2$ number of coins [2].

Divide the coins into three equal groups of four. Let us name the coins A, B, C, D, E, F, G, H, I, J, K, and L.

Divide each of the three groups into a main subgroup of 3 coins and then 1 coin.

Place the first two groups of 4 coins on either side of the scale and note the results. This is the first weighing.

Then, rotate the main subgroups—in other words, remove the main subgroup of the first group from the left pan of the scale, move the main subgroup of the second group from the right pan to the left, and keep the main subgroup of the third group on the right pan of the scale. Keep the single coins from the first two groups as they are on the scale. This is the second weighing.

The weighings are described in Table 7.

	Left Pan	Right Pan
Weighing 1 (W1)	A, B, C, D	E, F, G, D
Weighing 2 (W2)	E, F, G, H	I, J, K, H

TABLE 7 Configuration of Coins in the Two Weighings

Each of the weighings has three possible outcomes:

= means the two scales are equal.

< means the right pan is heavier than the left one.

> means the left pan is heavier than the right one.

Table 8 shows the nine possible outcomes of the two weighings.

Case	W1 result	W2 result	Probable odd coin(s)	Is the odd coin heavy or light?	Next step	How many more weighings needed?	Total number of weighings
1	=	=	L	Can't say yet.	Compare coin L with any of the good coins to know its relative weight.	1	3
2	<	<	D or H	Can't say yet.	Compare coins D or H with any of the good coins to know the relative weight of the odd coin.	1	3
3	>	>	D or H	Can't say yet.		1	3
4	=	<	I, J, or K	Heavy	This problem is reduced to the 3 coins problem, where the relative weight of the odd coin is known. Thus, solve the reduced problem.	1	3
5	=	>	I, J, or K	Light		1	3
6	<	=	A,B, or C	Light		1	3
7	>	=	A,B, or C	Heavy		1	3
8	<	>	D,E, or F	Heavy		1	3
9	>	<	D,E, or F	Light		1	3

TABLE 8 Possible Outcomes After the Two Weighings

The key aspect of this solution is that it tries to *maximize the amount of information gained in the least number of weighings*. In the first two weighings, 11 out of the 12 coins are weighed. The weighings are then configured in such a way so that after two weighings, the problem is reduced to a smaller problem that can be solved in just one more weighing, depending on the nine possible results. Also, we can leverage the information gained from the previous two weighings in the last weighing.

According to this solution, to solve a $(3^n - 3)/2$ coins problem in general, the following steps must be followed [2]:

Divide the coins into three equal main groups. Each is to be divided into $(n - 1)$ subgroups of $3^{n-2}, 3^{n-3}, \ldots, 3^0$ coins.

Place the first two main groups on each side of the scale. This is the first weighing.

Rotate only the largest subgroups, as described above in The 12 Coins Problem solution. This is the second weighing.

If the condition of the balance changes, as seen in the last six cases of The 12 Coins Problem solution above, the subgroup containing the odd coin will be identified, and the problem will be reduced to a smaller problem.

Continue the rotation of the next largest subgroups until there is a change in the condition of the balance or until there is only one coin on each side of the scale. Then rotate them and the odd coin, and its relative weight will be found.

4.4 HUMAN PROBLEM SOLVING

This problem was presented to a class of around 20 graduate students studying Artificial Intelligence. It was presented in two phases: as a 6 coins problem and then as The 12 Coins Problem. The choice of representation most students used was a search tree, with different branches of the tree signifying the different outcomes of the weighings.

Most students were able to solve the 6 coins problem in three weighings, with one of the students concluding that if the relative weight of the odd coin is known, only two weighings were sufficient.

The class struggled with The 12 Coins Problem because it is harder than the 6 coins problem. Most of them were able to solve the problem in four weighings, and one student solved it in the minimum three weighings. (This student's solution is shown in Table 8.) It used the information gained from the relative weights of two groups of coins compared in the first weighing to narrow down the number of possible odd coins.

From the analysis of The 12 Coins Problem, by reducing it into smaller problems, we learn more about the problem and get clues about how to solve the original problem. Also, decomposing a bigger problem into small parts and solving the smaller problems recursively help to solve the bigger problem. We have seen that problem reduction and recursion techniques were useful in solving The 12 Coins Problem.

4.5 HUMAN WINDOW ANALYSIS OF SOLUTIONS

When analyzing the solutions (Table 9), we can see some similarities in their rankings. First, note that each of them is extensional. The solutions we found are specific to The 12 Coins Problem. Since the solution is relatively small (three weighings), any method can depict the problem in its entirety. If the table contained a solution to the general *n coins problem*, however, it would most likely be classified as intensional.

Overall, their rankings of the solutions' extensionality are mixed. Those that used actual images depicting coins and scales were generally ranked higher, while those represented by text were ranked lower. However, not many of the solutions found used images as a means of representation.

The choices of knowledge representation used for the solutions are a mix between tables and text. The text solutions give a general description about each possible outcome for all three weighings. The tables simplify these explanations with the use and organization of symbols. In general, each solution uses the three weighings method similarly and emphasizes the subproblems generated by it.

Difficulty
3/10

Complexity
$O(n(\log_2 n))$

Name	Int or Ext?	Inlty/ Exlty	Rep.	HW?	Corr?	Grn Sz	Exec	Compr	Prob. Solv. Mthd	Flex	Mode of Conv	Opt?	Tot
B & Y	Ext.	2/10	Txt Desc	Y	Y	Ideal	8/10	8/10	Vis. Rep.; Subgoals	8/10	Txt Editor	Y	26/40
Duncanson	Ext.	4/10	Txt Desc	Y	Y	Ideal	7/10	6/10	Vis. Rep.; Subgoals	9/10	Txt Editor; Hand	Y	26/40
FA	Ext.	6/10	Tble	Y	Y	Ideal	10/10	7/10	Vis. Rep.; Subgoals	7/10	Tble Mkr; Txt Editor; Hand	Y	30/40
Generic Table	Ext.	7/10	Tble	Y	Y	Ideal	10/10	8/10	Tbl Rep.; Subgoals	8/10	Tbl Mkr; Hand	Y	33/40
Logically Enumerated	Ext.	3/10	Txt Desc	Y	Y	Small	7/10	5/10	Vis. Rep.; Subgoals	5/10	Graphic Img Mkr; Hand	Y	20/40
LogicFlow	Ext.	5/10	Logic Dgrm	Y	Y	Small	9/10	6/10	Vis. Rep.; Subgoals	7/10	Img Mkr	Y	27/40
Poskitt	Ext.	7/10	Txt; Tble	Y	Y	Ideal	8/10	5/10	Vis. Rep.; Subgoals	7/10	Tbl Mkr; Txt Editor; Hand	Y	27/40

Key

Int or Ext?: Intensional or Extensional—Is the solution intensional or extensional?

Intly/Extly: Intensionality/Extensionality—How intensional or extensional is it?

Rep.: Representation—How is the solution represented?

HW?: Human Window—Does the solution exist in the Human Window?

Corr?: Correctness—Is the solution correct?

Grn Sz: Grain Size—How much computation (large) or memory (small) does one need to solve the solution?

Exec: Executability—How executable is this solution?

Compr: Comprehensibility—How comprehensible is the solution? on?

Prob. Solv. Mthd: Problem-Solving Method—What method is used in the solution to solve the problem?

Flex: Flexibility—How flexible is this solution? (i.e., can this solution be represented in other ways)?

Mode of Conv: Mode of Conveyance—In what ways can this solution be reproduced/replicated?

Opt?: Optimal—Is the solution optimal?

TABLE 9 Ranking The 12 Coins Problem Solutions According to the Human Window

The rankings pertaining to how the solutions fit into the Human Window are mixed as well. In general, each of the solutions was given a high ranking for executability. Overall, it is easy to follow the steps of the three weighings regardless of the representation used. The comprehensibility of the solutions, however, was mixed. Those that used a text representation were generally ranked lower, while those represented by tables were ranked higher. Finally, it can be noted that each of the solutions used the same general problem-solving techniques, which entail looking for subgoals by employing using visual representations.

4.5.1 The Most Human Window–Compatible Solution

The solution assessed as MHWC is the "Generic Table Solution" (Figure 17). This solution is the same as the one in Section 4.3. It is represented as a table containing four columns. The first three columns are used to show the possible outcomes the scale may produce during any of the three weighings, with each column representing a different weighing. These outcomes contain letters that represent the coins and a conditional operator that represents the result of the weighing. The coins (letters) that are grouped together are those present on a specific side of the scale. The last column indicates the result of the third weighing, thus concluding whether a coin is heavy or light, or if the weighing is impossible.

This solution is comprehensible because it is concise and the columns in the table organize the solution well. This solution is also highly executable. When the result of the first weighing is found, the remaining possible results for the second weighing are directly adjacent to that result in the next column. This adjacency is also present for the second and third weighings. This makes it possible for the solution to be found easily and quickly, and it reduces the information needed to be found in the table overall.

Although the solution is comprehensible, the overall comprehensibility could be improved if a small picture of the actual scale were present next to each possible outcome to show if the scale is balanced or not. Additionally, it could be improved even further if the letters had circles around them, which would better indicate that they are in fact representing coins.

4.5.2 The Least Human Window–Compatible Solution

The solution assessed as LHWC is the "Logically Enumerated Solution" (Figure 18). This solution gives a textual description as to what to do at each weighing, given a particular outcome.

Weighing 1 ABCD ? EFGH	Weighing 2	Weighing 3	Result
ABCD = EFGH	ABC = IJK	A = L	Not possible as one of them is odd
		A > L	L is odd and light
		A < L	L is odd and heavy
	ABC > IJK	I = J	K is odd and light
		I > J	J is odd and light
		I < J	I is odd and light
	ABC < IJK	I = J	K is odd and heavy
		I > J	I is odd and heavy
		I < J	J is odd and heavy
ABCD > EFGH	ABE = CDF	G = H	Not possible as one of them is odd
		G > H	H is odd and light
		G < H	G is odd and light
	ABE > CDF	A = B	F is odd and light
		A > B	A is odd and heavy
		A < B	B is odd and heavy
	ABE < CDF	C = D	E is odd and light
		C > D	C is odd and heavy
		C < D	D is odd and heavy
ABCD < EFGH	ABE = CDF	G = H	Not possible as one of them is odd
		G > H	G is odd and heavy
		G < H	H is odd and heavy
	ABE > CDF	C = D	E is odd and heavy
		C > D	D is odd and light
		C < D	C is odd and light
	ABE < CDF	A = B	F is odd and heavy
		A > B	B is odd and light
		A < B	A is odd and light

Figure 17 The "Generic Table Solution"

While this solution shows each possible outcome and demonstrates how to solve the problem in the least number of weighings, a table representation may be better than a descriptive representation. This is because particular solutions to The 12 Coins Problem can be found instantly on a table, while they may be hard to find in the midst of a lengthy description.

In particular, this solution may not be very comprehensible, since the descriptions are grouped as small paragraphs. Within those paragraphs are representations of the coins, the coin groupings, and scales, which may be seen as inefficient. Each coin is given a name that corresponds to a particular group, such as X1, X2, Z3, and so on. To indicate that the coins belong to a particular group on the scale, the coins are concatenated using the "–" symbol.

Finally, the groups are indicated as being on the left or right side of the scale by separation using a conditional operator. Although this works for the "Generic Table Solution," it may not work in this type of representation.

- **Coin Groups:** {X1, X2, X3, X4}; {Y1, Y2, Y3, Y4}; {Z1, Z2, Z3, Z4}

- **Weigh X1-X2-X3-X4 against Y1-Y2-Y3-Y4.**

- **1st weighing: If X1-X2-X3-X4 = Y1-Y2-Y3-Y4**

The counterfeit must be in group Z. Take any of the X or Y coins as a control coin (i.e. X1).

Weigh Z1+Z2 against Z3+X1.

> - **2nd weighing: Z1+Z2 >Z3+X1.**
>
> Z1 or Z2 is heavy or Z3 is light. Weigh Z1 against Z2.
>
> (or if Z1+Z2 < Z3+X1, substitute heavy for light and vice versa in the following.)
>
> > - **3rd weighing: Z1 = Z2**
> >   Z3 is light.
> >
> > - **3rd weighing: Z1 > Z2**
> >   Z1 is heavy.
> >
> > - **3rd weighing: Z1 < Z2**
> >   Z2 is heavy.

> - **2nd weighing: Z1+Z2 = Z3+X1**
>
> Z4 must be the counterfeit.
>
> Weigh it against any of the control coins to determine whether it is heavy or light. (i.e. X1)
>
> > - **3rd weighing: Z4 < X1**
> >   Z4 is light.
> >
> > - **3rd weighing: Z4 > X1**
> >   Z4 is heavy.

- **1st weighing: X1-X2-X3-X4 < Y1-Y2-Y3-Y4 (analogous holds if X1-X2-X3-X4 > Y1-Y2-Y3-Y4; switch heavy for light and vice versa)**

One of the X's is lighter than the rest, or one of the Y's is heavier than the rest.

All the Z's can be taken as control coins

Weigh X1-X2-Y1-Y2 against X3-Y3-Z1-Z2.

> - **2nd weighing: X1-X2-Y1-Y2 > X3-Y3-Z1-Z2**
>
> **Y1 or Y2 is heavy, or X3 is light.**
>
> **Weigh Y1 against Y2.**
>
> > - **3rd weighing: Y1 > Y2**
> >   **Y1 is heavy.**
> >
> > - **3rd weighing: Y1 < Y2**
> >   **Y2 is heavy.**
> >
> > - **3rd weighing: Y1 = Y2**
> >   **X3 is light.**
>
> - **2nd weighing: X1-X2-Y1-Y2 = X3-Y3-Z1-Z2**
>
> **X4 is light or Y4 is heavy. Weigh X4 against Z1.**
>
> > - **3rd weighing: X4 < Z1**
> >   **X4 is light.**
> > - **3rd weighing: X4 = Z1**
> >   **Y4 is heavy.**

Figure 18 The "Logically Enumerated Solution"

4.6 BEST MACHINE SOLUTION

In general, there are no particular categories of algorithms or heuristics needed for a machine to solve The 12 Coins Problem. Any algorithm that implements the general method of solving The 12 Coins Problem in three weighings is guaranteed to find the optimal solution. If implemented correctly, the same technique can be used to solve any n coins problem in $[\log_3 (2k + 3)]$ weighings. Correctly implementing an algorithm will find a solution to the n coins problem in at most **O($n\log_3 n$)** time. The n represents the number of coins in the problem, and the $log_3 n$ represents the number of weighings. It is not simply $log_3 n$ because the algorithm must find a way to group every coin at each weighing. Although some coins are not used in the second and third weighings and will inevitably deal with fewer than n coins, they are still in the order of n.

4.7 PLAYABLE PROGRAM

You can find help playing The 12 Coins Problem at *http://www.mathplayground.com/coinweighing.html* (Figure 19).

Image published with permission from Novel Games Limited.

http://www.novelgames.com/en/spgames/coins/

Figure 19 The 12 Coins Problem

4.8 REFERENCES

1. Manvel, B. (1977). "Counterfeit Coin Problems." *Mathematics Magazine* 50: 90–92.

2. Bogomolny, A. (2013). *Odd Coin Problems: the 120 Marble Problem—Five Weighings from Interactive Mathematics Miscellany and Puzzles. Available at http://www.cut-the-knot.org/blue/OddCoinProblems.shtml.* Accessed on January 9, 2014.

CHAPTER 5

CRYPTARITHMS

```
    S   E   N   D

+   M   O   R   E
_____

    M   O   N   E   Y
```

FIGURE 20 The Send More Money Problem

5.1 BACKGROUND

A cryptarithm is a type of mathematical puzzle in which the digits are replaced by the letters of the alphabet or other symbols [1]. The first cryptarithm appeared in 1864 in *American Agriculturist* magazine. In 1931, Simon Vatriquant introduced the term *crypt-arithmetic* (*cryptarithme* in French) under the pseudonym MINOS in *Sphinx*, a Belgian recreational mathematics magazine [2, 3]. In 1955, J. A. H. Hunter coined the term *alphametic* to denote cryptarithms whose letters form meaningful words or phrases.

In Artificial Intelligence, cryptarithms are studied as a class of **constraint satisfaction problems**, where the goal is to assign the correct values (the digits) that belong to a domain (0 to 9 in the case of decimal numbers) to a set of variables (the alphabetic characters), while satisfying the constraints (the result of the arithmetic operations should be correct) of the problem [4].

The constraints are as follows:

Each alphabetic character represents one digit only, and each digit is represented by exactly one alphabetic character.

A numeric representation of a word does not start with the digit zero.

When alphabetic characters are replaced by digits, the resultant sum is arithmetically correct.

5.2 PROBLEM-SOLVING TECHNIQUES

Deduction, generate and test, backtracking, solving subproblems, and *solving linear equations* are some of the techniques that can be helpful for solving cryptarithmetic puzzles. Usually the problem itself contains some clues that provide more information and clues to solving other letters or symbols. In doing so, we can build a database of information that can further help in finding more clues and ultimately the solution. For example, it is easy to spot 0 and 9 in an equation because 0 added to any number is the same number, and 9 added to a number is also the same number with a carryover if there is a carryover from the previous column. Also, when two decimal digits are added, the carryover is a maximum of 1, and thus an extra digit in the sum means that digit is 1. Furthermore, when digits representing one of the two operands being added are from the extreme end of the domain of possible values (e.g., 0, 1, or 9), it is relatively easier to decipher the other operand if we know whether or not the sum results in a carryover. Thus, we are able to logically determine results from given information [5]. In this chapter, we consider two well-known problems.

Problem 1:

SEND + MORE = MONEY

This is perhaps the most classic cryptarithmetic puzzle. It was introduced by Henry Dudeney in *Strand Magazine* in 1924 [1, 6]. This problem is also an alphametic, since the words in the puzzle form a sensible phrase *SEND MORE MONEY* (Figure 20). One of the notable characteristics of this problem is the extra digit in the sum (i.e., the M), because it is an important clue. Another is that some of the letters, such as M, E, and N, are repeated, so the sooner they are deciphered, the more quickly the problem can be solved.

	S	E	N	D
+	M	O	R	E
M	O	N	E	Y

Problem 2:

DONALD + GERALD = ROBERT (Clue: D = 5)

This is another well-known problem, and it has been the subject of Newell and Simon's study of human problem solving using cryptarithmetic.

	D	O	N	A	L	D
+	G	E	R	A	L	D
	R	O	B	E	R	T

Note the hint that D = 5. This very helpful in finding more information about all the variables connected to D by the different constraints—namely, the T, the carryover to the second column, G, and R.

5.3 SOLUTION

Problem 1:

SEND + MORE = MONEY

Here is a solution that is very similar to many others available online. Since the sum has one digit more than the two numbers being added, we choose to start solving the problem from the left side. We will refer to the columns as first, second, third, and so on, starting from the right side. As we begin to find clues to the solution, we keep adding them to a Knowledge Table and refer to it to obtain additional clues.

c5	c4	c3	c2	
	S	E	N	D
+	M	O	R	E
M	O	N	E	Y

It is evident from the problem that **M = 1**, since it is a carry-over from the previous column and also because the sum cannot start with a leading 0. Figure 21 demonstrates this.

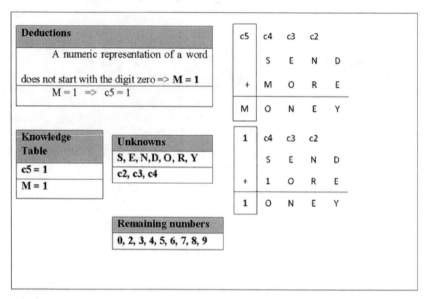

FIGURE 21 Step 1

Assuming there is no carryover from the third column, $S + 1 = 10$, and thus S can only be 9, which proves $O = 0$.

However, if there is a carryover from the third column, $1 + S + 1 = 10$—that is, $S + 2 = 10$, so $S = 8$, which gives $O = 0$, or $S = 9$, which gives $O = 1$, which is not possible because M is already 1. Thus, if there is a carryover, $S = 8$.

In any case, **O = 0. Figure 22 illustrates how we reach conclusions for O = 0, and S = 8 or 9.**

Deductions	
$c_5 = 1$	=> $c_4 + S + 1$ greater than 9
$S + 1$ greater than 9 => $\mathbf{S = 8}$ **if $c_4 = 1$**	
or $S = 9$ if $c_4 = 0$	
In both cases above, i.e. $S = 8$ or $S = 9$ =>	
$\mathbf{O = 0}$	

	1	c_4	c_3	c_2	
		S	E	N	D
+		1	O	R	E
1		O	N	E	Y

Knowledge Table	Unknowns
$c_5 = 1$	S, E, N, D, R, Y
	c2, c3, c4
$M = 1$	**Remaining numbers**
$O = 0$	2, 3, 4, 5, 6, 7, 8, 9
$S = 8$ if $c_4 = 1$ or $S = 9$ if $c_4 = 0$	

	1	c_4	c_3	c_2	
		S	E	N	D
+		1	O	R	E
1		0	N	E	Y

FIGURE 22 Step 2

We continue by moving to the third column from the right. Looking at Figure 23, we see that $E + O = N$, which is not possible because anything added to zero is itself. This means $c_3 = 1$. Therefore, $E + 1 = N$. The maximum that E can be is 9, and if $E = 9$, $N = 0$, which is not possible because $O = 0$. This means E is not equal to 9 and $E < 9$. Thus, $N < 10$, $c_4 = 0$, and $\mathbf{S = 9}$.

Continuing to the fourth column, we can see in Figure 24 that $N + R = E$ and $c_3 = 1$, so $N + R = E + 10$. This equation is valid if $c_2 = 0$.

In addition, we know that $E + 1 = N$. Substituting this in the above equation, we get $E + 1 + R = E + 10$, so $R = 9$. But $S = 9$, so our assumption that $c_2 = 0$ column is *incorrect*. Hence, the correct equation is

$1 + N + R = E + 10$

That is, $1 + E + 1 + R = E + 10$, which gives $\mathbf{R = 8}$.

FIGURE 23 Step 3

Continuing to the last column, we have $D + E = Y$, which generates a carryover to the next column (see Figure 24). Thus, $D + E = 10$. Now the numbers 0, 1, 8, and 9 are taken.

Hence, $12 = D + E = 17$

and D and E can be 2, 3, 4, 5, 6, or 7.

The following combinations of the above numbers have the sum between 12 and 17

$5 + 7 = 12$

$6 + 6 = 12$

$6 + 7 = 13$

$7 + 7 = 14$

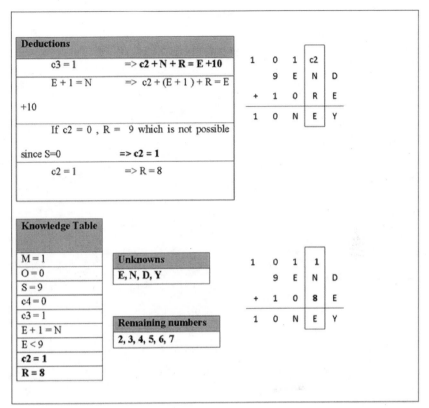

FIGURE 24 Step 4

Since D is not equal to E (a constraint of the problem), only the first and third equations are valid. Also, since E occurs more frequently in this problem, let us try the values 5, 6, and 7 for E first (see Figure 25)

If we assign E = 5, D = 7, Y = 2, and N = 6, we can see that each of these assignments are valid, and thus, have reached the solution.

FIGURE 25 Step 5

Trying E = 6, we get D = 7, Y = 3, and N = 7, which is not possible because D = 7.

Also trying E = 7, we get D = 6, Y = 3, and N = 8, which is not possible because we have proven R = 8.

Similarly, trying D = 5 leads to E = 7, so N = 8, which is again invalid because R = 8.

Thus, we conclude the problem is solved and there is no other solution.

Problem 2:

We name the carryovers $c_2, c_3, \ldots, c_6$ for the columns $2, 3, \ldots, 6$.

c_6	c_5	c_4	c_3	c_2	
D	O	N	A	L	D
+ G	E	R	A	L	D
R	O	B	E	R	T

Substituting the clue, we get $T = 0$ with a carryover to the second column. Thus, $c_2 = 1$ and $1 + L + L = R$, so **R is odd (see Figure 26).**

FIGURE 26 Step 1

Moving to the fifth column, $O + E = O$, which means if there is no carryover, $E = 0$, and if there is a carryover, $E = 9$ (see Figure 26).

Since T is already 0, **E = 9** and thus **confirming a carryover from the fourth column and a carryover to the sixth column—that is, $c_5 = c_6 = 1$.**

FIGURE 27 Step 2

FIGURE 28 Step 3

Since $A + A = 9$ (which is an odd number), there is a carryover from the second to the third column (see Figure 28). Also, there is no carryover from the third to the fourth column because it would mean $A + A + 1 = 9$, thus making A = 9. But 9 is already taken. So there is **no carryover from the third to the fourth column,** and thus **A = 4.**

Moving to the sixth column, we have $5 + G = R$ (see Figure 29).

Because R is odd, R = 7 or R = 9. But E = 9, so R = 7, which makes G = 1 because there is a carryover from the fifth column.

FIGURE 29 Step 4

In the fourth column, $N + 7 = B$ with a carryover to the fifth column (see Figure 30). Also, since there is no carry from the third column, N can be 2, 3, 4, 6, or 8. To generate a carryover, N has to be greater than 2. N = 3 or 4 makes B = 0 or 1, both of which are already assigned. N = 6 makes B = 3, and N = 8 makes B = 5, which is again invalid. Thus, **N = 6 and B = 3**.

Deduction

N + 7 = B and c5 = 1	=> N + 7 = B + 10
N + 7 = B + 10	=> N = B + 3
N = B + 3 => Of the remaining numbers, only N= 6 and B = 3 satisfy the equation.	

```
    1  1  0  1  1
    5  O  N  4  L  5
+   1  9  7  4  L  5
  ───────────────────
    7  O  B  9  R  0
```

Knowledge Table

D = 5
T = 0
c2 = 1
R is odd
2L + 1 = R or 2L + 1 = R + 10
E = 9
c5 = 1, c6 = 1
c3 = 1, c4 = 0
A = 4
R = 7
G = 1
N = 6
B = 3

Unknowns

O, L

Remaining numbers

2, 8

```
    1  1  0  1  1
    5  O  6  4  L  5
+   1  9  7  4  L  5
  ───────────────────
    7  O  3  9  7  0
```

FIGURE 30 Step 5

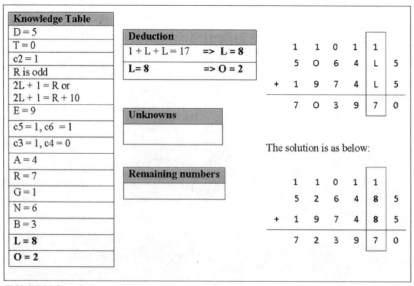

FIGURE 31 Step 6

Now we also have some new data for the second column: $1 + L + L = 7$ (see Figure 31). Because there is a carryover to the third column, $L = 8$ makes the sum $= 1 + 8 + 8 = 17$. The only remaining digit is 2, and the remaining alphabet is O. Thus, $O = 2$.

It is evident from the above two solutions that we also have computed the value of the carryovers, which are also known as auxiliary variables. Even though auxiliary variables are not directly a part of the solution, they help in the problem-solving process.

Let us consider Problem 1: SEND + MORE = MONEY.

The variables are S, E, N, D, M, O, R, and Y.

The domain for these variables is 0 to 9.

The auxiliary variables are c_1, c_2, c_3, and c_4 (the carryovers).

The domain for auxiliary variables is 0, 1.

The constraints are as follows:

All the variables represent different numbers.

The numbers do not start with digit 0.

$S = c_4$

$c_3 + S + M = O + 10*c_4$

$c_2 + E + O = N + 10*c_3$

$c_1 + N + R = E + 10*c_2$

$D + M = Y + 10*c_1$

If we conduct an exhaustive search for the solution through the problem state space, we soon realize that it is a herculean task, because if a problem consists of 10 different variables, there are $10! = 3,628,800$ possible assignments [4]. However, as observed previously, if we can decipher some of the variables using the clues inherent in the problem, such as an extra digit in the sum or a 0 or 9, we can reduce the number of possible combinations—but only to a certain extent.

Alternatively, we can formulate the problem as a search tree by considering one of the values found initially as the initial state and the goal state, being the situation where the value of every variable in the solution is known [4]. We can also divide the problem into subproblems. In this case, we can think of a column as a subproblem and consider solving one subproblem at a time by computing the values of the variables in that column. However, it is futile to consider a column in isolation because the carryovers from the sum in one column affect the sum in the next column, and thus the columns are connected to each other. This relationship between the columns—or, more specifically, between the variables—is evident from the list of constraints and can be more clearly seen via a *constraint hypergraph*, which George Luger developed for this problem [4]. Therefore, we have to consider the constraints that connect one column to the other. If we look closely, it is the auxiliary variables (i.e., the carryovers) that connect two columns. Fortunately, the domain of these auxiliary variables is very small, because the values are either 1 or 0. Thus, if we correctly identify these auxiliary variables, we may be able to prune the search tree and reduce the search effort and time. Additionally, we can assume one of the legal values for the auxiliary variable and find the values for the remaining variables in a particular column.

This heuristic, which involves considering the variables' fewest possible values, is called the *minimum remaining values (MRV) heuristic* [4]. Thus, after applying the "generate and test technique" to the variables with MRV, the domain of the other variables in the column is also reduced. We also consider the second possible value for the auxiliary values and compare the resulting domains of the variables in the column.

For example, in Problem 1, consider column 4 after substituting $M = c_4 = 1$:

$c_3 + S + 1 = O + 10$

If $c_3 = 1, S + 1 = O + 10$

Thus, $S + 1 = 10$, and the only possible legal value for S is 9 and for O is 0.

Similarly, if $c_3 = 1, S + 2 = 10$, and the only possible legal value for S is 8 and for O is 0.

Now the question is whether or not the order in which the two possible values of c_3 needs to be considered. In this case, the order does not matter because the domain of S is reduced to only one legal value (i.e., 8 or 9) in both cases (for both possible values of c_3)—that is, 1 or 0, respectively. In cases where testing a probable value for a variable results in a domain that is too small or null for its neighboring variable, such a variable is considered last. This heuristic, choosing the value that rules out the least possible values for the neighboring variables, is called the *least constraining value (LCV)* [4].

Thus, when using the MRV heuristic, we can find the value of O and can reduce the domain of S to two values: 8 and 9. This prevents us from having to test all other values from the domain for the variables, which would later fail anyway.

After choosing the LCV for a variable, we can start deriving possible legal values for the remaining variables and proceed further down the search tree toward the solution. This technique is called *forward checking*. Continuing this way, if we were to reach a dead end or a state where no legal values are left for a variable, we trace back to the last assignment. This technique is called *backtracking*.

5.4 HUMAN PROBLEM SOLVING

If we analyze the solution to Problem 1, we realize that it starts by assigning the value 1 to M, which is deduced from constraints 2 and 3. Then in column 4, the auxiliary variable c_3 is chosen as the MRV, since its domain is smaller compared to the other two variables. Thus, we are left with only two possible values for the letter S and only one value for O. Following the substitution of O = 0 in column 3, the relation between E and N is found, which helps find the value of R. After deciphering all the remaining auxiliary variables, the domain of the variables in the first column is reduced to just three numbers, due to an exhaustive search using a combination of the three values, and the application of constraints leads to the solution.

The solution to Problem 2 starts with a similar path, substituting the clue and deducing the values/parities of the related variables. The solution proceeds to finding the value 9 and the values of most of the auxiliary variables. Also, the columns are observed one by one, substituting the knowledge gained.

5.5 HUMAN WINDOW ANALYSIS OF SOLUTIONS

Overall, each solution we found follows the same general concept: show (at least) the completely encrypted and decrypted cryptarithm and give a step-by-step description of how the solution was found.

When analyzing the solutions we found (Table 10), we can see that they are all represented using text. This is because a mathematical arithmetic problem, along with any reasoning behind it, is easily understood by words rather than pictures or diagrams. Therefore, the choice of representation is less likely to play a role in determining the best solution. Rather, the organization, detail, and description of steps play a major factor in identifying the solution that would be considered the most compatible.

The majority of the solutions are extensional, mainly consisting of methods to solve the **SEND MORE MONEY** problem and the **DONALD GERALD ROBERT** problem. They are considered extensional because they explain the step-by-step procedure for solving either one of these two cryptarithms in their entirety. The intensional solutions found, such as the "Primer Solution," summarize the possible arithmetic constraints and techniques for solving any cryptarithm, even for those that involve arithmetic other than addition [7].

The rankings for both executability and comprehensibility are generally mixed. Since each solution uses text as a means representation, they were analyzed more profoundly, especially in terms of organization, detail, and description of steps, as mentioned before. However, it can be seen that the intensional solutions were generally ranked lower. This is most likely because they use general arithmetic techniques that one must remember to solve cryptarithms instead of the solution to a cryptarithm being readily available to the problem solver, as in the case of extensional solutions.

Difficulty
8/10

Complex.
O((n − (constrs + N/A))!)

Name	Int or Ext?	Intly/ Extly	Rep.	HW?	Corr?	Grn Sz	Exec	Compr	Prob. Solv. Mthd	Flex	Mode of Conv	Opt?	Tot
Ariels	Ext.	6/10	Txt	Y	Y	Ideal	7/10	6/10	Constr. Satisf.	9/10	Txt Editor; Hand	Y	28/40
Code	Int.	7/10	Code/ Algrthm	Y	Y	Ideal	6/10	4/10	Constr. Satisf.; Brute Force	8/10	Txt Editor	N	25/40
Donald	Ext.	9/10	Txt	Y	Y	Small	5/10	5/10	Constr. Satisf.	9/10	Txt Editor; Hand	Y	28/40
Knowl-edge Table	Ext.	8/10	Txt w/ Pics	Y	Y	Ideal	10/10	10/10	Constr. Satisf.	9/10	Txt Editor; Hand	Y	37/40
M and Cs	Ext.	8/10	Txt w/ Tables	Y	Y	Ideal	9/10	8/10	Constr. Satisf.	8/10	Txt Editor; Tbl Mkr; Hand	Y	33/40
Pavalli	Ext.	9/10	Txt	Y	Y	Ideal	7/10	9/10	Constr. Satisf	9/10	Txt Editor; Hand	Y	34/40
Primer	Int.	4/10	Txt	Y	Y w/ Cycles	Vry Large	6/10	5/10	Constr. Satisf.; Brute Force	8/10	Txt Editor; Hand	N	23/40

Key

Int or Ext?: Intensional or Extensional—Is the solution intensional or extensional?

Intly/Extly: Intensionality/Extensionality—How intensional or extensional is the solution?

Rep.: Representation—How is the solution represented?

HW?: Human Window—Does the solution exist in the Human Window?

Corr?: Correctness—Is the solution correct?

Grn Sz: Grain Size—How much computation (large) or memory (small) does one need to solve the solution?

Exec: Executability—How executable is this solution?

Compr: Comprehensibility—How comprehensible is this solution?

Prob. Solv. Mthd: Problem-Solving Method—What method is used in the solution to solve the problem?

Flex: Flexibility—How flexible is this solution (i.e., can this solution be represented in other ways)?

Mode of Conv: Mode of Conveyance—In what ways can this solution be reproduced/replicated?

Opt?: Optimal—Is the solution optimal?

TABLE 10 Ranking Cryptarithmetic Solutions According to the Human Window

Not surprisingly, each solution uses constraint satisfaction as a problem-solving technique. This method, along with the help of solving for subgoals, is almost crucial to cryptarithmetic. As for the intensional solutions, they use constraint satisfaction accompanied with the use of *brute force*. This is because, unlike the SEND

MORE MONEY problem, cryptarithms are not generally unique. Therefore, it is possible that a single letter or symbol can represent multiple possible values, and not a specific digit. To solve these types of cryptarithms, brute force must be used.

Finally, it is also important to note that the solutions' flexibility is ranked fairly high. Since they are represented using text, these solutions can be presented in many different ways.

5.5.1 The Most Human Window–Compatible Solution

The solution assessed as the MHWC is the "Knowledge Table Solution." This solution is the same solution presented in Section 5.3. This solution is a simple, yet detailed solution for the SEND MORE MONEY cryptarithm. We could consider it the MHWC for several reasons. One is because it is divided into steps, making the solution highly comprehensible. Another reason is because the solution divides the columns of the equation into subproblems, making it highly executable.

A third reason is because the equation is reiterated consistently at every step, showing the current values at that particular step in the solution and columns that are being analyzed. In addition, the symbols and values of the carryovers are displayed as well. This prevents the need to memorize or write down the values of the letters and carryovers and keeps the reader engaged.

A fourth reason is the level of detail of its description. This solution has just the right amount of detail in that it explains exactly why the letters are assigned their particular values. Also, the language of the description is very explicit, so even those without an advanced mathematical background can properly understand the solution.

The final, and most substantial, reason as to why it is considered the MHWC solution is because of the use of the Knowledge Tables. These tables display the letter values, deductions, and unknowns that remain at each particular step. As the solution proceeds further, more elements are added or removed from these tables. These tables are significant because it is a compact and concise way of organizing data. This makes the solution very comprehensible and very executable.

5.5.2 The Least Human Window–Compatible Solution

DONALD + GERALD = ROBERT

Solution:

```
  c1 c2 c3 c4 c5
  D  O  N  A  L  D
  G  E  R  A  L  D
  ----------------
  R  O  B  E  R  T
```

Steps:
1) T is even (D + D = an even number)

2) D $\geq$ 5 $\longleftrightarrow$ c5 = 1
   D $\leq$ 4 $\longleftrightarrow$ c5 = 0

3) L $\geq$ 5 $\longleftrightarrow$ c4 = 1
   L $\leq$ 4 $\longleftrightarrow$ c4 = 0

4) A $\geq$ 5 $\longleftrightarrow$ c3 = 1
   A $\leq$ 4 $\longleftrightarrow$ c3 = 0

5) c5 = 1 $\longleftrightarrow$ R is odd
   c5 = 0 $\longleftrightarrow$ R is even (L + L)
   R is not 0 (R and L cannot both be 0)

6) c4 = 1 $\longleftrightarrow$ E is odd
   c4 = 0 $\longleftrightarrow$ E is even (A + A = an even number)
   E not 0 (E and A cannot both be 0)

7) c2 = 0 $\longleftrightarrow$ E = 0
   c2 = 1 $\longleftrightarrow$ E = 9 and c3 + N + R > 9

8) c1 + D + G $\leq$ 9 (no carry)
   R $\leq$ D
   R $\leq$ G
      . . .
      . . .
      . . .
      . . .
      . . .

FIGURE 32 The "Donald Solution" (Shortened)

The solution assessed as the LHWC solution is the "Donald Solution" (Figure 42). This is a solution to the DONALD GER-ALD ROBERT cryptarithm, with a representation similar to one presented in [8]. The solution consists of equivalence functions that implicitly and briefly show the potential values of the letters and carryovers at each step. Although the solution is organized as steps, it shows how those values are obtained with only a brief mathematical explanation and a small amount of description. These factors could potentially lower both the executability and comprehensibility of the solution, especially for those who are not familiar with cryptarithms. Nonetheless, this solution may be suitable for those who are highly mathematically and/or logically inclined.

Another feature that could be an issue with this solution is the fact that, unlike the "Knowledge Table Solution," the cryptarithm is not reiterated in between steps. This further reduces the amount of guidance provided to the reader and thus may further reduce the comprehensibility of the solution.

Finally, you may notice that the solution begins by analyzing the letters in the rightmost column as opposed to the leftmost column. As seen in the previous solutions in this chapter, we usually begin by analyzing the letters in the leftmost column and then moving toward the rightmost column. This approach is more efficient because it is likely to determine the values of the carryover variable earlier in the process. However, beginning from the rightmost column may result in more steps, which is the case in the "Donald Solution." Therefore, this may also reduce the executability of the solution.

5.6 BEST MACHINE SOLUTION

Up to this point, we have only analyzed cryptarithms whose values contained up to 10 possible values (i.e., digits 0 to 9). That is, we have been solving for equations whose values are in base 10, which is essentially the number system we all use every day. However, the possibility of using different bases has most certainly been considered.

For a machine, determining if a cryptarithm has a solution is **NP-complete** when generalized to arbitrary bases [9]. This means there is no known algorithm that can guarantee a solution to a cryptarithm in an acceptable amount of time as the number of unknown digits (base) increases (a solution can be verified in polynomial time, however). For any cryptarithm whose values are of base n, the worst-case runtime for finding that solution is $O(n!)$. This is the case when all n digits are used in the equation and when there are no constraints that can be concluded by the use of mathematical arithmetic rules. However, it is more than likely that cryparithmetic problems will not contain every one of its n values and will contain mathematical constraints of some kind. Thus, the average running time would be **O((n – (constraints + unused digits))!)**.

Fortunately, most cryptarithmetic problems that are analyzed tend to contain letters with values in base 10 (e.g., the SEND MORE MONEY problem), since this is the base we are used to. For cryptarithms in base 10, we replace n with 10 and thus find that the worst-case running time is $O(10!)$ and the average case is **O((10 – (constraints + unused digits)) !)**.

Although this greatly reduces the problem space, 10! is still relatively large. For a machine, one of the most efficient algorithms for finding solutions to cryptarithms is a **parallel genetic algorithm**. This algorithm is essentially the same as a typical genetic algorithm (i.e., the "Code Solution" [10]) but is executed with the aid of multiple processors. In an experiment done at Shahid Chamran University, the time required to solve a cryptarithm with a parallel genetic algorithm increased proportionately as the number of unknown variables increased. After doing this experiment on a base 10 cryptarithm containing all 10 variables, it took 3.5 seconds to find the solution using a parallel generic algorithm, whereas the depth-first algorithm took a little more than an hour [11].

5.7 RELATED PROBLEMS

A problem that is related to cryptarithms is the "clockwork problem" [13]. It is not a cryptarithm problem per se but the process of solving this problem is very similar to how one would solve a cryptarithm problem. The problem is described as follows: The date and time is written in the format of HH:MM:SS DD/MM, so 6 minutes and 34 seconds past 5 on the afternoon of July 25th would be written as 17:06:34 25/07. Using all the digits 0-9 only once, what would be the earliest time and date which can be generated by the clock and what would be the latest?

The solution to this problem requires players to realize the constraints on the problem. The first constraint would be that the first digit of for the month can only be 0 or 1, and if it is 1, then the digit that follows could only be a 0 or 2, because there are only 12 months and digits cannot be repeated. The second constraint would be that the first digit for the date can only be 0, 1, 2, or 3, and if 3, only 0 or sometimes 1 for the second digit, due to that there are only 30 or 31 days for most months, except February. The third constraint is on the hour in which the first digit can only be a 0, 1, or a 2, and if it's a "2," then only "0," "1," or "3" for second digit, as there are only 24 hours in a day and 12 o'clock is usually written as "00" which would not be available due to repeating digits. The fourth constraint would be built on top of all previous constraints in that the numbers 6, 7, 8, or 9 can only be on the second digit in any of the 5 categories of the date and time. This is for the reasons stated above, and in addition, there can only be at most 59 minutes or seconds as once they reach 60, a reset to "00" occurs. Therefore, it is only possible that these four numbers can occur only for the second digit of any four of the five categories. The final constraint is the precedence of the categories. That is, month takes precedence over date, then follows hours, minutes, and lastly seconds. Following all these constraints, will eventually lead to the solution of 17:48:59 26/03 for the earliest time and date, and 17:56: 09 for the latest. Try it.

5.8 PLAYABLE PROGRAM

Today, there are many apps available on iPhone and Android phones that have kept the interest in cryptarithmetic alive. With the advent of modern computers a few decades ago, people started publishing computer-generated cryptarithms that were too complex to be solved by humans, leading to a decrease in interest in these games [12]. Cryptarithms that fall inside the Human Window are fun to solve and help in improving our problem-solving skills. However, keeping track of the knowledge table, the latest state of the problem, and the different variable possibilities using strictly a pen and paper can be a tedious job. This is where playing apps and computer games containing cryptarithms can help. We can choose the variables' values based on logic and heuristics, while the computer can do the complex calculations and memory management. One of the apps can be found at *http://www.letsgetwordy.com/#am_app* (Figure 33).

Image published with permission from Thomas L. Peterson, Eximietate, Inc.

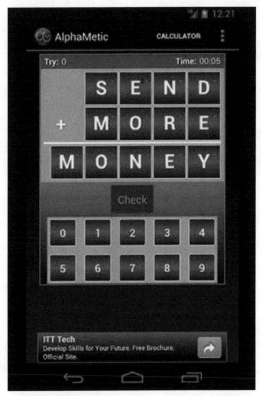

FIGURE 33 Alphabetic App
http://www.letsgetwordv.com/#am app

5.9 REFERENCES

1. Logicville. (2012). *Cryptarithm*. Available at *http://www.logicville. com/cryptarithm.htm*. Accessed on January 8, 2014.

2. Wikipedia. (2012). *Simon Vatriquant*. Available at *http://fr.wikipedia. org/wiki/Simon_Vatriquant*. Accessed on January 8, 2014.

3. Soares, J. (2012). The Sphinx Memorial. *http://cry ptarithms.award-space.us/sphinx.html*. Accessed on January 8, 2014.

4. Luger, G.F. (2008). *Artificial Intelligence: Structures and Strategies for Complex Problem Solving* 6th ed., Reading, MA: Addison-Wesley.

5. Polk, T.A., and Newell, A. (1995). "Deduction as Verbal Reasoning." *American Psychological Association* (102) 3: 533–536.

6. Elitmus Guide. (2012). *Guide to Solve Cryptic Multiplication Question*. Available at *http://elitmusguide.blogspot.in/2012/07/guide-to-solve-cryptic-multiplication.html*. Accessed on January 8, 2014.

7. Soares, J. (2002). *A Primer on Cryptarithmetic*. Available at *http://cryptarithms.awardspace.us/primer.html*. Accessed on January 8, 2014.

8. Moran, D.B. (2013). *Name Addition: DONALD + GERALD = ROBERT*. Available at *http://www.dougmoran.com/examples/puzzle-name-addition.txt*. Accessed on January 8, 2014.

9. Eppstein, D. (1987). "On the NP-Completeness of Cryptarithms." *SIGACT News* 18 (3): 38–40. Available at *http://www.ics.uci. edu/~eppstein/pubs/Epp-SN-87.pdf*. Accessed on January 8, 2014.

10. *Pachnekar, T (2011). Cryptarithmetic. Available at http://www.codeproject.com/Articles/176768/Cryptarithmetic. Accessed on January 8, 2014.*

11. *Abbasian, R., and Mazloom, M. (2009). Solving Cryptarithmetic Problems Using Parallel Genetic Algorithm. Available at Available at http://staff.science.uva.nl/~masoudm/Papers/mazloom,milad.pdf. Accessed on January 8, 2014.*

12. *Soares, J. (2003). Will Cryptarithmetic Survive Innovation? http:// cryptarithms.awardspace.us/survival.htm. Accessed on April 22, 2013.*

13. *"Murderous Maths Brainbenders" Available at http://www.murderous-maths.co.uk/books/BKMMPxbb.htm Accessed on February 20, 2016.*

CHAPTER 6

THE RED DONKEY PUZZLE

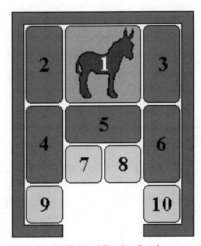

FIGURE 34 The Red Donkey Puzzle

6.1 BACKGROUND

Apart from being known as a variation of Dad's Puzzler, which is perhaps the earliest-known puzzle of its kind [1], **The Red Donkey Puzzle** (Figure 34) is credited as the third most sold sliding block puzzle (after The 15 Puzzle and Dad's Puzzler) in the book *Sliding Piece Puzzles* by L. Edward Hordern [2]. The earliest appearance of this puzzle was recorded in France, where it was known as *L'Âne Rouge* (The Red Donkey) and enjoyed great popularity. The English version of the puzzle, known as The Red Donkey, had surfaced in the early 1930s [1], while in Poland it was known as *Klocki* (wooden blocks) and in Japan as *Hakoiri musume* (Daughter in the Box) [3].

The Red Donkey Puzzle is a type of sliding block puzzle that consists of several tiles (or blocks) bounded by a set area in which the tiles must be organized into a specific arrangement. Specifically, The Red Donkey Puzzle is bounded by a 4" × 5" rectangular area and consists of 10 blocks: a 2" × 2" square block (known as the Donkey piece), four 1" × 2" vertical blocks, a 2" × 1" horizontal block, and four 1" × 1" square blocks. The constraints on the puzzle are as follows:

The blocks can only slide within the bounded rectangular area.

The blocks cannot be lifted from the area to be replaced.

The arrangement of the blocks in the initial state of the puzzle is shown in Figure 35 [4]. In its initial state, the 2" × 2" block, which is the largest block, is at the top center of the bounded area, and the goal is to move it to the bottom center. We have also numbered the blocks so they can be easily referenced and the solution is clearly understood.

FIGURE 35 The Red Donkey Puzzle

6.2 SOLUTION

In this section, we study a solution consisting of 81 moves, similar to the one provided by Martin Gardner in the March 1964 issue of *Scientific American*. For The Red Donkey Puzzle, any solution that reaches the goal state in 81 moves is considered optimal, as this is known to be the least number of possible moves required to solve the puzzle. An online game (available at *www. bsswebsite.me.uk*) is used to play the puzzle and to show some of the important stages in the solution. Here is the solution with numbers representing blocks:

10 (halfway), 6, 5, 7 (down), 4

9 (halfway), 7, 4, 5, 8 (up, left)

10, 4, 8 (right, down), 5, 10

8, 6, 4, 9, 7, 5, 8 (down, left), 4, 6, 3

2, 1, 10, 8, 4, 1, 2, 3, 6, 7, 8 (left, up), 5, 1, 4, 7

2, 10, 8 (up, right), 7, 4

1, 9 (left, down), 2, 10 (down, left), 3

6, 2, 10, 8 (halfway), 7, 4, 1, 9, 10 (down), 2

6, 3, 7, 8, 4, 1, 2, 8, 7, 3

6, 8 (right, up), 5, 10, 9

2, 7, 8, 5, 9 (up, right), 2

After some trial and error and after gaining some understanding of the problem, we realize that the empty space created by moving the unit square blocks must be shaped as either a horizontal or vertical rectangle to allow the larger blocks to move. Thus, the small square blocks are more flexible when compared with the larger blocks, since they can be used to create space for the larger blocks, either in a horizontal or vertical direction. Furthermore, one of the key observations is that the horizontal block in the middle is obstructing the movement of the donkey block and the vertical blocks. Hence, it would be a good idea to move this block away from the middle to the side. Thus, one of the important subgoals of the problem would be to move the horizontal block toward a corner or a side, away from the middle, enabling free movement of the other blocks.

The following moves lead to the state shown [1] in Figure 36:

10 (halfway), 6, 5, 7 (down), 4, 9 (halfway), 7, 4 and 5

In this state, we are able to move block 5 to a side. After five more moves, block 5 moves a row down with the help of the small blocks as shown in Figure 37 and after move 21, block 5 is in the lowest row (Figure 38).

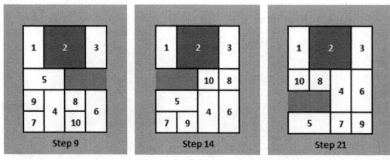

FIGURE 36 Step 9   **FIGURE 37** Step 14   **FIGURE 38** Step 21

We now have space to move the vertical blocks so block 2 can move laterally, as seen in Figure 39 after the 26th move. However, the small square blocks need to be adjacent to block 2 to help it move because the vertical blocks still restrict block 2's movement. The small square blocks are adjacent to the donkey block in Step 31 (Figure 40).

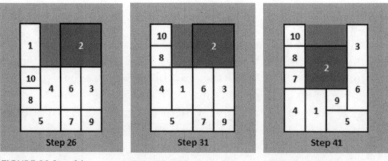

FIGURE 39 Step 26   **FIGURE 40** Step 31   **FIGURE 41** Step 41

By Step 41 (Figures 41 and 42), the horizontal block has moved to the bottom right corner, allowing vertical blocks 4 and 1 to move further down, making space for one of the two remaining unit square blocks to move up. It is very important to have one of the single unit square blocks remain at the bottom to avoid creating a unit square space, which can hinder movement of the larger blocks. With the three small square blocks on top, vertical blocks 4 and 1 can be moved to the left side so the donkey block can move a row down, as shown in Step 48 (Figure 43). An observation of the current state reveals that the donkey block is still constrained by the vertical blocks on both sides, and it is necessary to move them to the top to enable the donkey block to move freely farther down.

FIGURE 42 Step 41   **FIGURE 43** Step 48   **FIGURE 44** Step 52

Steps 48 to 71 concentrate on moving all the vertical blocks to the top, which is another important subgoal. This will clear the donkey block's path toward its goal at the bottom. After Step 48, the small blocks 8 and 10 can be arranged to create vertical space, enabling block 6 to move to the top. Then the donkey block can conveniently slide to its right to make space for the vertical blocks 1 and 4 to move to the top, as seen in Step 52 (Figure 44). At this point, block 10 can be moved back to the bottom. As seen in Step 60 onward (Figures 45 to 49), block 6 has to move down temporarily to get unit square blocks 7 and 8 down while the donkey block slides left.

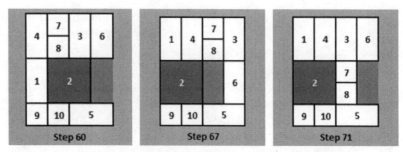

FIGURE 45 Step 60   **FIGURE 46** Step 67   **FIGURE 47** Step 71

With all four of the small square blocks adjacent to block 2 in Step 71, the donkey block can slide to the bottom row by displacing blocks 5, 9, and 10. The last step is achieved in the 81st move, when the donkey block moves right to the center.

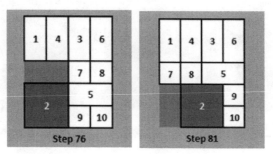

FIGURE 48 Step 76   **FIGURE 49** Step 81

6.2.1 Bidirectional Search

If we know the goal state, a bidirectional search is helpful by searching from both the initial state and the goal state to meet halfway when a solution path exists.

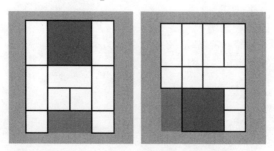

FIGURE 50 The Initial State   **FIGURE 51** The Goal State

The initial and goal states are shown in Figures 50 and 51, respectively. A careful observation of the goal state suggests that a significant milestone while working backward is when the donkey block is moved to the left and one row up, while the horizontal block moves to the bottom right. This is the state represented in Step 71 in the previous solution.

FIGURE 52 Subgoal 1 While Searching Backward from the Goal State

Moving back to the initial state, we can consider the state in Figure 52 as our intermediate goal state and work toward it. Thus, our new subgoal in our forward search is to move the donkey block and the horizontal block two rows below their current positions. The second of the two subgoals, if achieved optimally, can be done in 21 steps, as shown in Figure 52. Thus, the search technique of mean-ends analysis can be used to reduce the difference between the current state and the goal state [4, 5]. Kose (2012) solved the *Klotski* puzzle using the bidirectional search in 116 moves [6].

6.3 HUMAN PROBLEM SOLVING

This problem is too complex to be solved in 20 minutes, especially without any simulation tool like an actual game or a playable program. Therefore, some of the solutions available online were studied instead of the ones done by a class of students. From our experience with this problem, the puzzle is very difficult, and without a strategy, one gets stuck at dead ends, resulting in a fair amount of backtracking.

The solution studied in Section 6.2 divides the problem into several subgoals:

- Moving the horizontal block to the bottom to make space for the donkey block to move to the center

- Moving the small square blocks to the top to help move the vertical blocks out of the donkey block's pathway to the center

- Moving all the vertical blocks to the top once the donkey block is in the center

6.4 HUMAN WINDOW ANALYSIS OF SOLUTIONS

Although The Red Donkey Puzzle was once extremely popular, we were unable to find many solutions for our analysis. The solutions we have found, however, are very similar to one another.

When analyzing Table 11 that the solutions are all ranked similarly to one another in almost all fields. This is because, as the rankings for flexibility will show you, there are only so many ways The Red Donkey Puzzle can be represented. This is because the puzzle has fixed block sizes and shapes, which are key features that every representation must have.

From Table 11, we can see that each solution is represented extensionally. This is because they each use images of the actual puzzle and show every block movement made to achieve the end state. For a problem as difficult as The Red Donkey Puzzle, it is better to show the actual puzzle instead of describing the solution using words. As a result, the extensionality and executability of each solution are relatively the same, and they each use the same problem-solving technique of visual representation.

The attribute with the biggest difference in ranking is comprehensibility. While each solution uses the same representation, they all contain additional properties that set them apart from one another including block colors, numbering, and pictures. Therefore, the comprehensibility of a solution may be a definitive factor as to whether or not it should be considered MHWC.

Difficulty
9/10

Complexity
$O(b^{1/2})$

Name	Int or Ext?	Intly/ Extly	Rep.	HW?	Corr?	Grn Sz	Exec	Compr	Prob. Solv. Mthd	Flex	Mode of Conv	Opt?	Total
Donkey	Ext.	6/10	Pics	Y	Y	Ideal	9/10	9/10	Vis. Rep.; Subgoal	7/10	Img Mkr	Y	31/40
Gnome	Ext.	7/10	Pics	Y	Y	Ideal	9/10	5/10	Vis. Rep.; Subgoal	5/10	Img Mkr	Y	26/40
Hollow	Ext.	5/10	Pics	Y	Y	Ideal	8/10	4/10	Vis. Rep.; Subgoal	5/10	Img Mkr; Hand	N	22/40
Klajok	Ext.	7/10	Pics	Y	Y	Ideal	9/10	6/10	Vis. Rep.; Subgoal	5/10	Img Mkr	Y	27/40
Neon	Ext.	9/10	Pics	Y	Y	Ideal	9/10	8/10	Vis. Rep.; Subgoal	5/10	Img Mkr	Y	31/40

Key

Int or Ext?: Intensional or Extensional—Is the solution intensional or extensional?

Intly/Extly: Intensionality/Extensionality—How intensional or extensional is the solution?

Rep.: Representation—How is the solution represented?

HW?: Human Window—Does the solution exist in the Human Window?

Corr?: Correctness—Is the solution correct?

Grn Sz: Grain Size—How much computation (large) or memory (small) does one need to solve the solution?

Exec: Executability—How executable is this solution?

Compr: Comprehensibility—How comprehensible is this solution?

Prob. Solv. Mthd: Problem-Solving Method—What method is used in the solution to solve the problem?

Flex: Flexibility—How flexible is this solution (i.e., can this solution be represented in other ways)?

Mode of Conv: Mode of Conveyance—In what ways can this solution be reproduced/replicated?

Opt?: Optimal—Is the solution optimal?

TABLE 11 Ranking The Red Donkey Puzzle Solutions According to the Human Window

6.4.1 The Most Human Window–Compatible Solution

The solution we consider the MHWC is the "Donkey Solution" (Figure 53). An example of this type of representation can be found in [7]. Instead of showing each of the 81 steps, it has been shortened, displaying only the important subgoals. This solution has many qualities that make it highly comprehensible. Each tile is represented with a different shading and number, making them easily distinguishable from one another. This applies especially to the donkey piece, which has an actual image of a donkey on it. Additionally, above each image in the solution is a number that represents its corresponding step number. Finally, the quality that greatly increases the overall comprehensibility is the inclusion of the arrows. The arrows indicate which tile was moved from the previous state to get to the current state and in how many units it moved. This prevents the need to compare pictures for two consecutive steps to determine which tile has been moved. The picture of the current step can simply be viewed, and the arrangement of the previous step can be determined by it.

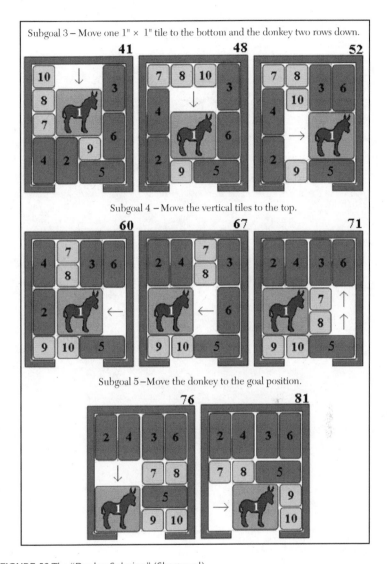

FIGURE 53 The "Donkey Solution" (Shortened)

6.4.2 The Least Human Window–Compatible Solution

The solution that was assessed as LHWC is the "Hollow Solution" (Figure 54). When analyzing this solution, it can be seen that the images that represent the puzzle are simply thin black lines that are put together in such a way as to make an image of the puzzle, including the tiles and the border. Although the tiles and border are spaced out efficiently enough to differentiate themselves from one other, the fact that all the tiles look almost the same can make them indistinguishable from one another, possibly reducing the comprehensibility of the solution. This applies especially when trying to identify the tiles that were moved from a previous step to achieve the arrangement of the current step. Additionally, the background color is the same as the tile color. This produces the effect that the tiles are hollow and can make the image look like a cluster of thin black lines, thus making the puzzle components even more indistinguishable from one another.

Initial State

Subgoal 1–Move the horizontal piece to the bottom.

FIGURE 54 The "Hollow Solution" (Shortened)

6.5 BEST MACHINE SOLUTION

Currently, no special heuristics can be used to solve The Red Donkey Puzzle. Similarly, there are no known algorithms that can solve the puzzle in the smallest number of possible steps. However, the two best-known solutions to solving the puzzle are the bidirectional search [6] and the simple breadth-first search.

The Red Donkey Puzzle has a relatively large state space, consisting of 25,955 possible block arrangements, along with 47,151 possible moves [8]. When analyzing these values in terms of a tree structure, the possible tile arrangements can be seen as the tree's nodes, while the tile movements can be seen as the arcs. Since The Red Donkey Puzzle can have a maximum of three possible moves per tile arrangement, the branching factor of the tree produced by a search is very small. However, given the large number of possible moves and tile arrangements, the depth produced can become quite large.

In his paper "Solving Klotski," Karl Wiberg shows the benefits of using the breadth-first search to solve The Red Donkey Puzzle. Just like any implementation of the breadth-first search, it analyzes every node in a specific depth k of the tree before analyzing every node in depth $k + 1$ in the tree. This search can find the solution in 116 steps [9].

Another, more sophisticated, search method that can be used to solve The Red Donkey Puzzle is the bidirectional search, which Erdal Kose developed. Interestingly enough, this search was able to find the solution in 116 steps, just like the breadth-first search [6]. However, this search is more sophisticated because it greatly reduces the number of nodes needed to be visited and expanded. This is because both ends of the search start with a parent node and meet each other at a common middle step (see Section 6.2).

Since solutions are found efficiently through the use of search algorithms, the complexity of The Red Donkey Puzzle can be evaluated in terms of a search tree. In the worst case, the runtime and space needed for the breadth-first search is $O(b^d)$, where b is the branching factor and d is the depth of the tree. For the bidirectional search, however, the runtime and space needed is $O(b^{d/2})$ [6]. This shows that the bidirectional search is more efficient than the breadth-first search, even though they find the solution in the same number of steps.

6.6 RELATED PROBLEMS

The same puzzle with different names and images on the pieces are available in different countries with a different name. However, these are basically one and the same game. On a different note, diverse versions of sliding block puzzles where there is a trapped piece(s) and the task is to transfer a block to a designated area of the puzzle, are related to this problem. There are many different versions of these types of games offered on the app store of most phones. Do note that these trapped pieces vary in sizes when compared to the original Red Donkey Puzzle. These can be found on apps developed for mobile platforms.

6.7 PLAYABLE PROGRAM

Many playable programs for The Red Donkey Puzzle are available online, where you can play the puzzle, become familiar with the problem, and learn to differentiate between good and bad moves.

It would be extremely difficult to memorize all the movements, so you would have to draw all the moves on a piece of paper. However, drawing the search tree can be difficult and tedious and would require a lot of space. This is why being able to solve the puzzle on a computer is preferable. Physical puzzles, such as those made of cardboard or wooden blocks, and virtual puzzles, such as games on a computer or a smart phone, are only some examples. These are the most extensional forms of representation of the problem, as the problem solver can physically or virtually manipulate the problem states. An online game can be found at *http://www.bsswebsite.me.uk/Puzzlewebsite/Reddonkey-puzzle/Reddonkeypuzzle.htm.*

6.8 REFERENCES

1. Gardener, M. (1964). "Mathematical Games." *Scientific American*, March: 133.

2. Brandeis. (2013). *Red Donkey.* Available at *http://www.cs.brandeis. edu/~storer/JimPuzzles/ZPAGES/zzzRedDonkey.html.* Accessed on January 8, 2014.

3. Bsswebsite. (2013). *Red Donkey Puzzle.* Available at *http://www.bss-website.me.uk/Puzzlewebsite/Reddonkeypuzzle/Reddonkeypuzzle. htm.* Accessed on January 8, 2014.

4. Sweller, J. (1988). "Cognitive Load During Problem Solving: Effects on Learning." *Cognitive Science* 12: 257–285.

5. Newell, A., and Simon, H.A. (1972). *Human Problem Solving.* Englewood Cliffs, NJ: Prentice-Hall.

6. Kose, E. (2012). *Comparing AI Search Algorithms and Their Efficiency When Applied to Path Finding Problems.* Ph.D. Thesis. New York, NY: CUNY, The Graduate Center, Department of Computer Science.

7. Whiting, R. (2009). *Red Donkey.* Available at *http://home.comcast. net/~l-whiting/attbi/Donkey_solution.html.* Accessed on January 8, 2014.

8. Blazewicz, D. (2011). *Red Donkey.* Available at *https://sites.google. com/site/klajok/klotski/huarong-trail/red-donkey.* Accessed on January 8, 2014.

9. Wiberg, K. (2009). *Solving Klotski.* Available at *http://www.treskal. com/kalle/klotski.pdf.* Accessed on January 8, 2014.

CHAPTER 7

THE 15 PUZZLE

FIGURE 55 The 15 Puzzle

7.1 BACKGROUND

The 15 Puzzle (Figure 55) was invented by Noyes Chapman, a postmaster who resided in Canastota, New York [1]. It is another example of a sliding block puzzle. However, unlike The Red Donkey Puzzle, which consists of different-sized tiles, The 15 Puzzle's tiles are all square and are the same size. Today, it is currently known as the earliest sliding puzzle created.

In 1874, Chapman developed a puzzle that involved "16 numbered blocks that were to be put together in rows of four." The goal of the puzzle was to arrange these blocks so the numbers on a row of blocks added up to 34. In 1879, a new and improved version of The 15 Puzzle spread throughout the United States after Chapman's son introduced the puzzle [1]. Eventually, the puzzle was popular all over the United States, and by 1880, it had spurred a puzzle craze. The puzzle eventually made its way to Canada and then to Europe. By July 1880, however, its popularity had begun to wane [2].

At one point Chapman unsuccessfully attempted to patent the puzzle. This is most likely because it was too similar to Ernest Kinsey's "Puzzle-Blocks" which was patented in 1878 [1].

The invention of The 15 Puzzle is often incorrectly accredited to American chess player, chess composer, and recreational mathematician Samuel Lloyd. Until his death, Lloyd insisted that he had invented the puzzle in 1891, and at one point, he revived its popularity when he introduced The 14-15 Puzzle, which was very similar, except two of the tiles were switched (see Section 7.2). However, despite these claims, it was in fact Chapman who invented The 15 Puzzle [1].

The 15 Puzzle consists of 15 square tiles numbered 1 to 15, bounded in a closed 4" × 4" area. The 15 tiles fill up 15 of the spaces in the area, while the 16th space is left empty so each tile has limited space to move. The goal is to reposition the squares so they are placed in numerical order by row.

7.2 PROBLEM-SOLVING TECHNIQUES

Unlike the problems we have analyzed so far, The 15 Puzzle does not have a specific predefined initial setup. Therefore, any arrangement of the tiles, including the goal arrangement, can be considered an initial state.

There are 16! * (2.09×10^{13}) arrangements in which the tiles can be placed. However, according to a study by Woosly Johnson and William Story, there are only 16!/2 possible positions in which the goal setup can actually be achieved. In 1879, Johnson and Story researched The 15 Puzzle and discovered that all puzzles with arrangements of even parity are solvable, whereas those of odd parity are not [3]. That is, if the number of tile interchanges (or permutations) needed to transform a particular arrangement into a solvable arrangement is even, then that particular arrangement itself is solvable. If it is odd, it is unsolvable. More than a decade after this discovery, Sam Lloyd presented a variation of the problem to the public that involved solving The 15 Puzzle where the tiles numbered 14 and 15 are switched. This was called The 14-15 Puzzle. Since this consists of one interchange, it is of odd parity, and therefore it is unsolvable [4].

Although the number of possible positions is lower than expected, 16!/2 (1.05 × 10¹³) possible initial tile arrangements is still a lot! However, finding the solution to The 15 Puzzle can be very straightforward. The most valuable problem-solving technique to use is solving subgoals. The subgoal is to achieve a completed row, and once that is accomplished, one can go on to the next step. However, as you will see (in Section 7.3), there are special situations, such as solving the fourth row, in which the completed third row must be *uprooted*.

Generally speaking, The 15 Puzzle is a type of n puzzle, with the value n representing an integer greater than 1. The rules and goal of any n puzzle are the same as The 15 Puzzle. The only difference is that it consists of n square tiles numbered from 1 to n placed in a closed $sqrt(n+1) \times sqrt(n+1)$ area, with the nth location left as an empty tile space. However, no matter how big the problem, the same problem-solving technique can be used. It may just take more moves to complete. In this book, we perform our analysis solely on The 15 Puzzle.

7.3 SOLUTION

A very common solution to The 15 Puzzle involves focusing on and solving individual tiles one by one in numeric order. Doing so will not only solve the puzzle in an orderly fashion, but it will also make it possible to solve for subgoals, as mentioned in Section 7.2. Specifically, a subgoal is the completion of a row. With the exception of the final step, once a row is solved, none of the tiles in the row need to be moved again.

Since there are so many possible initial tile arrangements, this solution will show general ways to solve each tile and therefore will not be based on an initial arrangement.

7.3.1 Solving the First Row

The first step is to move the 1 tile to the upper left corner of the board. This is a relatively simple step to achieve. Since the other tiles have not been properly positioned, it does not matter how they are moved as long as the 1 tile is placed in its correct position. Let's say the puzzle is arranged like in Figure 56.

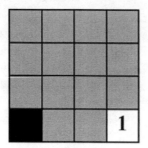

FIGURE 56 Initial State

The black square represents the empty tile space, and the gray squares represent tiles that we will not consider at this point.

First, arrange the tiles so the empty space is near the 1 tile (Figure 57).

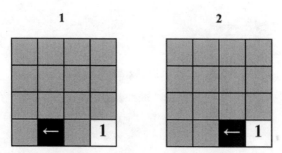

FIGURE 57 Move the Empty Space to the 1 Tile

Now, move the 1 tile to the upper left corner (Figure 58).

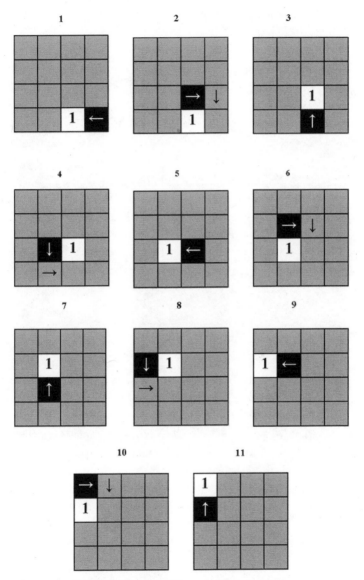

FIGURE 58 Move the 1 Tile to the Upper Left Corner

Basically, the general idea behind moving a target tile is to move all temporarily disregarded tiles around it until the empty space is in the general direction of the correct position relative to the target tile. Then use that empty space to move the target tile toward its goal position. Continue this until the target tile is in the correct position.

Figure 58 shows the general idea behind moving a tile throughout the board. From now on, future diagrams will only show moves that are significant to positioning a specific tile. To refresh yourself on how to move a tile around the board, refer back to Figure 58.

Next, we move the 4 tile to the upper right corner of the puzzle board. Just as we did with the 1 tile, this tile can be easily positioned by simply moving the temporarily disregarded tiles around. Position it as shown in Figure 59.

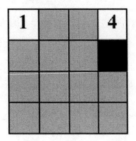

FIGURE 59 The 4 Tile Positioned

Now we position the 2 tile to the right of the 4 tile. Although the 4 and 2 tile positions are very close to each other, the 4 tile does not need to be disturbed from its correct position in order to position the 2 tile next to it. This can be done by moving the 2 tile and the empty spot to any position in the center "square" located in between the 1 and 4 tiles. For example, a sufficient tile arrangement would be as shown in Figure 60.

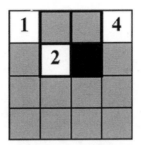

FIGURE 60 The Center "Square"

The center "square" we are referring to is indicated by the bolded borders. Now simply perform the movements in Figure 61.

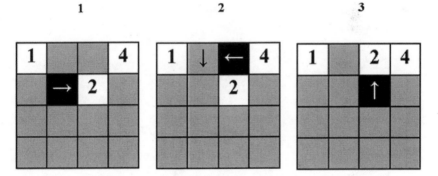

FIGURE 61 Positioning the 2 Tile

At this point, you have probably noticed that we have not placed the 2 tile in its correct position. However, temporarily placing it here will allow us to easily position the 3 tile.

Now, arrange the 3 tile and empty slot so they are in the positions shown in Figure 62.

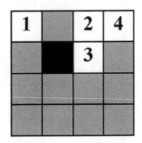

FIGURE 62 3 Tile Preferred Position

This should be very easy, since the 1, 2, or 4 tiles do not have to be moved to reach this state. Now perform the moves in Figure 63.

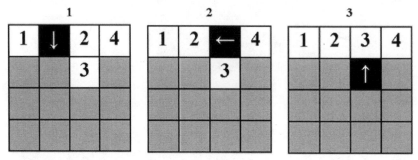

FIGURE 63 Positioning the 3 Tile

7.3.2 The Corner Technique

After positioning the 2 tile, the first row might look like Figure 64.

FIGURE 64 3 Tile Special Case

In this arrangement, the technique used in Figure 63 cannot be used. Instead, make sure the empty spot is located underneath the 2 tile and perform the moves in Figure 65.

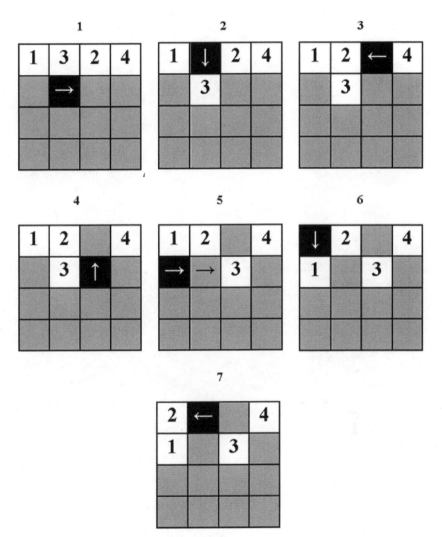

FIGURE 65 Positioning the 3 Tile (Special Case)

Now rotate the tiles in the "square" so they are arranged as in Figure 66.

FIGURE 66 1 and 2 Tiles Over the Corner

Then, reposition tiles 1 and 2 back in place, as in Figure 67.

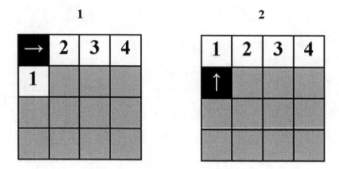

FIGURE 67 Reposition the 1 and 2 Tiles

We have now completed what we call the corner technique. It is named this due to the fact that we moved the 1 and 2 tiles over the corner of the board in order to create room for the 3 tile to move into position. This technique will be used again to complete row 4.

So now we have completed the first row. Furthermore, none of the tiles in the top row need to be moved again and will remain in place for the remainder of the solution.

7.3.3 Solving the Second Row

The next goal is to solve the second row. To do so, follow the same techniques that were used to solve the first row. Move the 5 tile to the upper left, the 8 tile to the upper right, the 6 tile to the left of the 8 tile, and use the same techniques that were used to solve the 3 tile to solve the 7 tile (Section 7.3.1 and Section 7.3.2). If done correctly the puzzle should look like Figure 68.

1	2	3	4
5	6	7	8
		■	

FIGURE 68 Row 2 Solved

At this point, the tiles in the second row do not need to be repositioned again. We are now halfway done, leaving us with two more rows to solve. As you can see, the amount of space is being reduced, and there is less room to move tiles. Positioning the last seven tiles will be a little trickier.

7.3.4 Solving the Third Row

Moving on, the next goal is to solve the third row. First, move the 9 tile to the leftmost position, and then move the 12 tile to the rightmost position, as in Figure 69.

1	2	3	4
5	6	7	8
9		■	12

FIGURE 69 Position the 9 and 12 Tiles

Next, we position both the 10 and 11 tiles simultaneously. To do this, it is important that the 10 and 11 tiles and the empty slot are located in the center square. Figure 70 shows a possible arrangement.

FIGURE 70 Acceptable Center "Square"

If this were the case, simply rotating the tiles in the "square" twice would complete the third row. However, this will certainly not always be the case. For example, you may have a position like the one in Figure 71.

FIGURE 71 Tile Positioned Badly

Notice how we have the empty space below the 9 tile. This would be acceptable if one of the temporarily disregarded tiles was to the right of it, but unfortunately that is not the case. With this arrangement, it would be impossible to solve the puzzle without moving the 9 tile. Follow the steps in Figure 72.

FIGURE 72 Moving the 9 Tile

Now, rotate the tiles in the center square so one of the temporarily disregarded tiles is next to the 9 tile and the empty slot is above it, as shown in Figure 73.

1	2	3	4
5	6	7	8
11		10	12
9			

FIGURE 73 Rotate the Center "Square"

Then perform the moves in Figure 74.

1

1	2	3	4
5	6	7	8
→	11	10	12
9			

2

1	2	3	4
5	6	7	8
9	11	10	12
↑			

3

1	2	3	4
5	6	7	8
9	11	10	12
	←		

FIGURE 74 Obtaining the Sufficient Center "Square"

Now we have obtained our requirement. Similarly, if the empty slot began under the 12 tile, perform a reflection of the above moves on the right side of the puzzle. Basically, it is vital that the 9 and 12 tiles have temporarily disregarded tiles underneath them to complete the third row.

As you can see, it is also possible that the 10 and 11 tiles are inconveniently placed occupying each other's target positions. Does this look familiar? Simply use the "corner technique" to properly position them. If done correctly the third row will be complete, as shown in Figure 75.

1	2	3	4
5	6	7	8
9	10	11	12

FIGURE 75 Third Row Complete

7.3.5 Solving the Fourth Row

We have only one row to deal with. At this point, the puzzle is either solved or positioned incorrectly, as in Figure 76.

1	2	3	4
5	6	7	8
9	10	11	12
	15	13	14

FIGURE 76 Incorrect Last Row

Let us assume the tiles in the last row are positioned incorrectly. Until this point, we have followed a basic strategy that prevented the need to displace any tiles that belong to a completed row. To proceed in finding the solution, that rule must be broken. To deal with this arrangement, we begin by once again using the corner technique. First move the 9 and 10 tiles so they are aligned vertically to each other. This involves moving the 9 tile into the last row and moving the 10 tile into the position where the 9 tile should be (Figure 77).

1	2	3	4
5	6	7	8
10	■	11	12
9	15	13	14

FIGURE 77 Shifted 9 and 10 Tiles

Then do the same to the 11 and 12 tiles (Figure 78).

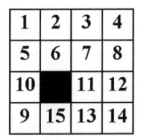

1

1	2	3	4
5	6	7	8
10	15	11	12
9	↑	13	14

2

1	2	3	4
5	6	7	8
10	15	11	12
9	13	14	←

3

1	2	3	4
5	6	7	8
10	15	→	11
9	13	14	12

FIGURE 78 Shifting the 11 and 12 Tiles

At this point, the tiles in the center "square" should only be those that belong to the final row (i.e., 13, 14, and 15). Arrange them as in Figure 79.

1	2	3	4
5	6	7	8
10	13	■	11
9	14	15	12

FIGURE 79 Rotate the Center "Square" Tiles

Finally, perform the moves in Figure 80.

1

1	2	3	4
5	6	7	8
10	13	11	12
9	14	15	↑

2

1	2	3	4
5	6	7	8
10	↓	11	12
9	13	14	15

3

1	2	3	4
5	6	7	8
9	10	11	12
↑	13	14	15

4

1	2	3	4
5	6	7	8
9	10	11	12
13	14	15	←

FIGURE 80 Solving the Last Row

At last, the puzzle is solved!

7.4 HUMAN WINDOW ANALYSIS OF SOLUTIONS

Like The Red Donkey Puzzle, we have not found many solutions for our Human Window analysis of The 15 Puzzle. Additionally, the majority of them are identical to the solution discussed in Section 7.3 and to one another. Therefore, they each use similar problem-solving methods and representations. Each solution demonstrates a general method in which descriptions are used, along with visual images as guidance, to solve The 15 Puzzle regardless of its initial arrangement. Therefore, the solutions can be considered intensional because of this generality. However, they are ranked relatively low on their intensionality because they are partially extensional (i.e., diagrams).

When analyzing the solutions' rankings for comprehensibility and executability (Table 12), we can see that they are generally mixed. Therefore, it is the features that affect these ranking categories that determine which solution should be considered the MHWC.

The only intensional solution that uses a somewhat different technique than the others is the "In-Place Solution." The subgoals required to solve it are the same, except that it guarantees that no tile that reaches its correct position will move again [5].

Finally, the only solution classified as extensional is the "Optimal Solution." which is discussed further in Section 7.4.2

Difficulty												
4/10												

Complexity												
$O(b^{d2})$												

Name	Int or Ext?	Intly/ Extly	Rep.	HW?	Corr?	Grn Sz	Exec	Compr	Prob. Solv. Mthd	Flex	Mode of Conv	Opt?	Total
In-Place	Int.	3/10	Descr. w/ Vis.	Y	Y w/ Cycles	Small	5/10	7/10	Sub-goals	7/10	Txt Editor; Img Maker; Hand	N	22/40
Jurgen	Int.	4/10	Descr. w/ Vis.	Y	Y	Ideal	4/10	6/10	Vis. Repr; Sub-goals	8/10	Txt Editor; Img Maker; Hand	N	22/40
Optimal	Ext.	3/10	Text	Y	Y	Ideal	9/10	5/10	Vis. Repr.	9/10	Txt Editor; Hand	Y	26/40
Real	Int.	9/10	Descr. w/ Vis.	Y	Y	Ideal	9/10	7/10	Vis. Repr; Sub-goals	7/10	Txt Editor; Img Maker; Hand	N	32/40
Tile	Int.	5/10	Descr. w/ Vis.	Y	Y	Ideal	10/10	9/10	Vis. Repr; Sub-goals	7/10	Txt Editor; Img Maker; Hand	N	33/40
W-how	Int.	5/10	Descr. w/ Vis.	Y	Y	Ideal	6/10	8/10	Vis. Repr; Sub-goals	7/10	Txt Editor; Img Maker	Y	26/40

Key

Int or Ext?: Intensional or Extensional—Is the solution intensional or extensional?

Intly/Extly: Intensionality/Extensionality—How intensional or extensional is the solution?

Rep.: Representation—How is the solution represented?

HW?: Human Window—Does the solution exist in the Human Window?

Corr?: Correctness—Is the solution correct?

Grn Sz: Grain Size—How much computation (large) or memory (small) does one need to solve the solution?

Exec: Executability—How executable is this solution?

Compr: Comprehensibility—How comprehensible is this solution?

Prob. Solv. Mthd: Problem-Solving Method—What method is used in the solution to solve the problem?

Flex: Flexibility—How flexible is this solution (i.e., can this solution be represented in other ways)?

Mode of Conv: Mode of Conveyance—In what ways can this solution be reproduced/replicated?

Opt?: Optimal—Is the solution optimal?

TABLE 12 Ranking The 15 Puzzle Solutions According to the Human Window

7.4.1 The Most Human Window–Compatible Solution

The solution considered the MHWC is the "Tile Solution," which is the same as the one in Section 7.3. It provides a step-by-step method on how to solve The 15 Puzzle with any initial arrangement. At each step, a simple description is given on what tiles to move and how to do it. Provided at each step is a picture of the puzzle itself, which contain tiles that are either shaded or numbered. The tiles that are shaded are unimportant at a particular step and can be ignored, while the numbered tiles are important or have been correctly placed. These images are used to show what the puzzle would look like after the execution of each step. Finally, arrows are used to show how certain tiles were moved at a step. These brief, but to the point, directions, along with the images, make the solution very comprehensible and executable.

To improve this solution even further, actual images of the puzzle can be used instead of a grid or a table. This will make the solution even more extensional. A solution that uses this approach is the "Real-Puzzle Solution" [6].

7.4.2 The Least Human Window–Compatible Solution

The solution assessed as the LHWC is the "Optimal Solution" (Figure 81). A representation similar to this was developed by B. MacKenzie [7]. It is referred to as such because it demonstrates how to solve The 15 Puzzle in the least number of possible steps. Optimal solutions may be feasible for machines by clever or precise algorithms, but for people, finding optimal solutions to nontrivial problems is usually very difficult, if not impossible.

Finding an optimal solution to The 15 Puzzle depends on the initial arrangement of the tiles. Of all 16!/2 possible initial tile arrangements, only 16 can be solved in 43 steps with multi-tile movements, which is considered optimal. Otherwise, the minimal number of single-tile moves required to solve the puzzle can average at around 80 steps [7]. However, as we have seen, optimal solutions will generally have little to do with the Human Window. Although this solution demonstrates a very efficient method in solving The 15 Puzzle in the least number of steps, we will only be analyzing the solution's representation.

This section analyzes 1 of the 16 possible arrangements that can be solved in 43 steps, which is optimal for The 15 Puzzle. This solution can be considered the LHWC for many reasons. One is because of its representation. Everything in this solution is in text, including the puzzle itself. The puzzle is represented as a collection of numbers that indicate the tiles. They are organized in such a way as to represent the actual puzzle (i.e., there are four rows and four numbers to a row). However, this may not be as comprehensible as an actual image of the puzzle itself.

Another reason this can be the LHWC is because of the way the steps are carried out. Each step consists of a letter and a number. The letter represents the direction in which the tiles should be moved relative to the empty space, and the number represents the number of tiles that must move in that direction. For example, "U2" means the first two tiles that are underneath the current empty space must move up into that space. This representation can be confusing, especially since there are no representations of the puzzle that correspond to each step. As a result, a person would most likely not be able to determine which step to backtrack to if he or she made a mistake and would have to start over.

Finally, it can be considered LHWC because this solution is extensional. For this solution, all the steps that solve this puzzle from beginning to end are shown, so it is classified as extensional. While the solution is very executable (since it provides the steps to solve an entire puzzle arrangement), this is a solution to only one specific tile arrangement. If a person were to attempt to solve The 15 Puzzle with a different arrangement, he or she may not have the required knowledge to do so.

The solution:

1	5	9	13
2	6	10	14
3	7	11	15
4	8	12	X

X = vacant position (empty tile space)

Moves (direction of X):

1. L1	11. R1	21. R3	31. R2	41. R2
2. U1	12. U1	22. D1	32. U1	42. D2
3. R1	13. R2	23. L3	33. R1	43. R1
4. U2	14. U1	24. D1	34. D2	
5. L3	15. L3	25. R2	35. L3	
6. D3	16. D1	26. U2	36. U1	
7. R2	17. R3	27. L1	37. R3	
8. U2	18. U1	28. D3	38. D2	
9. L2	19. L3	29. L1	39. L3	
10. D2	20. U1	30. U2	40. U2	

Key:

L = left

R = right

U = up

D = down

FIGURE 81 The "Optimal Solution"

7.5 BEST MACHINE SOLUTION

In the field of Artificial Intelligence, solutions to The 15 Puzzle, and the n puzzle in general, are usually modeled and studied with the application of search algorithms aided by heuristics. Although simple searches such as the breadth-first search would be able to find an optimal solution to The 15 Puzzle, the amount of space and time required to search every possible arrangement is incredibly large, even with the bidirectional search. Therefore, it is best to employ searches that use heuristics as a guide and to limit bad choices.

Heuristics give the search algorithm an estimate as to where the goal may be, greatly reducing the number of puzzle positions that need to be searched. The most commonly used search to find an optimal solution to The 15 Puzzle is the **A* search** equipped with an **admissible heuristic**. The A* Search combines the **uniform cost search**, which measures the number of steps it takes to reach a specific puzzle arrangement from the initial arrangement, with an admissible heuristic, which prevents the search from overestimating the goal [8]. These two properties, if practically operative, enable the A* search to find an optimal solution.

The A* search can use several admissible heuristics to solve The 15 Puzzle. One is the **best-first heuristic**, which maintains an open node queue and pursues the node at the front of the queue first but retains in memory the other nodes on the queue to pursue other possible paths [9]. Another is the **Manhattan distance heuristic**, which uses taxicab geometry to measure how far a specific tile is from its goal position. These heuristics, however, are slow and may still generate too many states, consuming a lot of memory [8, 9]. One solution to this problem is the use of the **iterative-deepening-A* search**. This search reduces the number of nodes normally searched by the A* search, thus reducing the need for space [8]. This search, however, is still slow.

Another, and better, heuristic that can be used is a **disjoint pattern database heuristic.** This works by finding the sum of the "number of needed moves to well order tiles" in a pattern of a given data structure. This structure is a priority minimum queue combined with a hash table. With this heuristic, fewer than 100,000 nodes are expanded, and any 15 Puzzle arrangement can be solved in less than 10 seconds [8].

Like The Red Donkey Puzzle, the worst-case runtime and space required to solve any arrangement of the puzzle is in the order of $O(b^{d/2})$ when using a bidirectional search. Given that the number of tiles that can move is limited, the branching factor is small. However, given the high number of possible arrangements, the depth can become very large. Fortunately, since the A° search with the disjoint pattern database heuristic greatly reduces the number of nodes expanded, a solution can be found with a complexity less than that of $O(b^{d/2})$.

For the general n puzzle, finding a solution to a legal tile arrangement can be done in polynomial time. However, the problem of always finding an optimal solution to a particular arrangement is **NP-Hard** [10].

7.6 RELATED PROBLEMS

Some problems related to the Fifteen Puzzle are ones that require a different ordering of the numbers 1-15, such as ordering according to columns or reversing the order. However, the basic solution is unchanged in these situations where getting the number 1 in the correct place first, followed by two and the remaining numbers. Some other similar problems are ones that has a different size than the 15 puzzle, such as the Eight Puzzle on a 3x3 board. These can be found on apps developed for mobile platforms since they fall into a classic puzzle genre that has immense popularity.

One popular usage of Fifteen Puzzle is to use it to test the efficiency of heuristic search algorithms. It has proven to be a good standard benchmark for evaluating heuristic search algorithms due to its well-understood properties [11]. To solve the Fifteen Puzzle, the distance of a tile from its initial state to its desired state is calculated. This distance is called the Manhattan Distance heuristic. The distance is calculated by the number of moves required by a tile to move horizontally and vertically, to reach its destination. Heuristic search algorithms calculate this number and choose the move with the smallest number of moves required for each tile to get into the desired state. A set of Fifteen Puzzles called the "Korf 100 Set" are used to test the algorithms due to it being the first set to be used for demonstration purposes. It has been used over and over again in subsequent similar tests performed by other algorithms researchers [11].

The fastest heuristic algorithm written in C++ could solve all the Fifteen Puzzles in the set in about 540 seconds and required a total of 27GB of memory [11]. Since The Fifteen Puzzle can easily be understood by all, it is a very effective tool to be used to test out a heuristic algorithm.

7.7 PLAYABLE PROGRAM

A playable 15 Puzzle game is available at *http://migo.sixbit. org/puzzles/fifteen/*. With a simple click, the player can move the tiles around into the empty space. Additionally, the player can perform multi-tile moves as well. Finally, there is an option to attempt the 14-15 Puzzle if you so choose. Good luck with that!

7.8 REFERENCES

1. Slocum J., and Sonneveld, D. (2006). *The 15 Puzzle*. Beverly Hills, CA: Slocum Puzzle Foundation

2. Slocum, J., and Weisstein, E.W. (2013)*15 Puzzle*. Available at *http://mathworld.wolfram.com/15Puzzle.html*. Accessed on January 9, 2014.

3. Johnson, W.W., and Story, W.E. (1879). "Notes on the '15' Puzzle." *American Journal of Mathematics* 2 (4): 397–404.

4. Grant, H. (2002). *The Fifteen Puzzle*. Available at *http://www.math. ubc.ca/~cass/courses/m308-02b/projects/grant/fifteen.html*. Accessed on January 9, 2014.

5. Yates, J. (2013). *Fifteen Puzzle Solution: How to Solve the Famous 15 Puzzle*. Available at *http://www.chessandpoker.com/fifteen-puzzle-solution.html*. Accessed on January 9, 2014.

6. Schmidt, W. (2013). *Wayne Schmidt's 15-Puzzle Solving Page.* Available at *http://www.waynesthisandthat.com/15puzzle.htm.* Accessed on January 9, 2014.

7. Norskog, B. (2013). The Fifteen Puzzle Can Be Solved in 43 'Moves.'" Available at *http://cubezzz.dyndns.org/drupal/?q=node/view/223.* Accessed on January 9, 2014.

8. Chiang, K-Y. (2013). *Finding Optimal Solution of 15 Puzzle.* Available at *http://www.cs.utexas.edu/~kychiang/files/Finding_Optimal_Solution_of_15_puzzle.ppt.* Accessed on January 9, 2014.

9. Lucci, S., and Kopec, D. (2013). *Artificial Intelligence in the 21st Century.* Dulles, Virginia: Mercury Learning Inc.

10. Ratner, D., and Warmuth, M.K. (1986). *Finding a Shortest Solution for the N × N Extension of the 15-PUZZLE Is Intractable.* National Conference on Artificial Intelligence. Santa Cruz, CA: University of California Santa Cruz.

11. Hatem, M., Burns, E., Ruml, W. (2013). *Faster problem solving in Java with heuristic search.* "IBM developerWorks" Available at *http://www.ibm.com/developerworks/library/j-ai-search/.* Accessed on February 20, 2016.

CHAPTER 8

THE KNIGHT'S TOUR PROBLEM

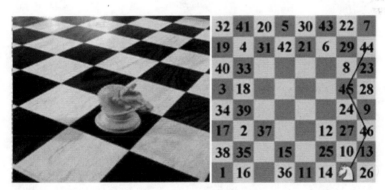

FIGURE 82 The Knight's Tour Problem

8.1 BACKGROUND

A *knight's tour* is a sequence of moves made by a chess knight, starting from any initial square on a chessboard (usually on the lower left corner), such that each square on the board is visited exactly once. While doing so, it must be taken into consideration that the knight is limited to the moves it would normally make on a chess board (i.e., the "L" shape).

The Knight's Tour Problem (Figure 82) entails finding the correct sequence of steps for the knight that will complete a knight's tour. The problem is normally solved on a standard 8" × 8" grid, similar to that of a standard chessboard. However, knight's tours have been studied on general $m \times n$ grids.

The concept of The Knight's Tour Problem dates back to around 2200 BC, but the earliest-known reference is around AD 900 in India. It was first introduced in a Sanskrit work on poetics titled *Kavyalankara*, by the Kashmirian poet Rudrata. In *Kavyalankara*, the pattern of The Knight's Tour was presented as an elaborate poetic figure called the *turagapadabandha*, which translates to "arrangement in the steps of a horse." The knight's tour was "apparently presented by a series of syllables on the squares that make sense when read in the sequence of the tour." The same verse in four lines of eight syllables can be read by following the path of the knight on tour, with each syllable being thought of as a square on a chessboard [1].

Over the years, The Knight's Tour Problem evolved as mathematicians began to take an interest. Leonhard Euler and H. C. Von Warnsdorff helped to develop notable solutions [2].

In general, there are two kinds of knight's tours. One is the open tour, which simply involves the knight visiting each square only once. The other is a closed (or reentrant) tour, which is like an open tour, except the knight must be able to go back to the square it started on after visiting all of the squares on the chessboard. This is a variation of a famous NP-Complete problem called The Hamiltonian Cycle Problem. The point is that for a given graph, it is impossible to determine apriori if a Hamiltonian Cycle of that graph (e.g., a closed knight's tour in this case) is possible.

Mathematician Allen Schwenk proposed a proven theorem that an $m \times n$ chessboard with $m \leq n$ has a closed knight's tour unless one or more of the following three conditions hold: m and n are both odd; $m = 1, 2,$ or 4; or $m = 3$ and $n = 4, 6,$ or 8 [3].

8.2 PROBLEM-SOLVING TECHNIQUES

Many solutions to The Knight's Tour Problem have been discovered on an 8" × 8" board with the use of several problem-solving techniques. One of them is *exhaustive enumeration*, but that would be very inefficient because an 8" × 8" board contains 4 × 10^{51} possible sequences. A more efficient problem-solving technique is *divide and conquer,* in which the chessboard is divided into smaller boards that are solved individually. The most efficient method is *solving subgoals,* and it is also the most commonly used technique. The solutions we have found use some of the more popular subgoal methods.

One method is a relatively straightforward method discovered by Abraham de Moivre. When starting at a corner square, the knight will first visit all of the squares around the edges of the board and then visit all of the remaining squares in the center. The heuristic is that at every choice point, the knight visits the square closest to the edge (i.e., the square with the smallest in-degree) first. A similar method is used in the solution presented in this chapter (see Section 8.3).

A second popular method is *square and diamonds.* This solution essentially divides the chessboard into four 4" × 4" subboards. In each of these subboards, four patterns are formed with the knight during the tour: a rhombus, a square, and a mirror image for each. This method is used in the "D&S Solution" [4].

A third method is *tessellation.* The basis of this method is to move the knight in a path that would trace the shapes of four polygons that, when combined together, form a tessellation. A tessellation is a group of shapes that can fit perfectly with one another on a plane without overlapping. With this method, the knight can start at any square on the board and form the polygon that the square is a part of. After completing that shape, the knight can simply move to another square that is a part of one of the other three polygons and travel along a path to trace its shape. The tour is complete after the knight traces the shapes of the four polygons. If done correctly, the tessellation method can create a closed tour. This method is used in the "Tessellation Solution," which was developed by Daniel E. Thomasson [5].

8.3 SOLUTION

This section presents a relatively simple solution, with steps and rules that are easy to follow and remember. It is based on the method developed by Abraham de Moivre, in which the knight travels on the outer edges of the chessboard. Using this method, we can still achieve a closed tour. However, there are specific points in the solution where the heuristic must be broken. This approach is similar to one developed by Andrew Joseph, a former student of Dr. Kopec's.

A closed knight's tour can be achieved by making the knight follow two general rules:

Rule 1: *Stick as close to the outer edges of the board as possible.*

Rule 2: *When the opportunity presents itself, corner squares must be taken.*

For this solution, our knight starts at the lower left corner of the board (Figure 83).

FIGURE 83 Initial State (Visiting Square 1)

The first general idea is to go in a spiral motion around the board, which is something the knight will be doing for most of the solution. We will start by traversing the outer squares of the board in a clockwise motion (Figures 84 and 85).

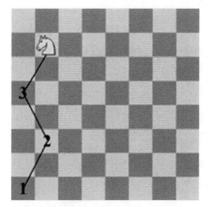

FIGURE 84 Visiting Squares 2–4

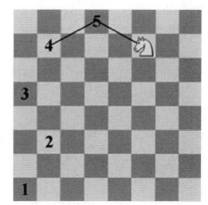

FIGURE 85 Visiting Squares 5 and 6

At this point, we have the opportunity to move into the upper right-hand corner of the chessboard. We will use this opportunity and have the knight move there (Figure 86).

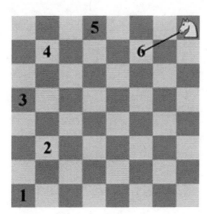

FIGURE 86 Upper Right Corner (Square 7)

Now proceed with Rule 1 as normal (Figure 87).

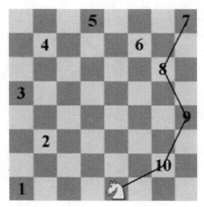

FIGURE 87 Visiting Squares 8–11

Landing on square 11 is one of two very important visits to take note of, as the rules will now be broken temporarily. Make the moves shown in Figure 88.

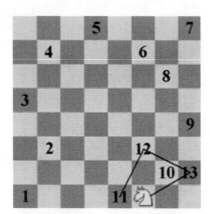

FIGURE 88 Break the Rules—First Time
(Visiting Squares 12–14)

Although this set of moves does not help the knight visit the lower right corner of the board, visiting squares 12 to 14 will help the knight with future moves. *For this "favored" solution, we recommend that the problem solver simply memorize this exception, as it will be necessary when we make a similar maneuver at square 36.* Until then, continue to follow the rules (Figures 89 to 92).

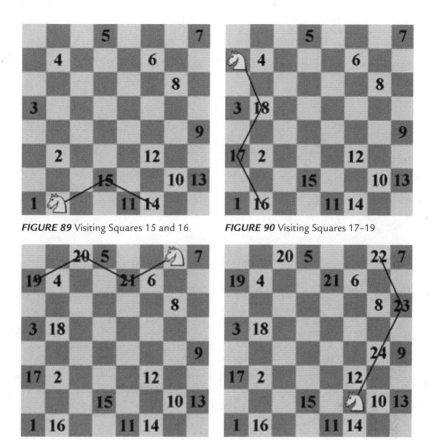

FIGURE 89 Visiting Squares 15 and 16   **FIGURE 90** Visiting Squares 17–19

FIGURE 91 Visiting Squares 20–22   **FIGURE 92** Visiting Squares 23–25

Again, we have an opportunity to visit a corner square. So we will take it (Figure 93).

FIGURE 93 Lower Right Corner (Square 26)

Now proceed to follow Rule 1. However, we will not continue moving in a clockwise spiral at this point. Instead, the knight will now start to traverse the board in a counterclockwise motion (Figures 94 and 95).

FIGURE 94 Visiting Squares 27–29   *FIGURE 95* Visiting Squares 30 and 31

We now have the opportunity to fill the final corner on the upper left of the board. We will take advantage of it (Figure 96).

FIGURE 96 Upper Left Corner (Square 32)

Then we proceed (Figure 97).

FIGURE 97 Visiting Squares 33–36

Now that we have reached square 36, we will once again break the rules. Move the knight to the squares shown in Figure 98.

FIGURE 98 Breaking the Rules—Second Time (Visiting Squares 37 and 38)

At this point, continue to follow the rules, with the knight once again traversing the outer squares of the board clockwise, as shown in Figures 99 to 102.

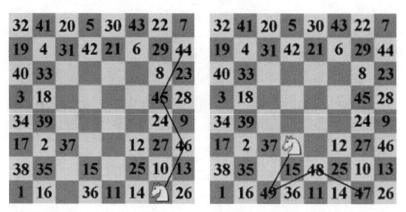

FIGURE 99 Visiting Squares 39–41   FIGURE 100 Visiting Squares 42–44

FIGURE 101 Visiting Squares 45–47   FIGURE 102 Visiting Squares 48–50

At this point, we have completed the knight's traversal around the board's outer squares. You will notice that one of the squares has not been visited. This is because it has been reserved so the knight can complete a closed tour.

Now the knight must visit each of the remaining center squares. The general idea now is to maintain subsequent moves in a clockwise direction (Figures 103 to 105).

32	41	20	5	30	43	22	7
19	4	31	42	21	6	29	44
40	33		52		8	23
3	18	51				45	28
34	39			53	24	9
17	2	37	50		12	27	46
38	35		15	48	25	10	13
1	16	49	36	11	14	47	26

FIGURE 103 Visiting Center Squares 51–54

32	41	20	5	30	43	22	7
19	4	31	42	21	6	29	44
40	33		57	52	55	8	23
3	18	51	54			45	28
34	39			56	53	24	9
17	2	37	50		12	27	46
38	35		15	48	25	10	13
1	16	49	36	11	14	47	26

FIGURE 104 Visiting Center Squares 55–58

32	41	20	5	30	43	22	7
19	4	31	42	21	6	29	44
40	33		57	52	55	8	23
3	18	51	54		58	45	28
34	39	60		56	53	24	9
17	2	37	50	59	12	27	46
38	35		15	48	25	10	13
1	16	49	36	11	14	47	26

FIGURE 105 Visiting Center Squares 59–61

The rest is now straightforward (Figure 106).

32	41	20	5	30	43	22	7
19	4	31	42	21	6	29	44
40	33	62	57	52	55	8	23
3	18	51	54	61	58	45	28
34	39	60	63	56	53	24	9
17	2	37	50	59	12	27	46
38	35		15	48	25	10	13
1	16	49	36	11	14	47	26

FIGURE 106 Goal State (Visiting Squares 62–64)

And thus we have completed our knight's tour. Additionally, since we are able to move the knight to its first position from its last position, it is a closed tour.

8.4 HUMAN PROBLEM SOLVING

In the Spring of 2013, The Knight's Tour Problem was presented to several college students. They were not observed when they were given the problem, so it is uncertain whether or not the students acquired their solutions by fair means. The majority of the students took an approach similar to that of the "Simple Solution" (see Section 8.5.1). They began by moving the knight around the outer squares of the board. Then, when they hit a point where they could not continue, they traversed some center squares so they could reach an outer square and continue traveling to the outer squares once again. Finally, after all the outside squares were visited, they moved the knight to the center and visited the remaining squares.

One student used his own approach after discovering a solution after some "trial and error." As explained in his description, his main approach was to "first eliminate the corner boxes [and] then the middle boxes." However, he did not follow this heuristic specifically. First, he traversed the outside squares, making any attempt to fill the corners. Then he entered the center and filled random corners until every square had been visited. Such an approach may work for the open tour (visit every square without consideration of where we started and ended), but it is not likely to work for the closed tour, since transition squares to extreme edge squares may well have already been visited.

8.5 HUMAN WINDOW ANALYSIS OF SOLUTIONS

We found several solutions for The Knight's Tour Problem. This is no surprise, since there are so many methods to finding a tour and it is a relatively popular problem. When analyzing the solutions (Table 13), we can see that there is a mix between extensional and intensional solutions. This is because solutions to The Knight's Tour Problem can be expressed in two possible ways: a solution can provide the general steps of a method that is used to find a knight's tour, classifying it as intensional, and a solution can also be represented by showing how a method is used to find a tour step-by-step, using actual diagrams of a chessboard and a knight, classifying it as extensional.

From looking at Table 13, we can see that the majority of the solutions are extensional. Additionally, they are ranked relatively high in extensionality. For an extensional Knight's Tour solution, the more it appears as an actual chessboard, the higher the extensionality. We can see that each of them uses similar problem-solving methods and representations as well.

They also rank relatively identical in terms of comprehensibility. The comprehensibility of the solutions depends on the amount of detail used for their representation (e.g., chessboard, path, numbering). From the rankings, it can be seen that no solution is highly comprehensible. However, it is possible that, when combining specific attributes from each solution, the MHWC representation can be produced.

Finally, we can see that the rankings for the executability of the solutions are generally mixed. It is apparent that the executability of the solutions depends on which method is used to find a knight's tour. While there are so many methods to use to find a tour, some can be carried out much more easily than others. Therefore, one of the factors that may determine if a solution is the MHWC is its executability, and thus finding the "best" method for solving The Knight's Tour Problem.

Difficulty
5/10

Complexity
O(n)

Name	Int or Ext?	Intly/Extly	Rep.	HW?	Corr?	Grn Sz	Exec	Compr	Prob. Solv. Mthd	Flex	Mode of Conv	Opt?	Tot
Algorithm	Int.	8/10	Code	Y	Y w/ Cycles	Ideal	8/10	7/10	Bcktrck w/ Heurist	7/10	Txt Editor	N	30/40
D&S	Int.	6/10	Vis. Repr. w/ Descr.	Y	Y	Ideal	9/10	6/10	Subgoals	7/10	Txt Editor; Img Mkr	Y	28/40
Green	Ext.	8/10	Grid/ Table; Img	Y	Y	Ideal	5/10	7/10	Vis. Repr. ; Subgoals	8/10	Img/Tbl Mkr	Y	28/40
Narayan	Ext.	7/10	Grid/ Table; Img	Y	Y	Ideal	8/10	7/10	Vis. Repr. ; Subgoals	7/10	Img/Tbl Mkr	Y	29/40
Semi-Magic	Ext.	7/10	Grid/ Table; Img	Y	Y	Ideal	4/10	7/10	Vis. Repr. ; Subgoals	7/10	Img/Tbl Mkr	Y	25/40
Simple	Ext.	8/10	Grid/ Table; Img	Y	Y	Ideal	8/10	9/10	Vis. Repr. ; Subgoals	8/10	Img/Tbl Mkr	Y	33/40
Tessella-tion	Ext.	8/10	Grid/ Table; Img	Y	Y	Small	10/10	7/10	Vis. Repr. ; Subgoals	8/10	Img/Tbl Mkr	Y	33/40
Wiki	Ext.	7/10	Grid/ Table; Img	Y	Y	Ideal	8/10	7/10	Vis. Repr. ; Subgoals	8/10	Img/Tbl Mkr	Y	30/40

Key

Int or Ext?: Intensional or Extensional—Is the solution intensional or extensional?

Intly/Extly: Intensionality/Extensionality—How intensional or extensional is the solution?

Rep.: Representation—How is the solution represented?

HW?: Human Window—Does the solution exist in the Human Window?

Corr?: Correctness—Is the solution correct?

Grn Sz: Grain Size—How much computation (large) or memory (small) does one need to solve the solution?

Exec: Executability—How executable is this solution?

Compr: Comprehensibility—How comprehensible is this solution?

Prob. Solv. Mthd: Problem-Solving Method—What method is used in the solution to solve the problem?

Flex: Flexibility—How flexible is this solution (i.e., can this solution be represented in other ways)?

Mode of Conv: Mode of Conveyance—In what ways can this solution be reproduced/replicated?

Opt?: Optimal—Is the solution optimal?

TABLE 13 Ranking The Knight's Tour Problem Solutions According to the Human Window

8.5.1 The Most Human Window–Compatible Solution

The solution we analyzed to be the MHWC solution is the "Simple Solution." This solution is the same as the one presented in Section 8.3. This solution is very comprehensible. It is represented using a grid, which makes the state space look like a chessboard. Also, like on a chessboard, the colors of the squares alternate between dark and light, which makes each square identifiable from others. Additionally, the entity that represents the knight is a figure of the actual knight piece. This is a reminder that the solution must follow the same move restrictions as a knight. This is especially helpful to who are those unfamiliar with chess. After each step, a line that represents the path the knight has taken so far is drawn, connecting the knight's previous positions to its current position. These lines remain for every step of the solution. The final image in this solution summarizes the entire tour. It shows the entire path the knight took, as well as numbers on each square that indicate the sequence of the moves the knight made in completing the tour.

Although the solution is comprehensible, it is possible that the representation can be improved to increase its overall comprehensibility. For example, another attribute that could be added are letters and numbers to indicate the names of rows and columns, respectively, akin to those of an actual chessboard. This can make the solution more traceable, and specific sequences and squares can be traced, memorized, or just identified.

What makes this solution the MHWC is the method used. Not only is the method highly executable, but it requires little to no memory to carry out, which is ideal for most human beings. Although there are a few rules to follow and some locations in which the heuristic must be broken, they are relatively easy to remember.

You may notice from Table 13 that the "Tessellation Solution," developed by Daniel E. Thomasson (see Section 8.2), has higher executability than the "Simple Solution." This is because the tessellation method not only produces a closed tour, but it also guarantees that a tour will be produced after moving the knight around the board so it traces the four polygons. No matter where the knight starts on the board, if those four shapes are traced, a tour will be created. Thus, the executability of the solution is very high. Unfortunately, to carry out this method, a decent amount of memory is required, as one would have to memorize each of the four shapes and which squares correspond to those shapes. Therefore, the grain size of the solution is considered small. The "Simple Solution," however, provides steps that are easy to remember.

8.5.2 The Least Human Window–Compatible Solution

The solution assessed as LHWC is the "Semi-Magic Solution" (Figure 107). The solution was also developed by Daniel E. Thomasson [6]. The method used to produce this knight's tour is the square and diamonds method (see Section 8.2), although it is implicitly used.

The solution shows the concept of the "Semi-Magic Tour," which is a knight's tour that results in the formation of a *semi-magic square*. An $n \times n$ matrix consisting of values from 1 to $n2$ is called a *magic square* if the numbers in each row, column, and diagonal add up to a single number known as the *magic constant* [7]. If the values of each row and column add up to this number, but the diagonals do not, it is considered a semi-magic square.

Finding a knight's tour can be thought of as producing an 8" × 8" square whose values range from 1 to 82. Each square in the chessboard can be assigned a value corresponding to the step number in which the knight landed on that square. After the tour is completed, if the values of the squares in each row, column, and diagonal add up to the same number, the entire chessboard is considered a magic square. It has been proven, however, that a magic square cannot be formed by a knight's tour on an 8" × 8" board. However, it is possible to find a tour that results in a semi-magic square [7]. The first original semi-magic square was discovered by Leonhard Euler, where each row and column of the chessboard added up to the magic constant of 260 [2].

The "Semi-Magic Solution" shows a method of how a semi-magic square is formed with the same magic constant of 260. Using the squares and diamonds method, two simultaneous knight's tours are produced: one that starts at square 1 and increases by step, and another decreasing by step. Both tours always visit squares vertical to one other, of which the step numbers add up to 49 and 81. Although this solution produces both a completed knight's tour and a semi-magic tour and reveals the symmetry behind it, we will analyze the representation of it in terms of the Human Window, as if it were intended to be shown to any audience (i.e., those unfamiliar with The Knight's Tour Problem). The solution is also shortened to save space, as it contains a total of 32 steps.

This solution may not be very executable for humans because there are too many goals to remember. The simultaneous squares and diamonds method is repeated for all four quadrants, and the values of the columns add up to 98. Afterward, the same process is continued, except the steps must be numbered to add up to 81. To carry out this solution, a person must remember exactly which shapes to produce at any given step and must remember the order in which they are formed.

The solution may also not be very comprehensible either. This solution does not have a knight to follow in the tour, nor is there a line indicating the path. It simply shows the numbers of the squares the knight would land on during a particular step. This may make the solution hard to follow and could take a person away from the fact that this is a solution to The Knight's Tour Problem. Finally, the squares are shaded differently to indicate the particular shapes (i.e., diamonds and squares) being formed. The mixture can make the solution hard to comprehend, even for the image that shows the completed knight's tour.

Initial State

Square 1Q3 (1-4)
Diamond 1Q3 (45-46)

Square 1Q4 (41-44)
Diamond 1Q4 (5-8)

Square 1Q1 (9-12)
Diamond 1Q1 (37-40)

Square 1Q2 (33-36)
Diamond 1Q2 (13-16)

Square 2Q1 (17-20)
Diamond 2Q1 (61-64)

Square 2Q2 (21-24)
Diamond 2Q2 (57-60)

Square 2Q3 (53-56)
Diamond 2Q3 (25-28)

Square 2Q4 (49-52)
Diamond 2Q4 (29-32)

FIGURE 107 The "Semi-Magic Solution" (Shortened)

Solution published with permission of Daniel E. Thomasson
http://www.borderschess.org/KTsemi.htm

8.6 BEST MACHINE SOLUTION

Many algorithms and heuristics have been developed for find-ing a knight's tour. One algorithm that can be used is a *divide-and-conquer* algorithm, which divides the chessboard into smaller pieces, finds sequences for those pieces, and combines them (see Section 8.2) [8]. There are also neural network solutions, in which the chessboard is implemented as a neural network and each square is represented as a neuron [9].

Given that there are about 4×10^{51} possible sequences on an 8" x 8" board, it is best to guide a computer to find a knight's tour through the use of heuristics to avoid the need to analyze each of these sequences. One of the most efficient and commonly used heuristics is one that is based on Warnsdoff's Rule, which was developed by H. C. Warnsdoff. The rule is to analyze the squares the knight can visit from its current position, and whichever square provides the knight with the fewest successor possibilities is the square it should move to [2].

The flaw with Warnsdoff's Rule, however, is that it does not always succeed in finding a complete tour, as it usually results in dead ends. Using the heuristic to find a knight's tour may sometimes result in failures, especially when a tour is to be found on larger chessboards. As the value of n for an $n \times n$ chessboard becomes large, the success rate of Warnsdoff's Rule declines [10]. One method to resolve this problem is to combine the heuristic with a *backtracking algorithm.* This algorithm will follow the Warnsdoff heuristic as usual, but when the knight reaches a dead end, the algorithm will then backtrack to a previous step and attempt to find a tour once again. This same type of algorithm is used in the "Algorithm Solution" [11].

A second and more efficient method has been analyzed by Luis Paris. This algorithm implements the Warnsdoff heuristic with the addition of a second heuristic that, in the case of a tie between the squares a knight may visit at a particular step, will "choose the lowest-valued square nearest to any of the four corners of the board, independently of n." According to an analysis done by Paris, this heuristic is always successful in finding a tour, no matter how large the chessboard is. This algorithm uses no backtracking and requires **$O(n^2)$** time [10].

(NEED IMAGE)

George Koltanowski, an International Chess Master with an ei-
detic memory, was famous for his "Knight's Tour" lectures. One
of the coauthors remembers the U.S. Open in Portland, Oregon,
in 1987, where he gave a demonstration in which he asked the
audience to attribute serial numbers on dollar bills, names of famous baseball players, and so on to the squares on a chessboard.
Koltanowski would then turn his back on the audience and study
the board for a few minutes. Then he would turn to the audience, performing a perfect knight's tour, while reciting all the information he had been given for each square. Not surprisingly,
Koltanowski also holds the world's official record for Blindfold
Chess—56 boards—which took place in San Francisco in 1960.

8.7 RELATED PROBLEMS

An extension to the problem discussed in this chapter is the
Knight's Tour on an infinite board. For this to happen, place the
knight at the center of the board. Make a move two squares down
and one square to the right to start and keep circling around the
center until every square is visited. Then make another move like
the first move to expand the outer perimeter of the tour and keep
circling around the inner portion until every block of that perimeter is visited. And once again make a move like the first move, and
keep repeating this for this infinite board.

8.8 PLAYABLE PROGRAM

A playable knight's tour game is available at *http://www.
kongregate.com/games/evgenykarataev/knights-tour.* In this
game, you get to control the knight and pick which square to
visit relative to its current position. The squares it can visit
and those it has already visited are indicated. Additionally, the
chessboard and the knight are presented three dimensionally,
giving the player the sense of using a real chessboard.

8.9 REFERENCES

1. Jelliss, G. (2002). *Early History of Knight's Tours*. Available at *http://www.mayhematics.com/t/1a.htm*. Accessed on January 9, 2014.

2. Jelliss, G. (2002). *Rediscovery of the Knight's Problem*. Available at *http://www.mayhematics.com/t/1b.htm*. Accessed on January 9, 2014.

3. Schwenk, A.J. (1991). "Which Rectangular Chessboards Have a Knight's Tour?" *Mathematics* 64: 325–332.

4. Frezco. (2009). *Solving a Knight's Tour Blindfolded*. Available at *http://www.frezcogames.com/Knights_Tour.php*. Accessed on January 9, 2014.

5. Thomasson, D. (2011). *Knight Tour Tessellations*. Available at *http://www.borderschess.org/KTtess.htm*. Accessed on January 9, 2014.

6. Thomasson, D. (2011). *Semi-Magic Square Knight Tours*. Available at *http://www.borderschess.org/KTsemi.htm*. Accessed on January 9, 2014.

7. Weisstein, E.W. (2003). *There Are No Magic Knight's Tours on the Chessboard*. Available at *http://mathworld.wolfram.com/news/2003-08-06/magictours/*. Accessed on January 9, 2014.

8. Parberry, I. (1997). "An Efficient Algorithm for the Knight's Tour Problem." *Discrete Applied Mathematics* 73: 251–260. *http://larc.unt.edu/ian/pubs/algoknight.pdf*.

9. Takefuji, Y., and Lee, K.C. (1992). "Neural Network Computing for Knight's Tour Problems." *Neurocomputing* 4 (5): 249–254.

10. *Paris, L. (2013). Heuristic Strategies for the Knight Tour Problem. Available at http://faculty.harrisburgu.net/~paris/papers/ppr_icai_knight_tour.pdf. Accessed on January 9, 2014.*

11. *Mička, P. (2013). Knight's Tour. Available at http://en.algoritmy.net/article/39907/Knights-tour. Accessed on January 9, 2014.*

CHAPTER 9

MASTERMIND

FIGURE 108 Mastermind

9.1 BACKGROUND

Mastermind (Figure 108) is a board game invented in 1970 by Mordecai Meirowitz, an Israeli postmaster and telecommunications expert. After being turned down by several leading toy companies, the rights to Mastermind were finally purchased by Invicta Plastics Ltd, a small English firm, and released in 1972 [1]. According to G. Darby, "Over 50 million copies later, the game is still marketed today" [2].

Mastermind is a type of "code-breaking" game. In the original Mastermind game, one player, known as the code-breaker, must guess a secret code chosen by another other player, known as the code-maker. This code is a sequence of four pegs that can be any of six different colors, with same-colored pegs allowed in the same sequence. The code-breaker must break this code by determining the exact colors and order of these pegs. To do so, the code-breaker must make a series of at most 10 guesses. After each guess, the code-maker gives the code-breaker a score in the form of two values: the number of pegs that are the right color and in the correct position and the number of pegs that are the correct color but *not* in the correct position. These numbers are represented by small black and white pegs, respectively. If in 10 guesses the code-breaker cannot determine the correct sequence, the code-maker wins. [2]

Since its release in 1972, there have been a wide variety of alternate versions of the original game. One version is called Mastermind44, which includes six colors, five pegs to a sequence, and as many as three code-makers [3]. Another version is Ultimate Mastermind, which includes eight colors and five pegs to a sequence [4].

9.2 PROBLEM-SOLVING TECHNIQUES

Like The 15 Puzzle, Mastermind does not have a specified initial state. However, unlike any of the problems we have analyzed in this book, this problem does not have a specified goal state. Additionally, for the other problems, we attempt to find methods of achieving the goal, while in Mastermind we try to find the goal itself. We could say that The Knight's Tour Problem is similar in that there is no specific set goal. However, we do know that the knight must visit all 64 squares, so it is not the same.

In the original Mastermind game, there are a total of $6 \times 6 \times 6 \times 6 = 1,296$ possible combinations, and the code-breaker must determine the one correct sequence of colors [5]! With only 10 guesses available, the key is to reduce the number of possible combinations as much as possible with each guess. This can be done by analyzing the score given at each guess and using deduction to determine which colored pegs to use and which not to use, and in which order they must be placed. Therefore, *deduction* is the most valuable problem-solving technique to use in solving for the correct sequence of pegs and winning Mastermind. This kind of logical deduction is also performed for the solution to the n coins problems to determine how to best split the number of coins for each weighing.

9.3 SOLUTION

Before beginning the solution, let's go over some notations:

- Instead of using colors, the pegs will be represented as letters from A to F. This notation is better than using actual color names because the different versions of the game may use different-colored pegs.

- A sequence of pegs will be represented by placing four of these letters in a line. For example, ABBC is a sequence of four pegs that contains peg color A, peg color B, peg color B, and peg color C, in that precise order.

- The score will be represented as a set of numbers in parentheses: (x, y). The variable x will represent the number of pegs that are guessed correctly and in the correct location (i.e., small black pegs), and the variable y will represent the number of pegs that are guessed correctly but are in the wrong position (i.e., small white pegs). For example, $(2, 1)$ means that 2 pegs are correct colors and in the correct location in the final sequence, and 1 other peg color is correct but is not in the correct location in the final sequence. This sequence has a total score of 3.

An example of a single guess may look like Figure 109.

FIGURE 109 Sample Guess

Since there is no one specific goal to achieve, there is no general solution to winning Mastermind. By taking the following steps, however, the code-breaker can solve the sequence in four to six guesses:

1. The first guess should always be the sequence AABB. This is not only the simplest guess, but it is also very important because, even in the worst case, this guess greatly reduces the number of possibilities remaining (in the worst case, it reduces the 1,296 possible guesses to 256). [5]

2. You must use the score of the first guess to make assumption(s) as to which of the pegs from the previous guess (i.e., pegs A and B) should be used for the next guess. For example, if the score is a total of 0, pegs A and B should not be used again for this game. If the score is a total of 1 or 2, use both an A and a B in the next guess to determine which A or B is in the sequence. If the score totals 3, use two A pegs and one B peg in the next guess. Finally, if the score happens to be 4, that means all four pegs are in the sequence and must simply be arranged to the correct order.

3. Repeat step 2 for future guesses until all the peg colors have been used (that is, if we do not wind up having a score of 4 before then). At this point there should be enough information from all the guesses already made to use deduction and solve for the sequence.

At first, the above steps may seem too broad and unclear. However, we will be providing five examples so you can understand them better.

9.3.1 Example 1

Let's start with an easy example. The goal sequence is CEDF. We start with the required first guess and get Figure 110.

```
1.  AABB    (0,0)
```

FIGURE 110 Ex. 1—Guess 1

We know from this that neither A nor B is in the sequence. Therefore, we will make a similar guess using peg colors C and D, reducing the number of choices even further (Figure 111).

```
2. CCDD     (2,0)

1. AABB     (0,0)
```

FIGURE 111 Ex. 1—Guess 2

We now have a score of 2. Even better, we have two pegs that are in their correct positions. However, because we don't know which pegs are correct, we need to make an assumption. We can pick any two, but it is best to have both colors included in the next guess. We will keep the first C and first D in the sequence, and, since there are two spots available, we will add two E pegs (Figure 112).

		Assumption:
3. CEDE	(3,0)	C_D_
2. CCDD	(2,0)	
1. AABB	(0,0)	

FIGURE 112 Ex. 1—Guess 3

Our score has increased to 3, with all three pegs in the correct position. From this, we can conclude three things: our assumptions about the inclusion and location of the C and D pegs were correct; peg E is in the sequence; and with one peg still incorrect and one color remaining, peg F must also be in the sequence. This means that one of the E pegs must be removed. We will make the assumption that the E in position 2 is correct and the E in position 4 should be replaced with an F (Figure 113).

		Assumptions:
4. CEDF	(4,0) *	CEDF
3. CEDE	(3,0)	
2. CCDD	(2,0)	
1. AABB	(0,0)	

FIGURE 113 Ex. 1—Guess 4

Thus, we have solved for the sequence. Of course, guess 4 was a lucky guess. If we had assumed the E in position 4 was correct instead of position 2, we would have Figure 114.

		Assumption:
4. CFDE	(2,2)	CEFE

FIGURE 114 Ex. 1—Alternate Guess 4

However, from this information we could simply determine the solution, and we would only need one extra guess to solve it.

When looking at the score, we can see that all four pegs exist in the final sequence, with two pegs in the correct position and two in the incorrect position. Since we already know that pegs C and D are in the correct place, we can easily conclude that pegs E and F must be switched.

9.3.2 Example 2

The goal sequence is EAFA. As always, we make our required first guess (Figure 115).

1. AABB   (1,1)

FIGURE 115 Ex. 2—Guess 1

We see that we have a score of 2, with one peg in the correct position and one in the wrong position. Having a score of 2 for the first guess makes it hard to determine which A or B is correct. Let's make the assumption that both colors are in the final sequence, and we will put both in the next guess. Let's assume the first A peg is the correct spot and that one of the B pegs is out of place. Move the B to position 2 and add two of the next color to the sequence (Figure 116).

		Assumption:
2. ABCC	(0,1)	AB _ _
1. AABB	(1,1)	

FIGURE 116 Ex. 2—Guess 2

We now have our score reduced to 1, with one peg being out of place. This gives us two conclusions: C is not in the final sequence, and either two A pegs or two B pegs are in the final solution, but not both. We know this because our score of 2 in the first guess has been reduced to 1. For guess 3, we will assume that two As are in the sequence. Now we will make some more assumptions based around this assumption. Since our current score indicates that we have one peg out of place, we know that A cannot be in position 1. Additionally, from looking at our score in guess 1, one of the A pegs must be in position 2, since there was a black peg. Therefore, let's assume that one A is in position 2. The second A can be placed in either position 3 or 4, so let's will assume it is in 3. Finally, we will now introduce peg color D (Figure 117).

		Assumption:
3. DAAD	(1,1)	_AA_
2. ABCC	(0,1)	
1. AABB	(1,1)	

FIGURE 117 Ex. 2—Guess 3

We once again have a score of 2, with one peg in place and one out of place. Unfortunately, with this guess, we cannot make any immediate conclusions. This guess can mean one of two things:

1. Both As are in the sequence, and the Ds do not belong. We would just need to move the A that is in position 3 to position 4.

2. The Ds are in the sequence, and our assumption about including the As was wrong, leaving the two Bs as a part of the final sequence.

Let's go with #1 and continue to assume that A is the correct color. From looking at our score, we can assume that the A in position 2 is in place because we have a black peg. We can also assume that A is in position 4, as mentioned before. Finally, the other two positions will be replaced by an E peg (Figure 118).

		Assumption:
4. EAEA	(3,0)	_A_A
3. DAAD	(1,1)	
2. ABCC	(0,1)	
1. AABB	(1,1)	

FIGURE 118 Ex. 2—Guess 4

This guess was very helpful. We have now come to three conclusions:

1. D is not included in the sequence, since we have an increased score, despite our removing them.

2. Thus, the two As are in the sequence and are in the correct place.

3. One E is in the sequence, and it is in the correct position.

With F being the only peg we have not used, we would normally conclude that F is the last missing peg. However, it is still possible that a third A peg is a part of the sequence (we have not disproved it). So for our next guess, let's assume that the correct E peg was the one in position 1 and that position 3 contains an F peg (Figure 119).

			Assumptions:
5. EAFA	(4,0) *		E*F*
4. EADA	(3,0)		
3. DAAD	(1,1)		
2. ABCC	(0,1)		
1. AABB	(1,1)		

FIGURE 119 Ex. 2—Guess 5

Thus, we have found our sequence. If position 3 had another A instead of an F, we would have only needed one extra guess to determine it.

9.3.3 Example 3

The goal sequence is EABC. As usual, the first guess is as shown in Figure 120.

FIGURE 120 Ex. 3—Guess 1

We begin with a score of 2, which means it may take a few guesses to determine which A and/or B is in the sequence. For the next guess, we will assume that both an A peg and a B peg are in the sequence. Additionally, since we have two black pegs, let's assume that the A peg is in position 1 and the B peg is in position 3. The remaining two positions will be Cs (Figure 121).

```
┌─────────────────────────────────────┐
│                     Assumption:       │
│                                       │
│  2. ACBC      (2,1)        A_B_       │
│                                       │
│  1. AABB      (2,0)                   │
│                                       │
└─────────────────────────────────────┘
```

FIGURE 121 Ex. 3—Guess 2

With this guess, we have increased our score to 3 with the addition of a white peg. Due to this increase from the last guess, we can make an obvious conclusion that at least one C peg is in the sequence. We can also use some logic to determine less obvious conclusions.

Let's say we keep our assumption that A and B are in the correct position. By this, we would have to say that there is one C peg in the sequence and it represents the white peg. However, this does not make sense. Thinking that switching the two Cs would get one in the correct position is unrealistic. In other words, switching the two Cs cannot suddenly produce a black peg, because nothing will change. With this single logical inference, we can come to four conclusions:

1. There is only one C in the sequence.

2. C represents the black peg and is in the correct position.

3. Based on #1 and #2 and the score for this guess, A and B are in the sequence.

4. One A or B is represented by the black peg, and the other is represented by the white peg. That is, one is in the correct position, and the other is in an incorrect position.

First, let's assume that the C peg belongs in position 2. We know that A and B exist in the sequence, and now we must determine where to place the A and B pegs. By analyzing the score from guess 1, in which there are two black pegs, we can assume that the A peg can only be in either position 1 or 2, and B can only be in either position 3 or 4. Based on conclusion #4, one A or B will remain in place, while the other will be moved to its next possible position. For our next guess, let's assume that A is represented by the black peg and is in place and that B is represented by the white peg and should be moved to its next possible position 4. Finally, position 3 will be given the D peg, as shown in Figure 122.

		Assumptions:
3. ACDB	(0,3)	AC_B
2. ACBC	(2,1)	
1. AABB	(2,0)	

FIGURE 122 Ex. 3—Guess 3

We continue to have a score of 3, but now every peg is out of position. This is not necessarily bad news, because we can now make four conclusions:

1. The C peg belongs in position 4.

2. The B peg belongs in position 3.

3. The A peg belongs in position 2.

4. Based on the fact that the score has not increased from the previous guess, the D peg does not belong in the sequence.

Conclusions #1 to #3 were easily determined because the A, B, and C pegs only had one of two possibilities, as we determined from our second guess. Since we chose wrong for all three pegs, we now know the correct positions for each. With this information, we can now construct our next guess. Position 2 will have peg A, position 3 will have peg B, and position 4 will have peg C. The remaining position will have the next type of peg we haven't used yet, which is E (Figure 123).

		Assumption:
4. EABC	(4,0) *	_***
3. ACDB	(0,3)	
2. ACBC	(2,1)	
1. AABB	(2,0)	

FIGURE 123 Ex. 3—Guess 4

And thus we have found the sequence.

9.3.4 Example 4

The goal sequence is FBFF. For our last example, we have a goal that is a little unusual, since we are now dealing with three of the same kind of peg.

We start with our usual first guess (Figure 124).

1. AABB	(0,1)

FIGURE 124 Ex. 4—Guess 1

We start a score of 1, with one peg out of place. We will assume that A is in the sequence and is out of place. We will first assume it is in position 3. The other three remaining positions will be filled with C pegs (Figure 125).

		Assumption:
2. CC AC	(0,0)	_ _ A_
1. AABB	(0,1)	

FIGURE 125 Ex. 4—Guess 2

With this guess we can make two conclusions: the A peg is not in the sequence, so the B peg must be, and C is not in the sequence.

Remembering that guess 1 had a score of 1 with a white peg, the B peg can only be in either position 1 or 2. We will first assume that peg B is in position 1. The other positions will be given D pegs (Figure 126).

		Assumptions:
3. BDDD	(0,1)	B_ _ _
2. CC AC	(0,0)	
1. AABB	(0,1)	

FIGURE 126 Ex. 4—Guess 3

With this guess, we have arrived at two conclusions: B is in position 2, and D is not in the sequence.

For the next guess, we will place the B peg in position 2. The rest will be given the E peg (Figure 127).

		Assumptions:
4. EBEE	(1,0)	_B_ _
3. BDDD	(0,1)	
2. CCAC	(0,0)	
1. AABB	(0,1)	

FIGURE 127 Ex. 4—Guess 4

We now have a black peg, which means our conclusion was correct and the B peg was in fact located in position 2. Additionally, we can also make two more conclusions: the E pegs are not in the sequence, and the remaining positions are F pegs, since it is the last type of peg available (Figure 128).

		Assumptions:
5. FBFF	(4,0)*	****
4. EBEE	(1,0)	
3. BDDD	(0,1)	
2. CCAC	(0,0)	
1. AABB	(0,1)	

FIGURE 128 Ex. 4—Guess 5

We have found our sequence.

9.4 HUMAN PROBLEM SOLVING

The Mastermind game was distributed digitally to students to analyze how the average person approaches the game and methods used to find the solution. The game was distributed to nine college students, and it did not have the original rules. In this version, there were eight colors, and no duplicate colors were allowed.

For the first guess, two students picked the first four colors that were presented as choices, while the rest picked four random colors. However, we cannot determine if any of the students would have picked the AABB guess if they had played the original game, although they may have picked the first four colors regardless.

Regardless of what the students picked as their first guess, all the students did fairly well on the game. Seven of the students used the right amount of deduction and logic to find the correct pegs and their order. One student was able to figure out the correct pegs but had difficulty determining their correct order. Eventually, this student was able to find the correct sequence in seven guesses. The other exception did a good job in deducing the correct order of the pegs but did not do so well in figuring out the correct pegs. This student used the same pegs that could have been reasoned out of the final sequence at an earlier guess. As a result, it took this student nine guesses to figure out the correct sequence.

On average, we can see that the students had solved the sequence with a fairly small number of guesses. One student solved the sequence in four guesses, three students in five guesses, two students in six guesses, two students in seven guesses, and one student in nine guesses. The mode is five guesses, which is also the average number of guesses it would take to solve the solution presented in Section 9.3.

9.5 HUMAN WINDOW ANALYSIS OF SOLUTIONS

Unfortunately, there was insufficient data for an analysis of the Human Window for this problem. Also, there were not enough solutions found that could be used to help in this analysis. What we *did* find were word descriptions to general strategies on solving Mastermind but no concrete solutions. This may be because, as mentioned before, this problem does not have a specific goal, so only general tips and strategies can be used to help find the goal. This, however, gives us an opportunity to use our Human Window analysis from other problems in the book to determine what kind of solution can be considered the MHWC for Mastermind.

Since the Mastermind problem does not have one specific goal to achieve, it is best to use a general, intensional solution, because this will help find the end goal to a Mastermind game regardless of what it is. Like the "Tile Solution," combined with examples like those in Section 9.3, a similar approach can be taken with a general solution to Mastermind. This solution can contain one or more examples that demonstrate a step-by-step method for solving for a particular goal sequence. Furthermore, there should be enough examples so that every scenario that can possibly occur can be explained. This will give the solution a high ranking of executability. Additionally, to increase the comprehensibility of the solution, images of the actual Mastermind game could be used at every step to give an idea of what the game should look like.

9.6 BEST MACHINE SOLUTION

The best solution to the Mastermind game for a machine so far is known as the *Five-Guess Algorithm*, which was developed and presented in 1977 in a paper titled "The Computer as Mastermind," by Donald Knuth. Knuth based his algorithm on a study he did on the original Mastermind game. It is called the Five-Guess Algorithm because it guarantees that any solution can be found in five or fewer guesses [6].

The algorithm is quite sophisticated and intricate. Here is a brief explanation:

1. Create a set P of remaining possibilities. At the beginning, P is always 1,296.

2. Make the first guess of AABB (the first guess as used in Section 9.3). Remove all possibilities from P that would give a lower score if they were the answer.

3. For each of the 1,296 possible guesses, calculate how many possibilities from P would be eliminated for each possible score. The score of the guess is the least of such values.

4. Play the guess with the highest score.

5. Repeat steps #2 to #4 until the sequence is found [6].

We repeat a historical note from Knuth [6]:

A game very similar to Mastermind, called "Bulls and Cows," has been popular in England for many years. The difference is that all the digits of the code in Bulls and Cows must be distinct, but any digits 0 through 9 are allowed. This version of the game became a popular computer demonstration after Frank H. King introduced a program for it in August 1968 at Cambridge University.

F.H. King, The Game of M00, University of Cambridge, Computer Laboratory, memorandum dated February, 1976.

9.7 RELATED PROBLEMS

As mentioned previously, one game that is very closely related to the Mastermind is Bulls and Cows. This game can be played with a 4-digit number from 0-9, or it could be played with a legitimate 4 letter word. The number version is explained here but the idea is the same with the word version. The chooser would write down a 4-digit number, and the guesser would try to guess that number. The guesser is given feedback after each guess, a bull denoting that a digit is correct and in the right position while a cow means a digit is correct but in a different (wrong) position. The game ends when the guesser guesses the correct number. The premise is the same with Mastermind except that it is a game that's played with numbers, or letters. The solution to these games is very similar to Mastermind.

9.8 PLAYABLE PROGRAM

A playable Mastermind game is available at *http://www.grayman.de/mastermind/index_en.php4*. Luckily, it follows the rules of the original game, so following the examples in Section 9.3 could be helpful. Additionally, the different pegs are not only colored individually, but they are numbered additionally as well.

9.9 REFERENCES

1. Nelson, T. (2000). *A Brief History of the Master Mind Board Game.* Available at *http://www.tnelson.demon.co.uk/mastermind/history. html.* Accessed on January 9, 2014.

2. Darby, G. (2013). *Mastermind Game.* Available at *http://www.delphi-forfun.org/Programs/Mastermind.htm.* Accessed on January 9, 2014.

3. *Mastermind44.* (1972). Available at *http://boardgamegeek.com/board-game/12467/mastermind44.* Accessed on January 9, 2014.

4. *Ultimate Mastermind.* (1972). Available at *http://boardgamegeek.com/boardgame/3874/ultimate-mastermind.* Accessed on January 9, 2014.

5. Nelson, T. (1999). *Investigations into the Master Mind Board Game.* Available at *http://www.tnelson.demon.co.uk/mastermind/.* Accessed on January 9, 2014.

6. Knuth, D. (1976). "The Computer as a Master Mind." *Journal of Recreational Mathematics* 9: 1–6. *http://www.dcc.fc.up.pt/~sssousa/ RM09101.pdf.*

CHAPTER 10

THE MONTY HALL PROBLEM

FIGURE 129 The Monty Hall Problem

10.1 BACKGROUND

The Monty Hall Problem (Figure 129) is one of the most well-known and widely studied problems in the area of puzzles. It is a probability-based puzzle where the chance of a favorable outcome is to be compared before and after an event occurs, and then the better of the two situations must be determined.

The problem is as follows: In a game show, the host asks a contestant to pick one door out of three, given that one of the doors has a car behind it. Each of the other two doors has a goat behind it. After the contestant picks a door, the host opens one of the other two doors to show a goat behind it. The contestant is then asked if he or she wishes to switch to the unopened door or stay with the original choice. Do you think the contestant has a better choice of winning if he or she switches?

Initially, it seems switching makes no difference because after the host opens the door with a goat, we still assume that the chances of the remaining unopened doors having the car are ½, the same chance as the original choice. Since the chances of winning seem equal with both remaining doors, there seems to be no benefit in switching.

Surprisingly, the correct answer is the contestant has a better chance of winning the car if he or she switches to the other door. We explain why this is true in the next section.

10.2 PROBLEM-SOLVING TECHNIQUES

It is clear that either of the two choices gives only a chance or probability of winning the car and does not guarantee a win. Therefore, probability-based analysis is the key to solving this problem. Also, this problem involves making decisions. Initially the contestant has to choose a door, which is very likely a random choice because all three doors have an equal probability (1/3) of having a car behind them. But after it is revealed that one of the doors has a goat, the situation changes. The contestant now has more information than when he or she picked one door out of three. Since the contestant's final decision of staying with or switching the chosen door depends on the original choice and the host's action, we create a decision tree to analyze the problem. A tabular version of the decision tree is shown in **Error! Reference source not found.**

Also, since this problem has a small state space in terms of all possible outcomes of the combination of the contestant's original decision, the host's choice of door, and the contestant's final decision, we can do an exhaustive enumeration of the solution state space as shown in **Error! Reference source not found.**

Error! Reference source not found. shows all the possible scenarios for this puzzle. The numbers 1, 2, and 3 represent the three doors. We consider the three possibilities of the car being behind each door one by one. In each of the three cases stated above, we further consider three cases or possibilities for the original choice.

Door with the Car	Initial Choice	Correct/ Incorrect	Host's Choice	Final Choice	Result
1	1	Correct	2 or 3	Stay	Win
				Switch	Lose
	2	Incorrect	3	Stay	Lose
				Switch	Win
	3	Incorrect	2	Stay	Lose
				Switch	Win
2	1	Incorrect	3	Stay	Lose
				Switch	Win
	2	Correct	1 or 3	Stay	Win
				Switch	Lose
	3	Incorrect	1	Stay	Lose
				Switch	Win
3	1	Incorrect	2	Stay	Lose
				Switch	Win
	2	Incorrect	1	Stay	Lose
				Switch	Win
	3	Correct	1 or 2	Stay	Win
				Switch	Lose

TABLE 14 The Monty Hall Problem

For each of the possible initial choices, the host will choose a door having a goat, thus reducing the number of doors possibly having a car to just two instead of three. This leaves the contestant with two choices: either to stay with the initial choice or switch to the door not opened by the host.

The final choice made by the contestant and the ensuing result are shown in the last two columns. It is evident that staying with the original choice guarantees a win if the original choice was correct. And the probability of the original choice being correct is 1/3 because only one door out of three has a car behind it. On the contrary, the probability of the original choice being incorrect is 2/3, so in this case switching leads to a better chance of winning.

We can look at it another way. Say instead of 3 doors, there were 10 doors with a car behind 1 door and goats behind 9 doors. The contestant chooses a door, and the host reveals 8 doors that have goats. In this case, should the contestant stay with his or her original choice or switch?

It is clear that initially the probability of opening the correct door is 1/10, which also means the probability of opening a door with a goat is 9/10. Since, we are more likely to open a door with a goat initially, switching is more likely to lead to a win—in this case, a 1/2 chance of winning.

10.3 SOLUTION

The solution as described in the previous section is that you have more chances of winning if you switch. This is because you have double the chances of having a wrong door with your initial choice. The host always opens a door (that you did not choose) with a goat behind it (as described in the problem). So after this event happens, we know the car is behind one of the two other doors and thus there is a 50% chance of the car being behind either of the two other doors. So staying with the original choice would mean 1/3 = 33.3% chance of winning, and switching would mean 2/3 = 66% chance of winning. This is clearly shown in **Error! Reference source not found.**

10.4 HUMAN PROBLEM SOLVING

The Monty Hall Problem first appeared in Marilyn vos Savant's column in *Parade Magazine*. vos Savant, who answers questions and solves puzzles submitted by readers, was once listed in the *Guinness Book of World Records* as having the highest IQ in the world.

The problem became very popular because it is loosely based on the popular game show *Let's Make a Deal* and was named after the show's host, Monty Hall. In response to the question of whether it was better to stay with the original choice or switch, vos Savant stated that switching was the better strategy. Her answer triggered around 10,000 responses, including from many PhDs, who insisted her answer was incorrect [1, 2]. This story garnered so much attention that it was featured in the *New York Times* [2].

10.5 RELATED PROBLEMS

A problem that is closely related to the Monty Hall Problem is the Bertrand Russell's "Box Paradox." Here is the statement of the problem: There are 3 identical boxes each having 2 drawers. One box contains a gold coin in each drawer, the other has a gold coin in one drawer and a silver coin in the other, while the last has a silver coin in each drawer. If a box is chosen at random and a drawer is open and a gold coin is found, find the probability that the other drawer also contains a gold coin. The answer is the same as with the Monty Hall Problem, 2/3. One explanation that is easy to understand is that there are 2 gold coins and 1 silver coin to be chosen from as there are only 2 boxes with gold coins, the probability that it would be gold is therefore 2/3.

Another problem related to the Monty Hall Problem is the "Three Prisoners Problem." The situation is that three prisoners are in jail awaiting execution and one of them will be pardoned. The guard knows which one will be pardoned but is not allowed to say who. Prisoner A asks the guard to tell him which one of the remaining 2 prisoners will be executed since only 1 prisoner can be pardoned. Guard replied B will be executed and A tells C about it. Find the probability that C is the one that would be pardoned. The answer is the same as Monty Hall Problem, 2/3. The reasoning is actually also the same as with Monty Hall Problem.

10.6 REFERENCES

1. Deaves, R.H. (2007). *The Monty Hall Problem: Behind Closed Doors. Lulu.com* Available at *http://www.amazon.com/The-Monty-Hall-Problem-Beyond/dp/1847530788.* Accessed on January 10, 2014).

2. Yanofsky, N. (2013). *The Outer Limits of Reason: What Science, Mathematics and Logic Cannot Tell Us.* Boston, MA: The MIT Press.

CHAPTER 11

RUBIK'S CUBE

FIGURE 130 Rubik's Cube

11.1 BACKGROUND

Rubik's Cube (Figure 130) is one of the most popular puzzles in history. It is a three-dimensional combination puzzle that was invented in 1974 by Ernö Rubik, a Hungarian architect and professor [1]. The cube is made up of 26 smaller cubes. When considering one of these smaller cubes as a unit, we can say that the whole cube has dimensions of 3" × 3" × 3", with 1 smaller cube missing from its center. Together, 9 smaller cubes that make up one of the faces of the whole cube can be turned into a "layer" that has the ability to rotate while staying in position. Rubik created the cube in an attempt to understand how blocks could move independently without [the entire structure] falling apart [2].

When the cube is unscrambled, each of its six faces will have one color. This is the cube's goal state. To arrive at this state, each of the smaller cubes must be moved into a certain position. However, this is not as straightforward as it sounds. A single small cube cannot be moved individually. Entire layers of the cube must be rotated to position it correctly. Unfortunately, this will inevitably reposition other smaller cubes, even if they are already in their correct positions. Therefore, specific algorithms must be used to correctly position smaller cubes without moving others out of place. After scrambling the model, Rubik took a month of trial and error to solve the puzzle himself [2].

In 1975, Rubik applied for a patent for his creation and began to look for a partner to help him market it [3]. He entered into a contract with the Hungarian toy manufacturer Politechnika to mass produce the cube. In 1977, the first version of the cube appeared in toy stores in Budapest as the *Büvös Kocka*, also known as the Magic Cube [4]. Eventually, the cube became popular throughout Hungary [3]. In 1980, the cube was taken to an international market and sold under the patent name, Rubik's Cube, making it well known throughout the world. Today, the puzzle is currently owned by Rubik's Brand Ltd. and is still widely popular. Rubik's Cube puzzle solvers, or "cubists," still practice and research the puzzle to this day [2]. Some of them are so dedicated that they have been able to set records by solving the cube in a matter of seconds.

Rubik's original cube was 3" × 3" × 3". Since then, several variations have been introduced. Two of the most popular variations are Rubik's Revenge (also known as the Master Cube), which is a 4" × 4" × 4" cube, and the Professor's Cube, which is a 5" × 5" × 5" cube [5, 6].

11.2 PROBLEM-SOLVING TECHNIQUES

The most valuable problem-solving technique for Rubik's Cube is *solving for subgoals*. There are many methods for solving

Rubik's Cube and more still waiting to be discovered. However, regardless of what steps the methods consist of and how different they are from one another, they will more than likely require the use of subgoals in their solution. Specifically, a subgoal is placing a particular set of smaller cubes into their correct positions.

As mentioned before, regardless of whether or not they are in their correct positions, it is inevitable that the smaller cubes will be moved after rotating the layers in an attempt to correctly position other small cubes. To overcome this, specific "algorithms" must be used. In the context of Rubik's Cube, an algorithm refers to a sequence of layer rotations that moves particular small cubes to specific locations and does not ultimately displace other small cubes that were already positioned correctly.

In general, a solution to Rubik's Cube may proceed as follows:

1. Use algorithm(s) to maneuver a particular set of small cubes into their correct positions.

2. Use other algorithm(s) to maneuver another particular set of small cubes into their correct positions without moving the cubes that were already arranged in the previous step(s). (It is all right if they are moved during the algorithm as long as they are returned to their correct positions when the algorithm is completed.)

3. Repeat step 2 until each of the smaller cubes is arranged in its correct position and the cube is solved.

It is possible for more than one algorithm to be used at a particular subgoal—in other words, one algorithm can be used to reorient the smaller cubes, while another correctly positions them.

11.3 SOLUTION

While there are many ways to solve the standard 3" × 3" × 3" Rubik's Cube, this section describes one of the easiest and most popular methods. This method uses seven subgoals to solve the cube. Before we begin, however, it is imperative that we provide some notations.

11.3.1 Cube Components

The Parts

As mentioned before, Rubik's Cube is made up of 26 smaller cubes. However, they are not identical, as there three different types of these smaller cubes.

The Corners (in white) (Figure 131)

There are a total of 8 corner cubes, each consisting of three colors.

FIGURE 131 Corner Pieces

The Edges (Figure 132)

There are a total of 12 edge pieces, each consisting of two colors.

FIGURE 132 Edge Pieces

The Center (Figure 133)

There are a total of 6 center pieces, each consisting of one color. The center piece is a very important piece to take note of when solving the cube, as it identifies the color of a particular face. This is because a center piece will never change position relative to the other center pieces.

FIGURE 133 Center Pieces

For this solution, we will name each smaller cube by the colors they contain and their type. Additionally, we will refer to them as pieces instead of smaller cubes. For example, an edge piece consists of the colors red and blue. We will call this the Red-Blue edge piece.

The Faces (Figure 134)

Just like any cube, there are a total of six faces (or sides) to the Rubik's Cube. Each face is identified by a different color, and that color is determined by the color of its center small cube. The configuration of the colors may differ from cube to cube, so for the solution here, we use a two-dimensional view of the cube and its colors:

R = Red

W = White

Y = Yellow

B = Blue

G = Green

O = Orange

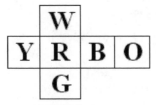

FIGURE 134 Cube Faces

The Layers

By *layers*, we are referring to the sections of the cube that can be rotated. A layer consists of 9 smaller cubes that can be rotated as much as 360 degrees two-dimensionally. The cube has a total of six layers, and each will be denoted by a single letter:

The Top (or Up) Layer = **U** (Figure 135)

FIGURE 135 Top Layer

The Bottom (or Down) Layer = **D** (Figure 136)

FIGURE 136 Bottom Layer

The Left Layer   =   **L** (Figure 137)

FIGURE 137 Left Layer

The Right Layer   =   **R** (Figure 138)

FIGURE 138 Right Layer

The Front Layer   =   **F** (Figure 139)

FIGURE 139 Front Layer

The Back Layer=   **B** (Figure 140)

FIGURE 140 Back Layer

The layers are named relative to the faces of the cube that are considered to be the front and top. For example, if we choose the White Face to be our Front Face and the Red Face to be our Top Face, then the layer considered as the Left will be different from the layer considered the Left if say the Blue Face was considered the Front Face.

These denotations will be used to show how a particular layer is to be rotated in an algorithm. When a letter is shown, that means that the layer it corresponds to is to be rotated 90 degrees clockwise. Furthermore, an apostrophe (') after the letter indicates that the same layer is to be rotated 90 degrees counterclockwise. A chain of these letters will make up an algorithm, and they must be followed in the order given. Here is an example of an algorithm:

U D F'

This algorithm indicates that the Top Layer should be moved clockwise, then the Bottom Layer, and finally the Front Layer should be moved counterclockwise. You will see that as more small cubes are put into place, the algorithms used to solve the remaining cubes become more complex. To begin this solution, we choose the Red Side to be the Top Face. The Front Face will be determined later.

11.3.2 Subgoal 1: The Top Cross

FIGURE 141 Subgoal 1

The first subgoal (Figure 141) is to place the top 4 edge cubes into their correct positions. As a result, the Top Side should look like a red cross.

Achieving this configuration is straightforward. The worst case occurs when an edge piece happens to be on an incorrect side. For example, let's assume that the Red-Green edge is a part of the Blue Face. We want to get it into its correct place on the Green Face. The first thing to do is rotate the layer that contains the Blue Face until this edge is on the Bottom Layer. Next, rotate the Bottom Layer until this edge piece is located on its corresponding Green Face. Finally, rotate the layer with the Green Face twice, and the Red-Green edge should be in its correct position. It could have been the case that the Red-Blue edge could have been in its correct position from the start, and our move displaced it. Fortunately, it is easy to put the Red-Blue edge back into place. After rotating the layer with the Blue Face enough to put the Red-Green edge to the Bottom Layer, rotate the Bottom Layer once so the Red-Green edge is away from the layer with the Blue Face, and then rotate that layer until the Red-Blue Side is back in place. It is possible you may end up with Figure 142.

FIGURE 142 Inverted Edge

Take note of the issue here. The Red-Green edge has its colors inverted. To fix this, a particular algorithm must be used.

First, consider the Front Side as the Green Face, with the Top Side remaining as the Red Face. Next, perform these moves:

F' U L' U'

This algorithm will reorient the Red-Green edge to its correct configuration, while keeping the other three top edges in place.

11.3.3 Subgoal 2: The Top Corners

FIGURE 143 Subgoal 2

The sub-goal in Figure 143 will not only put the 4 top corner pieces in the correct place, but it will also complete the Red Face and the entire Top Layer!

Let's say we want to begin by putting the Red-Blue-Green corner in its correct place. Our first step is to bring the corner to the bottom if it is not already there. First, locate one of the sides that the Red-Blue-Green corner is on and call that the Front Side. In our case, let's say that it is located in between the Yellow and White Faces. We can either choose the Front Face to be the Yellow Face or the White Face. Let's choose the White Face to be the Front Face. The Red-Green-Blue corner can now be located on the upper left corner of the Front Face. To get it to the bottom without displacing the Red-White edge, perform this algorithm:

F D' F'

If we had chosen the Front Face to be the Yellow Face instead, the Red-Green-Blue corner would be located on the upper left side, and we would have to perform this algorithm instead:

F' D F

Whichever algorithm was performed, our target corner should now be on the Bottom Layer, and the edge we positioned in sub-goal 1 should still be on the Top Layer. Rotate the Bottom Layer until the corner piece is located in between the Green and Blue Faces. At this point, we can have one of the three possible states shown in Figures 144 to 146.

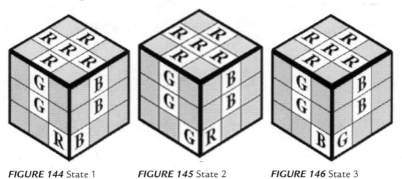

FIGURE 144 State 1   **FIGURE 145** State 2   **FIGURE 146** State 3

State 1: Make the new Front Face the face that contains the correct color (which in this case will be the Blue Face). Our target corner should now be a part of the lower left corner of the Front Face. Then perform the following algorithm:

L D' L'

State 2: As with State 1, make the new Front Face the face that contains the correct color (which in this case will be the Green Face). However, the target corner should now be a part of the lower right corner of the Front Face. Then perform the following algorithm:

R' D R

State 3: In this orientation, we cannot properly place the Red-Green-Blue corner in its correct position. We need to reorient the corner so it matches State 1 or State 2. Let's change it to State 1. First, pick the new Front Face that will make the target corner be a part of its lower left corner (in this case the Green Face). Then perform the following algorithm:

L D'D' L' D

After performing this, the corner piece will be back in between the Green and Blue Faces and will be oriented as it appears in State 1. Now simply perform the State 1 algorithm. Do these methods for all four corners, and you will have achieved subgoal 2.

Subgoal 3: The Middle Layer

FIGURE 147 Subgoal 3

Subgoal 3 (Figure 147) puts the four center edge cubes in their correct positions. By the end of this subgoal, the middle layer of Rubik's Cube will be completely solved. Before we begin, it is important to flip the cube upside down. Therefore, the new Top Layer is the Orange Face, now making the Red Face the Bottom Layer.

First, locate an edge on the Top Layer that does not contain the color of the top face (in this case Orange). Let's say we find the Blue-Green edge. Also, let's say that the vertical color of this edge happens to be Blue, while the horizontal is Green. Rotate the Top Layer until the vertical side of the edge piece matches its corresponding face. In this case, rotate the Top Layer until the Blue-Green edge is located on the Blue Face, which will now be considered the Front Face. The cube should now look like Figure 148.

FIGURE 148 Pre-Algorithm State

Take note of the top color of this edge piece. From the Front Face, look at the colors of the Left and Right Faces. Whichever color matches the target edge's top color determines which algorithm to use next. In this case, the Green on the top of the Blue-Green edge matches the Green Face, which is located on the Right Layer. Therefore, use the following algorithm:

U R U' R' U' F' U F

After performing this algorithm, the Blue-Green edge will be placed in its appropriate position in the middle row.

Alternatively, if it were the case that the Green Face was on the Left Layer, we would use this algorithm:

U' L' U L U F U' F'

One possible issue that can occur is that an edge piece will be placed in its correct position but oriented incorrectly, as in Figure 149.

FIGURE 149 Incorrect Orientation

To fix this issue, it must first be moved back into the Top Layer. This is done simply by using any one of the two algorithms above to place another edge piece in that spot. Specifically, this edge should have Orange on it, since it will be replaced anyway and will not misplace any other important edges. After it is removed from the middle row, appropriately use the above algorithms to put it back into its correct orientation. Do this for the four edges to successfully solve the middle layer.

11.3.4 Subgoal 4: The New Top Cross

FIGURE 150 Subgoal 4

We have successfully completed two-thirds of the entire cube. However, solving this Top Layer requires four subgoals.

This next subgoal is to make a cross on the now Top Face (Figure 150). It does not matter which edge pieces are used as long as the top of the edges are Orange and an Orange cross is made.

After the previous subgoal, the Top Face will be arranged in one of the four ways shown in Figures 151 to 154.

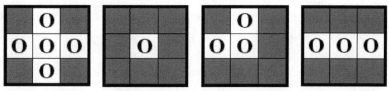

FIGURE 151 State 1   **FIGURE 152** State 2   **FIGURE 153** State 3   **FIGURE 154** State 4

In any of these four states, do not consider the color of the corners whether they are Orange or not. Also, this should still be considered the Top Face and not the Front Face. In carry out the following algorithms, you must pick a Front Face so the Top Face appears as one of these figures when you look at the cube from above.

State 1: The cross is already formed, and you can move on to subgoal 6.

State 2: The only part of the cross is the center. Use the following algorithm:

F U R U' R' F'

State 3: Only three pieces of the cross are in their correct places and form something like a right angle or a backward "L." Use the same algorithm as State 2 for this configuration.

State 4: Again, only three pieces of the cross are in their correct places, but this time they form a straight line. For this configuration, use the following algorithm:

F R U R' U' F'

Additionally, you may find that the Top Face looks like Figure 155.

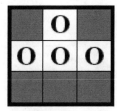

FIGURE 155 Alternate State

This is essentially like a combination of States 3 and 4. For this configuration, use one of the two above algorithms and it will reconfigure into one of the previous states. When this happens, use the appropriate algorithm that corresponds to that state. This completes this subgoal.

11.3.5 Subgoal 5: The New Top's Corners

FIGURE 156 Subgoal 5

Subgoal 5 (Figure 156) is to make the corners of the Top Face Orange, which will complete the Orange Face. Again, it does not matter if the corners are in the correct place or not as long as the tops of them are Orange.

After the previous subgoal, the Top (Orange) Face will have one of the three configurations shown in Figures 157 to 159.

FIGURE 157 State 1   **FIGURE 158** State 2   **FIGURE 159** State 3

Again, this is not the Front Face but the Top Face. However, make sure that you pick a Front Face so any of these configurations match what the Top Face looks like while looking at the cube from above.

For each state, the following algorithm will be used:

R U R' U R U U R'

State 1: Only the cross is present. It is important that you position the cube so the lower left corner piece has the Orange color on the outside left of it, just as the diagram depicts. In other words, while looking at the Left Face, you should see Orange on its upper right corner.

State 2: Any of the two corners on the Top Face has Orange. It does not matter how those two corners are oriented. What matters is that the lower left corner piece has Orange on the outside bottom of it, just as the diagram depicts. In other words, while looking at the Front Face, the upper left corner should be Orange.

State 3: Along with the cross, there is one single Orange corner. This is the state we are looking for. Orient the cube so this corner piece is on the lower left corner of the Top Face. Then use the above algorithm.

After continuously using the algorithm on these states, the entire Top Face will eventually be all the same color, and the subgoal will be achieved.

11.3.6 Subgoal 6: Correct Corner Positioning

FIGURE 160 Subgoal 6

Subgoal 6 (Figure 160) is to position the four Top Layer corner pieces into their correct orientations. At this point, there will be exactly two corners in correct orientation. From an overhead view of the cube, the Top Layer will be arranged in one of the two ways shown in Figures 161 and 162.

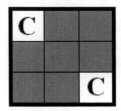

FIGURE 161 State 1 (Adjacent)　　　**FIGURE 162** State 2 (Diagonal)

The "C" indicates the corner pieces in their Correct orientation. They are indicated as such because this can apply to any two random corners in the Top Layer. To see which corners are in correct orientation, the entire cube must be analyzed. Fortunately, doing this is an easy task. First, analyze the four corner pieces as they appear. If you do not see that they are in their correct spots, then rotate the Top Layer 90 degrees and look again. If you still cannot determine them, rotate the Top Layer 90 degrees once again. Eventually, it will become obvious which corners are in correct orientation. However, it is important that once you discover the correct corners, you must rotate the Top Layer so they are placed in their correct locations relative to the entire cube.

For this subgoal, the following algorithm must be used in either case:

R' F R' B B R F' R' B B R R U'

State 1: It is possible that the two correctly oriented corner pieces will be directly next to each other. First, double check to see if they are in their correct positions relative to the cube. If not, you must rotate the Top Face until they are. This is easy to determine, since they are both adjacent and share two of the same colors. Then pick a Front Face so when you are looking at the Top Face from above, it will appear as in Figure 161 (i.e., the upper corner pieces). When looking at the Front Face, these pieces should be all the way in the back of the cube at the top.

State 2: It is also possible that the correctly oriented cubes are directly across from each other on the Top Layer. At this point we need to bring the cube into State 1. If the correctly oriented corner pieces appear as they do in Figure 162, simply use the algorithm above. It does not matter how the Top Layer is positioned or which face is chosen to be the Front Face as long as the Top Face we have been using remains as such (in this case the Orange Face). At this point, your cube will be ready for the final subgoal.

11.3.7 Subgoal 7: The Top Edges

FIGURE 163 Subgoal 7 (Goal State)

The final subgoal, subgoal 7, is to correctly position the four remaining Top Layer edge pieces (Figure 163). There are two algorithms that can solve the cube. At this point, the cube can be in one of two states:

State 1: One edge cube is in the correct position. It may be the case that one of the Top Layer edges is already in its correct position. The first thing to do is examine the cube and analyze the entire Top Layer to see which edge is in position. This is easy to determine because the edge that is in correct position will have completed one of the Side Faces. Then, orient the cube so the completed face is a part of what we will now consider the Back Layer.

The next step is to determine which algorithm to use. To do so, we must analyze the incorrect edge pieces and how they are positioned in relation to each other. First, look at two of the incorrect edges, preferably the one on the Front Layer and one on any Layer adjacent to it (i.e., Left Layer or Right Layer). At this point you will notice that one of the edges will have to either be shifted to the left or right to be correctly placed.

Let's say, for example, we have found the Blue Face to be a part of the Front Layer. Assume we have the configuration in Figure 164.

FIGURE 164 Orange-Blue Edge to the Right

We see that the Orange-Blue edge piece needs to be moved to the Front Layer from the Right Layer, meaning we need to shift it left. Therefore, use the following algorithm:

F F U L R' F F L' R U F F

This will shift the three target edge pieces in a clockwise direction relative to the Top Layer, which is why we can call this the "clockwise" algorithm

It may also be the case that the cube has the configuration in Figure 165.

FIGURE 165 Orange-Green Edge to the Right

Now, we see that the Orange-Green edge needs to be moved from the Front Layer to the Right Layer and shift it right. Therefore, we use what we call the "counterclockwise" algorithm:

F F U' L R' F F L' R U' F F

This will shift the three target edge pieces counterclockwise. Using either of these algorithms once should place these edges in their correct positions

State 2: None of the Top Layer edges are correct. It may be the case that all four Top Layer edges are not in their incorrect positions. If so, then use any one of the two algorithms above. It will not put all four edges in their correct positions, but it will put one edge in its correct position, bringing the cube into State 1. At this point, Rubik's Cube will be completely solved.

11.4 HUMAN PROBLEM SOLVING

Unfortunately, we have not been able to obtain a collection of test subjects to apply our Human Problem Solving analysis to Rubik's Cube. However, if you know anyone who is determined to solve a puzzle, that puzzle is probably Rubik's Cube. It may just be out of curiosity, but if you put a Rubik's Cube in a room with some people, someone (probably even a few people) is going to pick it up and try to solve it. Even if you are with a friend and we are having a conversation, he or she will pick it up and begin to solve it, either consciously or unconsciously.

Personally, we have never seen anyone solve the cube. If we observe someone trying, he or she always makes the fatal mistake of trying to solve one face at a time. First, without an attempt to use any algorithms, they struggle to solve one face. As soon as they solve it, they try to solve a second one, only to find that their first face becomes unsolved. Then they simply give up. If they had attempted to correctly position the small cubes instead of simply the faces, maybe they would have been more successful.

11.5 HUMAN WINDOW ANALYSIS OF SOLUTIONS

Difficulty
7/10

Complexity
O(n²/log)

Name	Int or Ext?	Intly/ Extly	Rep.	HW?	Corr?	Grn Sz	Exec	Compr	Prob. Solv. Mthd	Flex	Mode of Conv	Opt?	Tot
Adam	Ext.	3/10	Txt w/ Pics	Y	Y	Ideal	8/10	4/10	Subgoals	5/10	Img/Txt Editor	N	20/40
Animation	Ext.	9/10	Txt w/ Pics	Y	Y	Ideal	9/10	8/10	Subgoals	7/10	Img/Txt Editor	N	33/40
C&P	Ext.	4/10	Txt w/ Pics	Y	Y	Ideal	8/10	6/10	Subgoals	6/10	Img/Txt Editor; Hand	N	24/40
Cartoon Pics	Ext.	5/10	Txt w/ Pics	Y	Y	Ideal	8/10	7/10	Subgoals	7/10	Img/Txt Editor; Hand	N	27/40
Enemy	Ext.	8/10	Txt w/ Pics	Y	Y	Ideal	7/10	9/10	Subgoals	7/10	Img/Txt Editor	N	31/40
Magic Cube	Ext.	7/10	Txt w/ Pics	Y	Y	Ideal	7/10	8/10	Subgoals	7/10	Img/Txt Editor; Hand	N	29/40
Short	Ext.	6/10	Txt w/ Pics	Y	Y	Ideal	2/10	3/10	Subgoals	6/10	Img/Txt Editor; Hand	N	17/40
Simple Cube	Ext.	7/10	Txt w/ Pics	Y	Y	Ideal	8/10	9/10	Subgoals	7/10	Img/Txt Editor	N	31/40
Square	Ext.	7/10	Txt w/ Pics	Y	Y	Ideal	6/10	4/10	Subgoals	7/10	Img/Txt Editor	N	24/40

Int or Ext?: Intensional or Extensional—Is the solution intensional or extensional?

Intly/Extly: Intensionality/Extensionality—How intensional or extensional is the solution?

Rep.: Representation—How is the solution represented?

HW?: Human Window—Does the solution exist in the Human Window?

Corr?: Correctness—Is the solution correct?

Grn Sz: Grain Size—How much computation (large) or memory (small) does one need to solve the solution?

Exec: Executability—How executable is this solution?

Compr: Comprehensibility—How comprehensible is this solution?

Prob. Solv. Mthd: Problem-Solving Method—What method is used in the solution to solve the problem?

Flex: Flexibility—How flexible is this solution (i.e., can this solution be represented in other ways)?

Mode of Conv: Mode of Conveyance—In what ways can this solution be reproduced/replicated?

Opt?: Optimal—Is the solution optimal?

TABLE 15 Ranking Rubik's Cube Solutions According to the Human Window

Since Rubik's Cube is such a popular puzzle with so many methods to solve it, it only makes sense that such a large number of solutions exist for it. However, regardless of the fact that such a large number of solutions exist, their representations are substantially identical.

When analyzing the solutions, it can be seen that there are three key features for each that make up each of their representations:

Cube Depiction: Whether it is to show a goal arrangement, a subsequent step, or an arrangement to avoid, it is common for a solution to present images of the actual cube itself. Displaying images of the cube will show a clear depiction of what the cube should or should not look like at a particular step. This makes a solution highly comprehensible, especially to those who are using a physical cube, as they can simply match their cube to the image. It is possible for the cube to be described using words, but that would make things unnecessarily complex.

Text Descriptions: While pictures are beneficial, it is also important that a solution contains some description as well. This will help to emphasize and explain important features of a solution, such as its notations, the sides of the cube to focus on at a particular step, and what to look for or avoid at a step. A textual description provides a sort of guidance through the solution. A solution containing only images without descriptions will make it less organized and harder to follow and therefore may be less comprehensible.

Movement Notation: The feature that seems to be the most dissimilar between solutions is the representation of rotating layers of the cube when describing algorithms. The most commonly used representation is actual images of the cube, with indications as to which layer needs to be rotated and in which direction. Generally, this seems to be the best representation. Another representation is a small square with lines that represent layers and arrows on those lines that represent the direction of rotation (i.e. ,), as with the "Adam Solution" and the "C&P Solution." Finally, another representation uses letters that represent the layer to rotate and apostrophes to indicate that they will be moved counterclockwise, as with the "Cartoon Pics Solution," the "Short Solution," and the solution presented in this chapter (Section 11.3).

These features are the main determining factors of how comprehensible a solution is. As you can see from the table, the rankings are generally mixed. Some solutions had more diagrams and no text, others had too much text and too few diagrams, some were just right, and so on. For a solution to be ranked high in comprehensibility, it should have just the right amount of text and diagrams. The movement notation, however, can vary, depending on how the solution is conveyed.

The most commonly used algorithms and subgoals are those used in the solution presented in this chapter. Some solutions, however, provide similar subgoals but with different algorithms. Others give completely different algorithms and subgoals altogether. It is these criteria that determine a solution's executability ranking. Longer and more complex algorithms that are used may generally be harder to carry out correctly and may require more memory.

Finally, none of the analyzed solutions are optimal. Since the solutions are found by achieving particular subgoals, the number of moves needed to achieve these subgoals may very well be more than the shortest number of possible moves. More advanced solutions are most likely to be optimal, since they show more precise algorithms (see Section 11.6).

11.5.1 The Most Human Window–Compatible Solution

The solution assessed as MHWC is the "Animation Solution," which was developed by Ryan Heise. This solution contains animations, so it is difficult to reproduce it on paper. However, it can be found in reference [7]. This solution uses the same subgoals, steps, and algorithms as the solution depicted in this section. It depicts the subgoals so they are easy to understand, while the descriptions are short and clearly explain how to achieve these subgoals, making this solution highly comprehensible. The solution also includes every possible case at particular subgoals and how to correctly resolve them.

The most notable feature of this solution, and one of the main reasons this solution is considered the MHWC, is the fact that both the Cube Depiction and Movement Notation are combined together. The solution depicts three-dimensional images of the cube to show final subgoal arrangements and what the cube would look like at particular cases, increasing the solution's comprehensibility and extensionality. The most noteworthy feature of these images is that they are also animated, so when they are clicked, the layers rotate to show how the specific algorithms are carried out on command. This increases the solution's comprehensibility and executability even further.

To improve this solution even more, the steps of each algorithm should be depicted along with the animated cubes. This will give the solver a choice between watching the animation and following the steps of the algorithms as they are commonly followed.

11.5.2 The Least Human Window–Compatible Solution

Step 1: The Cross

Step 2: Bottom Layer Corners
Each algorithm moves a corner from the top layer to the bottom layer right below.

R U R'   F' U' F   R U2 R' U' R U R'

Step 3: Middle Layer
- First, position the edge from the top layer to the middle layer in the front.

- Second, position the edge from the top layer to the middle layer in the back.

R' U' R' U' R' U R U R   **R U R U R U' R' U' R'**

Step 4: Edges
If Orange pieces form a line on top, apply the first algorithm. Then apply the second.

  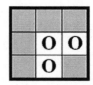

F (R U R' U') F' U2 F (U R U' R') F'

Step 5: Corners
View the top layer.
Algorithm: R U R' U R U2 R'

If ONE corner is Orange, move it to the bottom left. Then apply the algorithm.

 or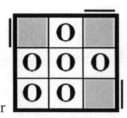

If TWO corners are Orange, rotate top layer until a Yellow sticker is on the bottom left, facing front. Then apply the algorithm.

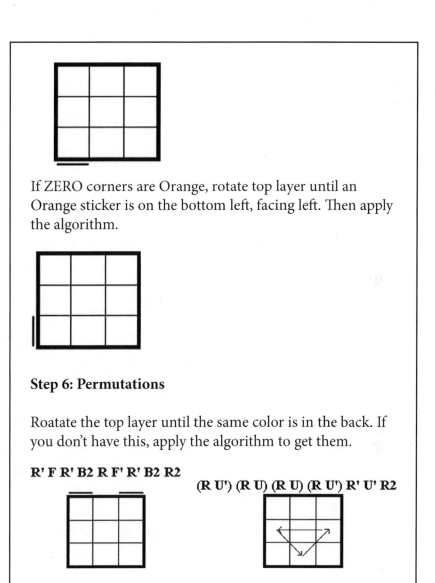

If ZERO corners are Orange, rotate top layer until an Orange sticker is on the bottom left, facing left. Then apply the algorithm.

Step 6: Permutations

Roatate the top layer until the same color is in the back. If you don't have this, apply the algorithm to get them.

R' F R' B2 R F' R' B2 R2

(R U') (R U) (R U) (R U') R' U' R2

FIGURE 166 The "Short Solution"

The solution assessed as LHWC is the "Short Solution" (Figure 166). (A representation similar to this can be found in reference [8].) Although it was intended to be a reference to those who already understand the solution, we will view this solution in terms of the Human Window as if it were intended for those who do not know how to solve the puzzle.

This solution also uses the common subgoals like those presented in Section 11.3. However, unlike the "Animation Solution" and the solution presented in Section 11.3, this solution is excessively shortened. The subgoals are briefly described and have little detail in their description, which may possibly decrease both the comprehensibility and executability. It also shows the possible layer arrangements for a subgoal and the algorithm used to resolve it, but it fails to show every possible case, which may also reduce executability.

Finally, it is important to take note that the first subgoal does not depict any description or algorithms. It merely shows the final arrangement and the arrangement to avoid. If a person is new to solving Rubik's Cube, he or she will be unaware of which algorithms to use.

11.6 BEST MACHINE SOLUTION

Rubik's Cube has approximately 43 quintillion possible arrangements, so from the start we could disregard any kind of brute force algorithm [9]. Despite this incredibly large number, we have already shown that the cube can be solved in a reasonable amount of steps by solving for subgoals. The question now is how efficiently can a machine solve the cube?

In 1981, mathematician Morwen Thistlethwaite developed a complex algorithm that could solve the cube with 52 or fewer moves. Since a fair amount of memory is required, this algorithm is more efficient for a machine. Unlike the algorithms we have seen in this chapter, Thistlethwaite's algorithm "works on all the pieces at the same time, restricting them to fewer and fewer possibilities until there is only one possible position left for each piece" [10]. There are four phases:

$G0 = \{L, R, F, B, U, D\}$

$G1 = \{L, R, F, B, U^2, D^2\}$

$G2 = \{L, R, F2, B2, U^2, D^2\}$

$G3 = \{L2, R^2, F^2, B^2, U^2, D^2\}$

$G4 = \{1\}$

These groups represent the subgoals that are to be achieved. They are depicted as sets, which represent every possible arrangement that can be achieved, given certain restrictions on layer movements. The letters contained in the brackets represent these restrictions. Each letter represents a layer of the cube, and those with an exponent next to them are restricted to 180-degree turns only.

To achieve a particular subgoal, the cube must be arranged in one of the positions contained in the set of positions of the next subgoal. For example, say the cube is in one of the arrangements of set G1. This means that to achieve subgoal G2, the cube needs to be repositioned into a position contained in subgoal G2, which essentially means a position in which the Front, Back, Up, or Down layers no longer need to be rotated 90 degrees. However, to achieve such a position, we must follow the rules of G1, and whenever the Up or Down face is to be moved, they are strictly to be turned 180 degrees and not 90 degrees. To determine whether or not the next subgoal is met, the current position of the cube is matched with a table [10].

Despite the improvements made to Thistlethwaite's algorithm, its biggest flaw was that the number of phases meant the table had to be quite large. One person who addressed this problem and improved the algorithm was Herbert Kociemba. First, he reduced the algorithm to just two phases:

$G0 = \{U, D, R, L, F, B\}$

$G1 = \{U, D, R^2, L^2, F^2, B^2\}$

$G2 = \{1\}$

The consequence of reducing the number of phases is that it greatly increases the number of moves available and the size of the table per phase. To fix this, he decided "to make pruning tables and use IDA* to solve each phase," greatly reducing the state space [11]. To improve the algorithm further, Kociemba added a feature that continues the IDA* search even after the solution is found for a particular phase. This allows the algorithm to find the solution with the shortest number of steps possible [11].

Although Kociemba's algorithm is efficient, it is not optimal. In 1995, Michael Reid analyzed this algorithm and discovered that it takes at most 29 moves to solve the cube with the algorithm [12]. However, in 2010, Tomas Rokicki, Herbert Kociemba, Morley Davidson, and John Dethridge proved that Rubik's Cube can be solved in at most 20 moves, no matter what the position is. Although there is no specific algorithm that can solve the cube in 20 moves, this was proven by doing extensive research to solve all 43 quintillion possible arrangements. By using simple mathematics programming and by partitioning these arrangements into particular sets, it took approximately 35 CPU years to solve every position of Rubik's Cube, discovering that it only takes at most 20 moves to solve the cube from any arrangement. This number is now referred to as "God's Number," since it is the optimal number of moves, indicating that "God's Algorithm" would result in 20 moves [12]. The term "God's Algorithm" refers to an algorithm that solves Rubik's Cube, or any other combinatory puzzle, in the shortest number of steps. Some algorithms have come close, but none have received the title.

Regardless of which algorithm is used to solve Rubik's Cube, the complexity for any algorithm in the worst case was found to be $\Theta(\ n2/\log(n)\ )$, according to a research paper on algorithms for Rubik's Cube titled "Algorithms for Solving Rubik's Cubes" [13].

11.7 PLAYABLE PROGRAM

A playable Rubik's Cube game is available at *http://activeden. net/item/cube-assembler/full_screen_preview/3131480*. The game depicts a three-dimensional cube with layers that can be rotated with a simple stroke of the mouse. Also, the cube itself can be rotated at will by shifting one of two scrollbars, allowing the player to get a full view of the cube. Additionally, the player can choose between solving the easy 2" × 2" × 2" cube up to the more difficult 5" × 5" × 5" cube. Finally, the player has the option to change the colors of the cube faces to any color he or she desires.

11.8 REFERENCES

1. *The History of Rubik's.* (2013). Available at *http://www.rubiks.com/ world/history.php.* Accessed on January 9, 2014.

2. MSKIFF. (2013). *The Rubik's Cube: A Brief History.* Available at *http://azscitechfest.org/blogs/rubik's-cube-brief-history.* Accessed on January 9, 2014.

3. Goudey, Christophe. (2013). *The Rubik's Cube History.* Available at *http://cubeland.free.fr/infos/infos.htm.* Accessed on January 9, 2014.

4. Rosenberg, J. (2013). *History of the Rubik's Cube.* Available at *http:// history1900s.about.com/od/1980s/a/rubikscube.htm.* Accessed on January 9, 2014.

5. TheRubiks4×4×4—"RubiksRevenge."(2013).Availableat*http://www. rubiks.com/products/3d_puzzles/rubiks_cube-4×4.php.* Accessed on January 9, 2014.

6. *The Rubiks 5 × 5 × 5—"Professor's Cube."* (2013). Available at *http://www.rubiks.com/products/3d_puzzles/rubiks_cube-5×5.php.* Accessed on January 9, 2014.

7. Heise, Ryan. (2013). *Beginner's Rubik's Cube Solution.* Available at *http://www.ryanheise.com/cube/beginner.html.* Accessed on January 9, 2014.

8. BADMEPHISTO. (2013). *Rubik's Cube Solution: Printable Cheat Sheet.* Available at *http://badmephisto.com/begsoln/.* Accessed on January 9, 2014.

9. Dillow, C. (2010). "God's Number Revealed: 20 Moves Proven Enough to Solve Any Rubik's Cube Position." *Popular Science.* Available at *http://www.popsci.com/science/article/2010-08/gods-number-revealed-20-moves-will-solve-any-rubiks-cube-position.* Accessed on January 9, 2014.

10. Jaap. (2013). *Thistlethwaite's 52-Move Algorithm.* Available at *http:// www.jaapsch.net/puzzles/thistle.htm.* Accessed on January 9, 2014.

11. Jaap. (2013). Computer Puzzling—Kociemba's Algorithm. Available at *http://www.jaapsch.net/puzzles/compcube.htm.* Accessed on January 9, 2014.

12. Rokicki, T., Kociemba, H., Davidson, M., and Dethridge, J. (2013). *God's Number Is 20.* Available at *http://www.cube20.org/.* Accessed on January 9, 2014.

13. Demaine, E.D., Demaine, M.L., Eisenstat, S., Lubiw, A., and Winslow, A. (2011). *Algorithms for Solving Rubik's Cubes.* Cambridge, MA: MIT Computer Science and Artificial Intelligence Laboratory.

THE PRISONER'S DILEMMA

DENY EVERYTHING ƎNIHTYЯƎVƎ YИƎO

FIGURE 167 The Prisoner's Dilemma

12.1 THE TRADITIONAL PROBLEM*+

In the movie *The Postman Always Rings Twice*,** the two lead characters fall in love and decide to "eliminate" the husband

---

°   This section is based on Lucci and Kopec (2013). *Artificial Intelligence in the 21st Century.* Mercury Learning. Dulles, Virginia, pp. 130-132.

°° The 1981 version is a reproduction of an earlier movie based on the novel by James M. Cain (1934) that stars Jack Nicholson and Jessica Lange.

of the female character. The police have insufficient evidence to obtain convictions. However, after the murder, the lovers are apprehended by the police and held for questioning in separate interrogation rooms, where each is offered the same proposition: "Tell the truth and incriminate your partner, and we'll go easy on you." Acquiescing to this request is called "defecting." Both perpetrators know that their accomplice is being offered this same deal. What should each prisoner do? This predicament is intriguing in that neither person is privy to their counterpart's thoughts (they are in isolated cells). In an ideal world, both would remain loyal to each other (as per their original agreement in perpetrating the crime) and without the existence of further evidence and supporting testimony against them would probably be convicted of a lesser crime. However, if either accomplice defects, then the other would certainly be better off by defecting as well, rather than serving a murder sentence.

This so-called **Prisoner's Dilemma** (Figure 167) was first formulated in game-theoretic terms by Merrill Floyd and Melvin Dresher at the RAND Corporation in 1950 [1]. At the time, most countries were involved in a Cold War with two nuclear super-powers: the Soviet Union and the United States. Should these two countries cooperate with each other and work toward mutual disarmament (aware at all times that the other side might renege), or should each continue to create new and more lethal armaments? This is the dilemma that confronted our planet for four decades, from the end of World War II until the eventual end of the Cold War in 1989 with the fall of the Berlin Wall. The Prisoner's Dilemma aptly models that era of mistrust. This dilemma can also be modeled by the **payoff matrix** in Figure 168. A payoff matrix specifies the return to each player for every combination of actions by the two game participants.

Assume that the two players (that is, the prisoners) in this game are rational and want to minimize their jail sentences. Each prisoner has two choices (as did the two characters in

The Postman Always Rings Twice): cooperate with their partner in crime and remain silent or defect by confessing to the police in return for a lesser sentence.

Prisoner B

		Cooperate (remain silent)	Defect (betray partner)
Prisoner A	Cooperate (remain silent)	A: 1 Year B: 1 Year	A: 10 Years B: 0 Years
	Defect (betray partner)	A: 0 Years B: 10 Years	A: 5 Years B: 5 Years

FIGURE 168 Payoff Matrix for The Prisoner's Dilemma

You might notice that this game differs in an important aspect from the games discussed earlier in this book. To determine a course of action in the other games and puzzles discussed, you need to know your opponent's course of action. For example, if you are moving second in a game of tic-tac-toe, you need to know where the other player has placed the initial X. This is not the case in The Prisoner's Dilemma. Suppose you are the A player and you choose to defect. However, the B player decides to remain loyal and chooses the cooperation strategy. In this case, your decision results in no prison time as opposed to the one-year term had both of you chosen to cooperate. If your partner chooses to defect, your outcome is still superior if you choose to defect. In game-theoretic terms, defecting is a **dominant strategy**. Because you assume that your opponent in this game is rational, he or she will arrive at the same strategy.

The strategy {Betray, Betray} shared by the two participants is referred to as a **Nash Equilibrium**. A change in strategy by either player results in a lesser return to them (i.e., more jail time).

As shown in Figure 168, if each player acts more on faith than rationality (faith that their partners would remain loyal), then the total payoff would exceed the total of 10 prison years accorded by the Nash Equilibrium of {Defect, Defect}. This strategy of {Cooperate, Cooperate} yields the best possible outcome in terms of total payoff to the two players. This optimal strategy is referred to as **Pareto Optimal**. It should be noted that The Prisoner's Dilemma is not a zero-sum game. *Why not?* In such games, Nash Equilibrium does not necessarily correspond to a Pareto Optimal game [2].

12.2 THE ITERATED PRISONER'S DILEMMA

If you play The Prisoner's Dilemma only once, defecting is a dominating strategy for either player. In another version of this game, you play repeatedly—*n* times—where there is some memory of previous actions. When having more than one turn, each player is not as quick to defect, knowing that *revenge* from the opponent is forthcoming. One strategy might be to start with a single cooperation to give your opponent a chance to act *compassionately*. If your opponent chooses to defect anyway, you can counter by continually defecting. If your opponent eventually chooses to cooperate, you can return to a more *magnanimous* policy. It is interesting that with The Prisoner's Dilemma and its iterations or variations, we can ascribe words to numbers representing behaviors. Behaviors could include, for example, betrayal, defection, cooperation, trust, revenge, magnanimity, compassion, and so on. These concepts are fully discussed in Robert Bram's excellent treatise "Theory of Moves" [3]. The exercises at the end of this chapter discuss other two-person games that are similar to The Prisoner's Dilemma.

12.3 APPLICATIONS IN DIVERSE AREAS

The Prisoner's Dilemma allows us to address and depict problem situations in the social sciences—for example, economics, political science, psychology, philosophy—in a numerical way such that they may be better understood and solutions can be effectively represented in a convenient way. In addition, through the "Iterated Prisoner's Dilemma," generations of the problems under consideration can be simulated. The difference between The Prisoner's Dilemma and the other problems that we have discussed to this point is that it is concerned with considerations of "What if?" In other words, actions and responses to them are considered and evaluated in as realistic a way as the "matrix system" allows. Chapter 13 presents the problem "Ten Pirates and Their Gold." This problem is similar to The Prisoner's Dilemma, since to determine what course of action should be taken, you must consider a number of possible "moves" and scenarios several steps ahead.

The following are well-known problems that have been posed in Lucci and Kopec's book (page 132). Consider whether they are instances of essentially the same problem as The Prisoner's Dilemma. If you conclude that a problem is equivalent to The Prisoner's Dilemma, then design an appropriate payoff matrix. Comment on the existence of a Nash equilibrium and Pareto Optimal in each case.

Example 1: Linux is a version of Unix that has been developed under the GPL. Under this agreement, you are given free software and may study the source code, which is modifiable. You can defect by keeping these improvements to yourself, or you can cooperate by distributing the improved version of the code. In fact, cooperation is forced by making it illegal to distribute only the source code without your improvements.

Solution: In this problem, higher numbers mean more success.

If you **cooperate/cooperate** by distributing the source code with your improvements, there is mutual benefit. This is essentially a variation of The Prisoner's Dilemma. If you defect either by making no improvements or by distributing the software illegally, these actions are represented by cooperate/defect (10, 0) or defect/cooperate (0, 10), respectively. Finally, if you distribute the software AND make no improvements to it, you are performing defect/defect, which means you are a thief and a liar.

UNIX and GPL	Cooperate	Defect
Cooperate	(5, 5)	(10, 0)
Defect	(0, 10)	(1, 1)

TABLE 16 Example 1

The Nash Equilibrium is represented by (0, 10) and (10, 0) as in the original Prisoner's Dilemma.

Example 2: Cigarette companies were at one time allowed to advertise in the United States. If only one company decided to advertise, an increase in sales invariably followed. However, if two companies launched advertising campaigns, their ads would essentially cancel each other out, and no increase in revenue resulted.

Solution:

This is akin to the original Prisoner's Dilemma, but with a twist. If both companies advertise, the Nash Equilibrium is if either company advertises. If both companies advertise or neither company advertises, then the result is the status quo (1, 1).

Cigarette Advertising	Advertise	No Advertising
Advertise	(1, 1)	(10, 1)
No Advertising	(1, 10)	(1, 1)

TABLE 17 Example 2

Example 3: In New Zealand, newspaper boxes are left unlocked. One can easily steal a paper (defect). Naturally, if everyone did this, no papers would remain [2]. Clearly this is an example of the Iterated Prisoner's Dilemma, because even though at first it may seem that the "stolen" newspapers have little effect, over time there would be no newspapers left to sell.

Example 4 (Tragedy of the Commons): A village has n farmers, and grassland is limited. Each of these farmers may decide to keep a sheep. Each farmer obtains some utility from these sheep in the form of wool and milk. However, the common grassland (the Commons) will suffer somewhat from the sheep grazing there.

Solution: The solution is described below. It was first described by Hardin in *The Tragedy of the Commons* [5].

When multiple individuals act independently and they apply their own self-interest, they will deplete a shared resource. This will occur even though it is in no one's long-term interest. Originally formulated in terms of sheep and common grassland, it can readily be applied to many contemporary conundrums. Global climate is one such arena. It is cheaper to manufacture products if little or no attention is paid to pollution and emission control, but it is certainly detrimental to the earth's long-term health. A nice example for this scenario is available at *www.skepticalscience. com.*

12.4 RELATED PROBLEMS

A problem which seems to resemble The Prisoner's Dilemma most closely is the game of Chicken. This is a situation where two drivers are on a collision course with one another. They are given a choice of steering away (avoidance) or staying on course. If both stay on their course, the worst possible outcome, a crash, occurs. It seems interesting that although both participants may be aware of the worst possible outcome and best one, some people will still choose not to cooperate. This might be due to the rationale that both drivers would think that the other driver is going to steer away to avoid collision.

This also reminds one of the kind of the "escalation" which can occur when there is a false nuclear alert. Each party may raise the level of its response in such a situation without knowing what level of reaction the other party is at. This is a very dangerous state of affairs [6].

12.5 REFERENCES

1. Merrill, F., and Dresher, M. (1961). *Games of Strategy: Theory and Applications.* Upper Saddle River, NJ: Prentice Hall.

2. Poundstone, W. (1992). *Prisoner's Dilemma.* New York: Doubleday.

3. Brams, S. (1994). *Theory of Moves.* Cambridge, UK: Cambridge University Press.

4. Lucci, S., and Kopec, D. (2013). *Artificial Intelligence in the 21st Century.* Dulles, Virginia: Mercury Learning Inc.

5. Hardin, G. (1968). "The Tragedy of the Commons." *Science* (162) 3859: 1243–1248.

6. Kopec, D. *Human and Machine Representations of Knowledge,* 1980. University of Edinburgh

PROBLEMS REQUIRING COMPUTER SOLUTIONS

CHAPTER 13

SUDOKU

2	1	4	8	6	7	5	9	
3	9	7	5	1	4	2	8	6
6	5		2	9	3	4	7	1
1	4	5	3		9	7	6	8
9	7		4	8	6	1	2	5
	6	2	1	7	5	9	3	
7	3	1	6	5	2	8		9
4	8	9	7	3	1	6	5	2
5		6	9	4	8	3	1	7

FIGURE 169 Sudoku

13.1 BACKGROUND

Sudoku is a logic puzzle featuring a 9 × 9 number grid with nine 3 × 3 sub-grids. Each row, column, and sub-grid must contain all the digits from 1-9, with no digit appearing twice in any of those regions [1]. A ready to play game comes with some of the squares already filled in, and the objective is to fill the entire grid. The creator of a particular puzzle can control the difficulty level, the more "hints" being given, the easier the game is to solve. A "well composed" puzzle, however, will always have just one unique solution, even those that start with fewer filled squares [2].

The most basic ancestry of the Sudoku puzzle can be traced back to the "Magic Square" Puzzle found in China as early as 650 BC, which consisted of a square grid of numbers, in which each row, column, and the diagonal must equate to the same number. The Magic Square Puzzle eventually spread to Persia, Arabia, and India, and even made its way to Europe [3].

The mathematician Leonard Euler worked on a more complex Magic Square, called a Greco-Roman Square. The use of numbers as well as any requirements regarding the diagonal were discarded, replaced by combining Greek and Roman letters in each box in such a way that they all occur once in every row and column [3]. This idea was very similar in concept to the Sudoku of today. A complete Greco-Roman Square might have looked like this:

Aα	Bγ	Cδ	Dβ
Bβ	Aδ	Dγ	Cα
Cγ	Dα	Aβ	Bδ
Dδ	Cβ	Bα	Aγ

FIGURE 170 Greco-Roman Square

In 1979 in New York, the "Dell Puzzle Magazine" published a game it called "Number Place" which introduced the 9 × 9 number grid with the extra twist of adding the constraint of the 3 × 3 sub-grids, as well as the requirement that there be only one unique solution. Its conception is popularly attributed to Howard Garnes [3].

Over the course of the next few decades, the game gained immense popularity in Japan, where it was printed and circulated by the magazine "Nikoli" under the name Su Doku, which is translated as "number single" (i.e. each number appears only once). Nikoli also introduced the criterion of "symmetry," the requirement that the initial setting of the game be of a form that will retain its basic shape even if it is rotated. This makes it more aesthetically appealing as well as generally easier to solve. It may be that the nature of the Japanese language, which is not very well suited for crossword puzzles and other word puzzles, led to the strong appeal of a number game [4].

A New Zealand judge by the name of Wayne Gould became enamored with Sudoku after seeing it in a Japanese publication, and he was instrumental in getting the "Times" of London to begin publishing it in 2004. As a result, Sudoku became wildly popular in England, swiftly spreading to the United States and the rest of the world [4].

Preceding an in depth discussion about Sudoku, let us define the terms we will use to describe positions and entities within the puzzle: The "grid" is the entire 9 × 9 environment of the game. A "cell" is the smallest box unit in which one number is placed. "Rows" and "columns" are self-explanatory, containing 9 cells each. Each row will be labeled with a number 1 - 9(i), and each column will be 1 - 9(j). A particular cell can be described by its (i, j) position. There are 9 "blocks", comprising the sub-grids that each contain 3 × 3 cells and are themselves 3 × 3 arrays. A block will be called by the location of its upper left cell. "Sub-rows" and "sub-columns" are segments of a row or column containing 3 cells and contained within one block. Finally, a "band" refers to a row of blocks, and a "stack" refers to a column of blocks.

13.2 MATHEMATICAL ANALYSIS

For many years, it was known that there existed legitimate Sudoku puzzles that were initialized with just 17 filled cells, while no one had ever succeeded in composing a 16 clue puzzle with a unique solution. It was therefore conjectured that no such puzzle existed. Only recently, (January 1, 2012) in a proof posted online by Gary McGuire of University College Dublin, and approved by mathematicians at a conference a few days later (January 7), was it demonstrated that the minimum number of clues needed to complete a puzzle is 17; puzzles with 16 or fewer clues cannot have a unique solution. Most newspaper puzzles have around 25 clues, with the difficulty of the puzzle decreasing as more clues are provided [5].

The strategy for the proof was to come up with an algorithm that could check a complete Sudoku grid for all the "n-clue" setups that yield that grid as their unique solutions. The idea was to iterate through every possible fully filled in Sudoku puzzle, and apply the algorithm for n=16 to see if any complete grid is the unique solution of 16 clues. The algorithm used the notion of "hitting-sets" which, in brief, searches for "unavoidable sets," or arrangements of numbers which can be rearranged, to come up with clues that force those sets to stay in place. Both the algorithm itself and its application in searching for all possible Sudoku grids are computations that are impossible to carry out by hand. Hence, computers were enlisted for the task. Even so, it took millions of core hours on supercomputers to conclude that no 16 clue puzzle exists [6].

Another interesting mathematical problem related to Sudoku, which also used computer assistance in its solution, is the question of how many unique, complete, Sudoku grids exist. Using elementary counting techniques, even a layman can construct a rough estimate of the number of possible ways to fill an empty Sudoku grid. Beginning with the (obviously simplistic) assumption that each cell has **no more** than nine possibilities, this yields a total "upper bound" of 9^{81}, or 2×10^{77}, or, in words, two hundred quattuorvigintillion [7]. That's not far from the number of atoms in the universe, which is estimated to be between 10^{79} and 10^{80}! [8]

When we apply the row, column, and block restrictions,° however, that allows us to start with nine possibilities for any arbitrary starting square (let's assume top left for convenience). Now we can construct 3 grids, each representing a focus on one restriction. The number of possibilities for each cell will be represented by the number in that cell.

Grid 1 (Figure 171) will have all the top cells represented as nine possibilities, decreasing one at a time as you proceed down each column. As such:

9	9	9	9	9	9	9	9	9
8	8	8	8	8	8	8	8	8
7	7	7	7	7	7	7	7	7
6	6	6	6	6	6	6	6	6
5	5	5	5	5	5	5	5	5
4	4	4	4	4	4	4	4	4
3	3	3	3	3	3	3	3	3
2	2	2	2	2	2	2	2	2
1	1	1	1	1	1	1	1	1

FIGURE 171 Grid 1

Grid 2 (See Figure 172) will have nine possibilities for each left-most cell, decreasing by one as you proceed across the row.

° To give a sense of sale, the game of chess is estimated to have 10120 possible legal games.

9	8	7	6	5	4	3	2	1
9	8	7	6	5	4	3	2	1
9	8	7	6	5	4	3	2	1
9	8	7	6	5	4	3	2	1
9	8	7	6	5	4	3	2	1
9	8	7	6	5	4	3	2	1
9	8	7	6	5	4	3	2	1
9	8	7	6	5	4	3	2	1
9	8	7	6	5	4	3	2	1

FIGURE 172 Grid 2

Finally, grid 3 (See Figure 173) will have each block filled up (starting with nine options for the top left of each block and decreasing as you sweep across each sub-row within the block).

9	8	7	9	8	7	9	8	7
6	5	4	6	5	4	6	5	4
3	2	1	3	2	1	3	2	1
9	8	7	9	8	7	9	8	7
6	5	4	6	5	4	6	5	4
3	2	1	3	2	1	3	2	1
9	8	7	9	8	7	9	8	7
6	5	4	6	5	4	6	5	4
3	2	1	3	2	1	3	2	1

FIGURE 173 Grid 3

For our final grid (Figure 174) we ascribe to each cell the smallest number found in the first three grids for that cell, representing the number of possibilities for a cell considering the most restrictive rules acting on it.

9	8	7	6	5	4	3	2	1
6	5	4	6	5	4	3	2	1
3	2	1	3	2	1	3	2	1
6	6	6	6	5	4	3	2	1
5	5	4	5	5	4	3	2	1
3	2	1	3	2	1	3	2	1
3	3	3	3	3	3	3	2	1
2	2	2	2	2	2	2	2	1
1	1	1	1	1	1	1	1	1

FIGURE 174 Grid 4

For our final rough estimation we multiply the numbers in the above grid to find the total number of possibilities. The result is approximately 1.5×10^{31}, a number much easier to fathom, and a lot closer to the correct value [9].

In 2005, Bertram Felgenhauer and Frazer Jarvis computed the actual total number of ways a Sudoku grid can be filled conforming to all the rules. The calculations used are quite complex, and they discovered that the number of possible 9×9 Sudoku grids is $N = 6,670,903,752,021,072,936,960$ which is approximately 6.671×10^{21} [10].

The analysis involved filling up the top left block, and computing how many ways it would then be possible to fill the rest of the top band, and eventually each stack, to finally complete the grid.

This number is then multiplied by the number of possibilities for the top left block.

A brief synopsis of the technique used: Begin with the fact that there exist 9! possibilities for the top left block. This comes from employing the basic multiplication rule, allowing nine possibilities for the first cell and decreasing by one for every subsequent cell. Looking at any one of those setups, use 6 taken 3 at a time (which is 20) to compute how many ways the remaining six numbers for the top row can be split into the two empty sub-rows. Two of those 20 are called "pure" top rows (with 4,5,6 in one sub-row and 7,8,9 in the other), and the other 18 are called "mixed." For every pure top row there are $(3!)^6$ ways to fill up the top band and for every mixed top row there are $3 \times (3!)^6$ options. This gives us $2 \times (3!)^6 + 18 \times 3 \times (3!)^6 = 2,612,736$ possible ways to fill the top band for each completed top left block.

It would still be a monumental task to calculate all the grid completions for each of those top bands, so programmers set out to simplify that number. They succeeded in considering various permutations and operations that would result in equal numbers of solution sets (for example, if one were to switch the top middle and top left blocks, the solutions would require swapping those entire stacks, but would be exactly the same otherwise). This allowed them to reduce the total number of top bands necessary to consider to a mere 44. A computer program aided in determining the number of solutions for each of those possibilities. Each one of those results was multiplied by the number of top bands that shared that solution set, and this number was then multiplied by 9! (the number of possibilities for completed top left blocks) for a grand total of 6,670,903,752,021,072,936,960! (exclamation point, not factorial!)

There exist, however, "symmetrical solutions," which are essentially similar to each other in structure but some simple operation can be performed to the first option that transforms them into another option. The use of a computer program was enlisted here as well, to enumerate the classes of symmetries and use them to refine the total. Through this method it was further calculated that there are 3,546,146,300,288 **essentially different** Sudoku grids [10].

13.3 PROBLEM SOLVING TECHNIQUES AND STRATEGIES

So how does one go about solving a partially filled out grid (such as the ones found in magazines and newspapers)?

The simplest algorithm that anyone on the street can come up with would involve trial and error and brute force. Fill in the first available cell with the smallest available number, proceed to the next cell, and do it again. If you get stuck, backtrack to the last cell in question and try a different number before proceeding. This method is guaranteed to eventually find a solution, if one exists. However, actually attempting to solve a Sudoku puzzle in this manner by hand would surely get very messy and take a very long time.

Instead, let us begin with some basic rules that will enable us to fill empty cells, then we can move on to broader techniques that allow us to eliminate some numbers, and finally, we can analyze complete strategies or algorithms for implementing those rules in an attempt to solve the entire grid. The following rules are our own although inspired by those found on *SudokuDragon.com* as well as at:

http://www.math.cornell.edu/~mec/Summer2009/meerkamp/Site/Solving_any_Sudoku_II.html.

The Only Number Rule - This is perhaps the simplest rule of all. It focuses on one cell and lets us fill it if there is only one number that can go there (based on the rest of the row, column, block, or some combination of the above). To illustrate this, notice that cell $(1,1)$ has only one possible number that can reside in it. That number is 1, since 6 and 7 already appear in that row.

FIGURE 175 The Only Number Rule

The Only Cell Rule - Instead of focusing on a specific cell, our focus is on a specific number. We broaden our scope to an entire row, column, or block. Within that region, we see if there are any numbers that are restricted to a particular cell. For example, the number 3 might have only 3 open spots in a row, 2 of which can be eliminated based on column and/or block considerations. Look out for a row or column that is pretty full and you may be able to eliminate a number from two out of three subsections, and in the third it may be restricted to one of the three cells.

In this example, the 3 is forced into the (3,1) cell using the only cell rule, since the bottom sub- column is full, the middle one has a 3 in its block, and there is already a 3 in the top row.

FIGURE 176 The Only Cell Rule

The Two Out Of Three Rule - A broader usage of the Only Cell Rule: The strategy is to scan an entire band or stack at a time. Check if any number already appears in two out of three rows or columns. If there is such a number, it is now narrowed to one sub-row or sub-column. (Only one row/col is available and only one block as well). Very often, the number is restricted to one of those three cells.

In this example, in the top band, the last number 1 is limited to row 2, and further to the right-most sub-row. Finally, we see it is restricted to the cell (2,9).

FIGURE 177 The Two Out Of Three Rule

Some rules don't actually fill cells, but rather serve to eliminate some numbers to narrow the options for a cell or group of cells:

Sub-Group Exclusion Rule - Within a row or column, one can sometimes restrict a certain number to one of the three sub-sections. This, in turn, disqualifies that number from going anywhere else in that block. This can actually allow one to fill in a cell that previously had two options.

In this example, for row 6, the number 3 is eliminated from the first and third sub-rows, narrowing it down to the middle one, or the gray shaded cells. This disqualifies 3 from the red cells.

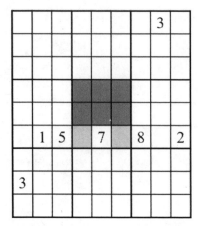

FIGURE 178 Sub-Group Exclusion Rule

Twin Exclusion Rule - If n elements are narrowed down to n cells (such as 2 to 2 or 3 to 3, etc.), that narrows the remaining free elements to the other open cells.

FIGURE 179 Twin Exclusion Rule

This rule is much easier to illustrate with a 4×4 square. Notice that the two numbers 2 and 3 are disqualified from the red shaded cells and forced into the two grey cells, leaving the red available to only 1 and 4. (Now we can actually fill both red cells since 4 can't go in (1,2) and 1 can't go in (2,2)!)

Actually Solving a Complete Puzzle

Before starting, I like to write down the numbers 1 through 9 somewhere on the side of the page to keep track of the values still available. Once every row, column, and box contains any of those numbers, it can be crossed off of the tally.

Stage One

Now we are ready to start. Always begin using the first set of rules ("only number" and "only cell," implementing "two out of three" to make "only cell" more powerful). Scan the grid carefully using either rule, and when no more cells can be filled, switch to the other. If any more cells are filled, you can switch back to the first one, as it may yield more answers now that the grid is more complete. Continue switching back and forth until you have filled in as many cells as possible.

Stage Two

Many Sudoku puzzles can be entirely solved using just the above rules. If your grid is full, congratulations! If not, use a pencil to mark the bottom of each empty cell with all of the possible numbers that can reside there. We can now apply the last two rules, "sub group exclusion" and "twin exclusion." These exclusion rules can be used to cross out possibilities written in some of the cells, and very often this will lead to more cells being solved. Keep in mind that any time a new cell is filled, stage one can be revisited to see if any elementary rules became pertinent. In fact, most puzzles can be entirely completed by this stage.

Stage Three

If any cells are still empty, we must now revisit the very simple algorithm we began with, while modifying it to make it more practical and efficient. Firstly, we began by employing other methods to fill up a big portion of the grid. That in itself drastically reduced the number of possibilities for the remaining cells, and in Stage Two we reduced that number even further. Now, instead of blindly filling in each cell with any available number and continuing until a problem arises, we can proceed with some forethought. If one cell has two possibilities and others have more, always begin with the cell with the fewest options. Additionally, great care must be taken to keep all the work neat and to keep track of the progress. I find that using multiple pencils with different colors helps tremendously.

Once a cell is selected to work with, randomly choose one of its possibilities and pencil it in. If you can now complete the grid, you are done! If cells remain with more than one possibility, you must branch out, make a new guess, and proceed (preferably with a different color). If at any point you get stuck, you have confirmed that the last number you chose at random is not an option and you must erase all of the tentative entries of the current color and try another number. (If you are not in the first level of guessing, you may exhaust all of your possibilities without any solutions, in which case you must go back and modify the level before.) While this last stage sounds slow and tedious, you did everything possible beforehand to set the stage and simplify everything as much as possible, and the good news is that you are guaranteed to (eventually) come to the solution!

13.4 A REAL LIFE EXPERIMENT

To get an idea how the Sudoku puzzle and the above solution play out in real life, a subject was found who did not have much exposure to the game and had never actually attempted to solve one. The goal of the experiment was to observe the initial attempt to see how the subject would try to work out the puzzle. The subject would then read the previous section and only after that attempt a different puzzle of comparable complexity. Then it would be seen if there was any marked improvement over the course of the trial.

The subject was a 23 year old female who seemed to be quite intelligent. She was given the "puzzle of the day" from *sudokuto-day.com* which had a rating for the category "easy." After working for about twenty minutes, and hitting a few dead ends, she assumed that she would need some sort of time consuming trial and error methodology to proceed. At that point she called it quits, having completed approximately half of the grid.*

---

*   Incubation – see Chapter 2.

It was very interesting to see how she naturally and spontaneously employed some combination of the "only cell" and the "only number" rules. This is really quite intuitive, as these rules spell out the most basic ways of filling in cells, which is the immediate goal at every step of the game. However, she was more or less pushing on without a clear picture of what she was doing, which led to some blunders early on, such as filling a cell with a number that was not completely forced into that position.

She was eager for some guidance so she immediately read the previous section and claimed that it made a lot of sense to her. Due to the fact that she had not solved the original puzzle on her first attempt, she was given an unfilled copy of the same puzzle for her second try. The difference was drastic. This time around she systematically and accurately filled in most of the cells by switching off between the first few rules, and then she wrote out the remaining possibilities for clarity and successfully completed the puzzle in around twenty five minutes.

Here is a step-by-step depiction of the puzzle used in the experiment and its solution:

This is the empty puzzle. In the next step we will show how all nine nines can be filled in using the "two out of three rule."

FIGURE 180 Empty Puzzle

FIGURE 181 Step 1

For example, we could have started with the middle band. The two existing 9's are in the top 2 rows and the left 2 boxes. That restricts the remaining 9 to the rightmost lower row. One cell is taken, and the rightmost column already has a 9, leaving only cell (6,7).

Using just the "two out of three rule," we can solve for all of the sixes, sevens, and nines, as shown. This rule is exhausted for now.

				6	7	5	9	
	9	7			4		8	6
6			2	9			7	
	4		3		9	7	6	
9	7				6			5
	6	2	1	7	5	9	3	
7	3		6		2			9
	8	9	7			6	5	
		6	9	4				7

FIGURE 182 Step 2

Notice that row 6 has only 4 and 8 missing. The standard "only cell rule" puts the 4 in (6,9). The "only number rule" puts the 8 in the remaining (6,1) cell.

				6	7	5	9	
	9	7			4		8	6
6			2	9			7	
	4		3		9	7	6	
9	7				6			5
8	6	2	1	7	5	9	3	4
7	3		6		2			9
	8	9	7			6	5	
		6	9	4				7

FIGURE 183 Step 3

"Only cell" can also be used on column 8 to put a "4" in (7,8), on the top right box to put a "4" in (3,7), and on row 8 to put a 4 in (8,1) and a 2 in (8,9).

			6	7	5	9		
	9	7			4		8	6
6			2	9		4	7	
	4		3		9	7	6	
9	7				6			5
8	6	2	1	7	5	9	3	4
7	3		6		2		4	9
4	8	9	7			6	5	2
		6	9	4				7

FIGURE 184 Step 4

We can now actually fill up the entire grid by switching between the rules "only cell," "only number," and "two out of three." It may be helpful to fill-in some possibilities "if we get stuck, although for a game like this it is not really necessary.

2	1	4	8	6	7	5	9	3
3	9	7	5	1	4	2	8	6
6	5	8	2	9	3	4	7	1
1	4	5	3	2	9	7	6	8
9	7	3	4	8	6	1	2	5
8	6	2	1	7	5	9	3	4
7	3	1	6	5	2	8	4	9
4	8	9	7	3	1	6	5	2
5	2	6	9	4	8	3	1	7

FIGURE 185 Step 5

This experiment clearly demonstrated that even if one may be very intelligent, the complex nature of the Sudoku puzzle makes it very hard to tackle without a clear and systematic approach. It also indicates that the approach we developed above is one that is simple enough to be learned relatively quickly, and that it seems to work when utilized.

13.5 ALGORITHMS FOR COMPUTER SOLUTIONS

It has been determined that most suitable algorithm for a computer to use is quite similar to the aforementioned "simple algorithm" that goes through all the cells, setting each to the first number that it can, and proceeds in that manner throughout the grid. If it ever gets stuck, it goes back to the last changeable cell and tries a different number. While this method is far too slow and messy for humans to consider, it is very appropriate for a computer in its simplicity and effectiveness. This type of algorithm is known as "backtracking" and is implemented by recursively traversing every cell of the grid and checking if it will lead to a solution [11]. An example of a program that uses backtracking can be found on the CD-ROM.

13.6 HUMAN WINDOW ANALYSIS OF SOLUTIONS

| Difficulty 5/10 | | | | | | | | | | | | | |
| Complexity $O(n^m)$ | | | | | | | | | | | | | |

Name	Int or Ext?	Intly/ Extly	Repr	HW?	Corr?	Grn Sz	Exec	Compr	Prob Solv Mthd	Flex	Mode of Conv	Opt?	Tot
Tips	Int.	9/10	Desc w/. Grids	Y	Y	Small	3/10	6/10	CS; Deduction; Vis Rep	8/10	Grid Generator; Hand	N	26/40
Frequency	Ext.	9/10	Desc w/. Grids	Y	Y	Ideal	9/10	8/10	CS; Deduction; Vis Rep	8/10	Grid Generator; Hand	N	34/40
No Think	Int.	8/10	Desc w/. Grids	Y	Y	Ideal	10/10	9/10	Costr. Satisf; Vis. Rep.	8/10	Grid Generator; Hand	N	35/40
Crosshatch	Int.	5/10	Desc w/. Grids	Y	Y	Ideal	9/10	9/10	CS; Deduction; Vis Rep.	7/10	Grid Generator; Hand	N	30/40
Simple	Int.	9/10	Desc w/. Grids	Y	Y	Very Small	8/10	5/10	CS; Deduction; Vis Rep	6/10	Grid Generator; Hand	N	28/40
Random	Int.	10/10	Desc w/. Grids	Y	Y	Small	5/10	5/10	Deduction; Vis Rep	8/10	Grid Generator; Hand	N	28/40
Pencil First	Int.	10/10	Desc w/. Grids	Y	Y	Ideal	6/10	4/10	Deduction; Vis Rep	7/10	Grid Generator; Hand	N	27/40
Step-by-Step	Ext.	9/10	Desc w/. Grids	Y	Y	Ideal	10/10	10/10	CS; Deduction; Vis Rep.	9/10	Grid Generator; Hand	N	35/40

Key

Int or Ext?: Intensional or Extensional—Is the solution intensional or extensional?

Intly/Extly: Intensionality/Extensionality—How intensional or extensional is the solution?

Rep.: Representation—How is the solution represented?

HW?: Human Window—Does the solution exist in the Human Window?

Corr?: Correctness—Is the solution correct?

Grn Sz: Grain Size—How much computation (large) or memory (small) does one need to solve the solution?

Exec: Executability—How executable is this solution?

Compr: Comprehensibility—How comprehensible is this solution?

Prob. Solv. Mthd: Problem-Solving Method—What method is used in the solution to solve the problem?

Flex: Flexibility—How flexible is this solution (i.e., can this solution be represented in other ways)?

Mode of Conv: Mode of Conveyance—In what ways can this solution be reproduced/replicated?

Opt?: Optimal—Is the solution optimal?

TABLE 18 Ranking Sudoku Solutions According to the Human Window

The Sudoku puzzle does not have one particular method for obtaining a solution. Therefore, there are many different techniques and problem solving methods available for analysis under the Human Window. Consequently, we can see that the rankings between each solution we have obtained (Table 18) vary on most criteria.

First, let's analyze the criteria which were ranked similarly among all solutions in the table. When looking at the solutions, we can see that they are all represented using descriptions accompanied with grids. This is no surprise, since the Sudoku puzzle is a 9 × 9 grid and the various techniques used to solve the puzzle can only be clearly explained in detail. One such technique that is most commonly used among all solutions, for example, is "crosshatching" which is utilizing the puzzle's given values to determine the values of empty squares in a particular quadrant. Another commonly used technique is called "penciling in," which is indicating the possible choices for each square to keep track of the remaining numbers without having to remember them. In order to be understood, techniques such as these must be explained descriptively alongside images.

Second, we can take note that the problem solving methods used in these solutions are primarily constraint satisfaction and deduction. This does not come as a surprise either because finding solutions to any Sudoku puzzle involves the same process: solving the remaining squares by the process of elimination through the constraints of the provided values and the rules of Sudoku.

Next, we can observe that the majority of solutions are intensional, while very few are extensional. The intensional solutions provide various techniques that may be applied to any puzzle, depending on the state of the puzzle. As a result, the Grain Size for these solutions is relatively small on average given that the solver must remember these techniques in order to complete a puzzle. Additionally, the executability is relatively low due to the fact that most of the intensional solutions do not follow a step-by-step procedure. The extensional solutions, on the other hand, provide step-by-step guidelines on how to solve one particular puzzle. These solutions are ranked higher in most criteria and have an ideal Grain Size because they are more straight-forward than intensional solutions.

However, despite their higher rankings, extensional solutions may not be the best approach given that most of them apply to only one solution among the many possible Sudoku puzzles. Therefore, it may be best to provide general steps and techniques which can be applied to any puzzle's solution. After analyzing the solutions from the table and their rankings in detail, a possible ideal solution would be one that provides general techniques which can be used to solve any Sudoku puzzle. However, these techniques should require little memory. Additionally, an ideal solution might demonstrate these techniques by solving a puzzle step-by-step as an example, thus making a solution more executable.

Finally, we can see that the rankings for the solutions' comprehensibility are relatively mixed. Since all the solutions are represented using grids (i.e. pictures of the Sudoku puzzle) and descriptions, a solution's comprehensibility is most likely measured through the detail of the grids at every step and how clear the descriptions are. Thus, an ideal solution might have clear and labeled grids representing the puzzle's state at each step, accompanied by simple but concise descriptions of techniques and how those techniques are applied.

13.6.1 The Most Human Window-Compatible Solution

Puzzle

	6		1		4		5	
		8	3		5	6		
2								1
8			4		7			6
		6				3		
7			9		1			4
5								2
		7	2		6	9		
	4		5		8		7	

Step 1: Fill in the "Missing Squares"

Enter the numbers 1 through 9 in a "tic-tac-toe" pattern in every blank box.

Step 2: Erase "Rows"

The first number (in the upper right corner) is a "6". Erase every penciled "6" in that row Do the same for all other provided numbers for all rows.

Step 3: Erase "Columns"

39	6	23 9	1	23 789	4	278	5	3 789
149	12 79	8	3	12 4 79	5	6	12 49	79
2	35 789	3 459	678	3 456 789	39	45 78	3 46 89	1
8	123 5 9	123 59	4	123 5 9	7	123	123 9	6
149	125 789	6	78	12 45 789	29	3	12 4 89	5 789
7	23 58	235	9	23 56 3	1	258	23 68	4
5	13 789	13 49	678	13 46 789	39	14 78	13 46 89	2
134	13 58	7	2	13 45 3	6	9	13 48	358
13 69	4	125 9	5	123 6 9	8	12	7	39

Now, for that same number "6", erase the corresponding penciled "6"'s in every box in the same column. Do the same for all other provided numbers for all columns.

Step 4: Erase "Quadrants"

39	6	23 9	1	2 789	4	278	5	3 789
149	179	8	3	2 79	5	6	2 49	79
2	35 79	3 459	678	6 789	9	4 78	34 89	1
8	123 59	123 59	4	235	7	125	12 9	6
149	125 9	6	8	258	2	3	12 89	5 789
7	23 5	235	9	23 568	1	258	28	4
5	13 89	139	7	134 79	39	148	15 468	2
13	138	7	2	13 48	6	9	13 48	358
13 69	4	123 9	5	13 69	8	1	7	3

Erase all the penciled "6"s in the same quadrant as the initial "6". Do the same for all other provided numbers for all quadrants

Step 5: Locate answers

	6	23/9	1	2/789	4	278	5	3/789
39								
149	179	8	3	2/79	5	6	2/49	79
2	35/79	3/459	678	6/789	9	4/78	34/89	1
8	123/59	123/59	4	235	7	125	12/9	6
149	125/9	6	8	258	2	3	12/89	3/789
7	25/5	235	9	23/568	1	258	28	4
5	13/89	139	7	134/79	39	148	13/468	2
13	138	7	2	11/45	6	9	15/48	358
13/69	4	123/9	5	13/69	8	1	7	36

At this point, some blocks may only have one penciled number is left. That remaining value is the answer for that block.

Step 6: Other Eliminations

	6	23/9	1	2/789	4	278	5	3/789
59								
1	7	8	3	2/79	5	6	2/49	79
2	5	4	6	6/789	9	4/78	3	1
8	123/59	123/59	4	3	7	125	12/9	6
4	125/9	6	8	5	2	3	12/89	7
7	23/5	235	9	6	1	228	28	4
5	13/89	139	7	1	9	148	6	2
15	138	7	2	4	6	9	13/48	5
6	4	2	5	9	8	1	7	3

Look at the remaining penciled values across each row. If you find a number that only appears once in a row, then that is the answer for that square. The same applies for columns and quadrants.

Step 7: Repeat

39 6	23/9	1	2/789	4	278	5	3/789
1	7	8	3 2/79	5	6	2/49	79
2	5	4	6 6/789	9	4/78	3	1
8 123/39	125/39	4	3	7	125	12/9	6
4 125/9	6	8	5	2	3	12/89	7
7 23/5	235	9	6	1	258	28	4
5 15/39	139	7	1	9	148	6	2
13 138	7	2	4	6	9	13/45	5
6	4	2	5	9	8	1	7 3

At this point, no matter how difficult the puzzle, we will have even more numbers than what we started with. Thus, if we repeat our previous actions, we can find the values of even more empty squares with our newly founded values.

Repeat steps 1 to 6 until the puzzle is solved.

FIGURE 186 The "No Think" Solution

The solution assessed as MHWC is the "No Think Solution" (Figure) (A good example of this solution can be found at [12].) This solution involves the use of one technique, which involves penciling in each empty square with all possible values, then eliminating those possibilities using deduction based on the provided values and the rules of Sudoku.

Generally, the solution proceeds as follows:

1. Pencil in the numbers 1 through 9 in all empty squares within the puzzle.

2. Eliminate any of these penciled values based on the initial values provided with the puzzle. If this results in an empty square with one penciled value left, then the value of the square is the value of that placeholder.

3. Search through all empty squares to see if any remaining placeholder values are unique to a row, column or quadrant. That unique placeholder value means that the value of the empty square is that remaining value.

4. Repeat steps 2 and 3. The new values obtained will allow you to eliminate more placeholder values. Repeat this until the values of all empty squares are found.

This solution is considered the MHWC because it is an intensional solution that provides a straightforward technique that can be applied to any Sudoku problem and guarantees the puzzle's completion, regardless of its state. Although the technique is tedious, it requires little memory to no memory (or no thinking as the name suggests) to execute, thus resulting in an ideal Grain Size. In addition, the descriptions at each step are concise and a detailed image of the puzzle is provided at each step showing its current state, thus increasing the solution's overall executability and comprehensibility.

13.6.2 The Least Human Window-Compatible Solution

GETTING STARTED

		7	9					1
	2	3	8			6	7	
		6		2	7			
	7	8		5				
	5		2		6		3	
			1		9	5		
			6	3		8		
	8	4			9	2	1	
2					1	3		

To solve a regular Sudoku puzzle, place a number into each cell of the diagram so that each row across, each column down, and each block within the larger diagram (there are 9 of these) will contain every number from 1 through 9. In other words, no number may appear more than once in any row, column, or block.

...

The basic elimination process used in the example above results in a Direct Solve. The best way to work through a Sudoku puzzle is to tackle the Direct Solves first, since they are the easiest.

...

Finding the candidates to eliminate is where advanced solving techniques—called Deductions—come in. Below are several different deductive techniques:

LOCKED CANDIDATE

7	2	1	349	34 69	14	34 59	45	8
5	34 639	34 69	1	234 69	8	23 49	7	349
39	8	349	239	7	5	6	124	13 49
239	5	23 79	239	1	234	23 47	8	6
8	139	239	7	23 49	6	12 34	124	5
4	136	23 67	5	8	23	12 17	9	137
12 39	139	8	4	5	12 37	179	6	179
136	7	346	8	36	9	145	145	2
12 69	14 69	5	26	26	127	8	3	14 79

In a locked candidate, a value must appear at the intersection of a particular block and row or column, and can therefore be removed as a candidate from the rest of that block and row or column. In the example, the 6 in Row A can only be in Quadrant 2 (in other words, none of the cells in Row A in either Quadrant 1 or Quadrant 3 have 6 as a candidate). Therefore, 6 can be eliminated as a candidate from all other cells in Quadrant 2—that is, the 6 can be eliminated from Row B, Column 5.

NAKED PAIR

579	379	37	1	2	4	678	36 78	358
125 79	8	237	567	69	79	4	123 67	135
6	147	247	57	8	3	9	127	15
3	69	1	4	5	2	68	689	7
79	2	67	3	69	8	1	5	4
4	5	8	67	1	79	3	69	2
78	37	9	2	4	1	5	378	6
127	17	5	8	3	6	27	4	9
28	346	23 46	9	7	5	28	123 8	138

In a naked pair, two cells in a row, column, or block each contain the same two candidates, and only those candidates. If a naked pair appears in a row, column, or quadrant, those two candidates can be eliminated from every other cell in that row, column, or block. In the example, the only possible candidates for cells Row I, Column 1 and Row I, Column 7 are 2 and 8, forming a "naked pair." Since 2 and 8 must be in those cells none of the other cells in Row I can be either a 2 or an 8 (or we could not give values to both cells). Therefore, 2 and 8 can be eliminated from all other cells in Row I.

FIGURE 187 The "Tips Solution"

The solution assessed as LHWC is the "Tips Solution" (Figure) (A good example of this solution can be found at [13].) This solution is a collection of techniques that can be applied to any Sudoku puzzle to find missing values. Such techniques include Locked Candidate, Hidden Pair, X-Wing, Swordfish, etc. Choosing a particular technique to apply to the puzzle highly depends on the puzzle's current state. In other words, the techniques that can be used at any given step are determined by the positions of the initial and newly discovered values available at that step.

The solution is ranked highly intensional due to how implicit the solution is on the whole. However, this solution is considered the LHWC for several reasons. First, as mentioned before, the determining factor as to whether or not the provided techniques can be carried out depends on the current state of the puzzle. Since the number of techniques this solution provides is limited, it may be possible for the puzzle to be in a state that none of the techniques can be applied to, thus lowering the solution's executability. Second, the solution does not provide a step by step procedure on how to achieve the puzzle's final goal. Instead, these techniques are applied to different puzzles, thus lowering the solution's executability even further. Third, the techniques provided are complex, and may not be best for those who are inexperienced with Sudoku, thus lowering the solution's overall comprehensibility. Finally, since the solution requires the solver to not only remember the techniques, but the states in which the puzzle needs to be in to make these techniques applicable, the solution's Grain Size is ranked as Small.

A possible way to improve the solution is to provide a step-by-step procedure on how to solve a single puzzle as an example from beginning to end, while demonstrating the techniques which may apply at the appropriate times in the procedure. This may increase the solution's overall executability. Additionally, combining these complex techniques with a technique similar to that of the "No Think Solution" will allow the solver to solve the puzzle even if it is in a state that the complex solutions cannot be applied to, thus increasing the solution's executatbility even further.

13.7 PLAYABLE ONLINE

Two well-known sites where Sudoku can be played are:

-sudokudragon.com

-sudokutoday.com

13.8 REFERENCES

1. *Sudoku.* (2015). Available at *http://www.merriam-webster.com/dictionary/sudoku.* Accessed on February 7, 2016.

2. *Sudoku Puzzle.* (2015). Available at *http://www.sudokudragon.com.* Accessed on February 7, 2016.

3. Ibid, *Origin of Sudoku.*

4. Smith, D. (2005). *So You Thought Sudoku Came From the Land of the Rising Sun...* Available at *http://www.theguardian.com/media/2005/may/15/pressandpublishing.usnews.* Accessed on February 7, 2016.

5. Reich, E.S. (2012). *Mathematician Claims Breakthrough in Sudoku Puzzle.* Available at *http://www.nature.com/news/mathematician-claims-breakthrough-in-sudoku-puzzle-1.9751.* Accessed on February 7, 2016.

6. McGuire, G., Tugemann, B., and Civario, G. (2013). *There Is No 16-Clue Sudoku: Solving the Sudoku Minimum Number of Clues Problem via Hitting Set Enumeration.* Available at *http://www.math.ie/McGuire_V2.pdf.* Accessed on February 7, 2016.

7. *Wolfram Alpha.* Available at *http://www.wolframalpha.com/input/?i=2x10%5E77.* Accessed on February 7, 2016.

8. Villanueva, J.C., (2009). *How Many Atoms Are There In the Universe?* Available at *http://www.universetoday.com/36302/atoms-in-the-universe/.* Accessed on February 7, 2016.

9. *Mathematics and Sudokus.* (2009). Available at *http://www.math.cornell.edu/~mec/Summer2009/meerkamp/Site/Counting_Sudokus_2.html.* Accessed on February 7, 2016.

10. *Felgenhauer, B., and Jarvis, F. (2005). Enumerating Possible Sudoku Grids. Available at http://www.afjarvis.staff.shef.ac.uk/sudoku/sudoku.pdf. Accessed on February 7, 2016.*

11. Zelenski, J. (2008). *Exhaustive Recursion and Backtracking.* Available at http://see.stanford.edu/materials/icspacs106b/H19-RecBacktrackExamples.pdf. Accessed on February 7, 2016.

12. delgaudm (2006). *Solve Sudoku (Without Even Thinking!).* Instructables.com. Available at http://www.instructables.com/id/Solve-Sudoku-Without-even-thinking!/. Accessed on January 23, 2016.

13. SOLVING TIPS (2012). *PennyDell SudokuSolver.* Available at http://www.pennydellsudokusolver.com/help/tips.html. Accessed on January 23,2016

14

MAP COLORING AND THE CHROMATIC NUMBER

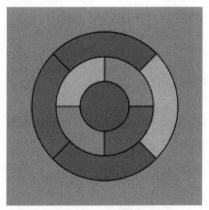

FIGURE 188 Map Coloring Problem
*(https://commons.wikimedia.org/wiki/
File:4CT_Non-Counterexample_2.svg)*

14.1 BACKGROUND

The Map Coloring problem is one that has intrigued mathematicians for nearly two centuries. The mathematician and astronomer August Ferdinand Möbius mentioned the problem in his lectures as early as 1840 [1]. The question is as follows: Given a map with any number of entities, each of any random shape, what is the minimum number of colors that can be used to paint each entity such that no two colors share a border with each other?

This number is called the Chromatic Number. It is interesting to note that this map centered problem is rarely pertinent to actual map-makers, as using the minimum coloring is not conducive to an aesthetically pleasing map that is clear and easy to read [2].

The earliest recorded hypothesis was presented on October 23, 1852, when Francis Guthrie noticed that only four unique colors were necessary to color a map of the counties of England. This was to become known simply as "The Four Color Theorem." At the time, Guthrie's brother, Frederick, was a student of the renowned mathematician Augustus De Morgan at University College in London. Francis inquired with Frederick regarding the problem, who then took it to De Morgan [3]. In De Morgan's own words:

"A student of mine [Guthrie] asked me to day to give him a reason for a fact which I did not know was a fact — and do not yet. He says that if a figure be any how divided and the compartments differently colored so that figures with any portion of common boundary line are differently colored — four colors may be wanted but not more — the following is his case in which four colors are wanted. Query cannot a necessity for five or more be invented. . . " [4].

In the year 1854 the problem was posed in the London based literary magazine "The Athenaeum" by a certain "F.G." presumably one of the Guthrie brothers. De Morgan himself presented the question again in the same magazine in 1860 [5].

The problem can be stated more concisely and mathematically in graph theory terms. A graph contains points called *vertices* which are connected with lines called *edges*. A planar graph is one in which none of the edges are forced to intersect. Any map can be converted into a planar graph by allowing entities to be represented as vertices and the edges between them to represent borders. Using these terms, the Four Color Theorem can be restated as follows: "every planar graph is four-colorable" [3], which is to say that four colors can be assigned to the vertices in such a way that no edge connects two vertices of the same color.

14.2 ILLUSTRATING THE THEOREM

Figure 189, shows a map of the United States of America filled in with only four colors. Although not so pleasing to the eyes, each region is clearly well defined, with no two colors bordering each other.

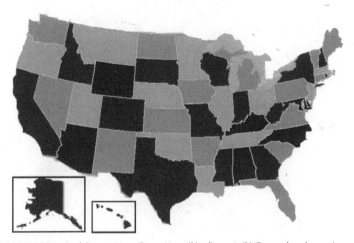

FIGURE 189 United States Map *(https://en.wikipedia.org/wiki/Four_color_theorem)*

Figure 190 shows that even unusual shapes and regions conform to the Four Color Theorem.

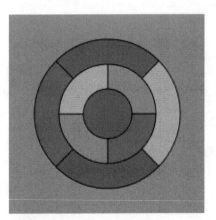

FIGURE 190 Unusual Shapes 1 *(https://commons.wikimedia.org/wiki/File:4CT_Non-Counterexample_2.svg)*

Figure 191 is another example of a complex map with very unusual shapes that can be colored with only four colors.

FIGURE 191 Unusual Shapes 2 *(https:// en.wikipedia.org/wiki/Four_color_theorem)*

Figure 192 depicts a "map" of four regions with five borders, and illustrates how it can easily be transformed into a graph with four vertices and five edges. Note that the graph is planar (none of the edges intersect).

FIGURE 192 Five Border Map *(https://en.wikipedia.org/wiki/Four_color_theorem)*

14.3 EARLY ATTEMPTS AT PROOF

De Morgan himself believed that the basis for the Theorem could be simply and logically stated as a fact about any four regions, and he did not believe that it could be derived from anything more basic. As he stated, "I soon made out the following - which was at first incredible - then certainly true - then axiomatic - for I cannot make it depend on anything I see more clearly." [6]

Over the course of the following few decades, there were repeated failed attempts to prove the Four Color Theorem. In 1879, Alfred Kempe put forth one alleged proof that was widely accepted. This was closely followed by another in 1880, given by Peter Guthrie Tait. Each erroneous proof stood unchallenged for eleven years, until in 1890 Percy Heawood showed Kempe's proof to be false, and in 1891 Julius Peterson showed Tait's to be incorrect. Throughout this noble academic process in pursuit of the truth, however, there were some useful and accurate discoveries. These include the discovery of Kempe chains, a proof to the Five Color Theorem, generalization of the Four Color Theorem to other types of surfaces, and the discovery (by Tait) that the Four Color Theorem is equivalent to the statement that a specific type of graph (called a snark) must be non-planar, opening a whole new field of research within graph theory [3].

It was only in the second half of the Twentieth Century that real progress on a successful proof actually began. In the sixties and seventies, the German mathematician Heinrich Heesch developed the use of a method called *discharging* to be used in conjunction with computer programs. In a nutshell, discharging involves assigning "charges" to the vertices in a planar graph and designing and implementing "charge functions" with rules that allow for proving that all graphs of a certain category contain some subgraph from a prearranged list. He also extended the concept of reducibility (that a given configuration can be replaced with something smaller without affecting its chromatic number) and developed computer-based methods for testing it. Due to technical and financial limitations, however, he was unable to carry out the process himself [3].

On June 21, 1976, Kenneth Appel and Wolfgang Haken of the University of Illinois announced that they had finally solved the query that had stumped the mathematical world for over a century. The method they used was based on the idea that if there existed a planar graph that required more than 4 colors, a minimal counter example containing the fewest possible regions had to exist, and some impossibility would then have to be true. The two concepts used to develop this proof by contradiction were the "unavoidable set" and "reducible configurations." The former is the set of configurations that, if there existed a minimal non-four-colorable graph, it must conform to something in this group. A "reducible configuration," however, is a map that can be reduced to a smaller map in such a way that the chromatic number is not affected. The Appel and Haken proof proceeded by developing an "unavoidable set" of 1476 configurations, and subsequently proving that all 1476 are reducible configurations, which in effect shows that there exist no planar graphs that are not four colorable [3].

The novel and groundbreaking aspect of this proof however, was not in the strategy. It was the way in which the proof was actually calculated. For although the unavoidability set was created and checked by human hands (filling over 400 pages of microfiche), proving that each configuration was reducible required the use of a computer and even then took over 1000 hours of computing time! Naturally, news of this proof took the world by storm. On one hand, one of the most famous and elusive mathematical puzzles had finally been solved. On the other hand, although the problem itself is so simple that any schoolchild could understand it, the solution was so complex that part of it could not really be checked by hand, and the part that ostensibly could, was still extremely long and tedious. In Appel and Haken's own words:

> "This leaves the reader to face 50 pages containing text and diagrams, 85 pages filled with almost 2500 additional diagrams, and 400 microfiche pages that contain further diagrams and thousands of individual verifications of claims made in the 24 lemmas in the main sections of text. In addition, the reader is told that certain facts have been verified with the use of about twelve hundred hours of computer time and would be

extremely time-consuming to verify by hand. The papers are somewhat intimidating due to their style and length and few mathematicians have read them in any detail" [7].

Over the years, however, the proof seems to have endured the test of time, and although there are still those who oppose it, it has become more or less accepted as valid. The 741 page magnum opus that Appel and Haken published in 1989 definitely helped by rigorously clarifying the proof and defending it against many of the claims of its imperfection. Reference for Appel and Haken.

In recent years there have been further improvements on the proof which have brought it ever closer to widespread acceptance. In 1996, Neil Robertson, Daniel Sanders, Paul Seymour, and Robin Thomas, of Georgia Tech and the University of Ohio, developed a proof similar to Appel and Haken's, yet simplified to feature an unavoidable set of only 633 configurations that were proven to be reducible [8]. While this version seems a lot better, it is still close to impossible to check by hand, and is therefore still subject to the criticism that the veracity of the proof was at the mercy of a computer program. Robertson, Sanders, Seymour, and Thomas came out with an alternative proof in 2001 by proving the Snark Theorem, which, as mentioned before, is equivalent to the Four Color Theorem [9].

The final piece in the puzzle was filled in 2005, when Benjamin Werner and Georges Gonthier used a computerized proof assistant called Coq to actually verify both the unavoidable set and the reducibility sections of the existing proofs. In Gonthier's own words:

> "Our work can be seen as an ultimate step in this clarification effort, completely removing the two weakest links of the proof: the manual verification of combinatorial arguments, and the manual verification that custom computer programs correctly fill in parts of those arguments. To achieve this, we have written a formal proof script that covers both the mathematical and computational parts of the proof. We have run this script through the Coq proof checking system, which mechanically verified its correctness in all respects. Hence, even though the

correctness of our proof still depends on the correct operation of several computer hardware and software components (the processor, its operating system, the Coq proof checker, and the Ocaml compiler that compiled it), none of these components are specific to the proof of the Four Color Theorem. All of them come off-the-shelf, fulfill a more general purpose, and can be (and are) tested extensively on numerous other jobs, probably much more than the mind of an individual mathematician reviewing a proof manuscript could ever be." [10]

One can see that the proof process, however it is interpreted, is long and complicated.

14.4 SUMMARY OF EVENTS THAT LED TO THE DEFINITION AND SOLUTION TO THE FOUR COLOR PROBLEM

Problem Identification and Definition

1840 Mathematician and astronomer August Ferdinand Möbius mentioned the problem in his lectures.

1852 Francis Guthrie noticed that only four unique colors were necessary to color a map of the counties of England; the hypothesis was brought before the renowned mathematician Augustus De Morgan and became known simply as "The Four Color Theorem."

1854 The problem was posed in the London based literary magazine "The Athenaeum" by a certain "F.G." (probably Francis Guthrie). De Morgan presents the same problem again 1860.

Repeated Failed Attempts at Proofs

1879 Alfred Kempe put forth one alleged proof that was widely accepted.

1880 Another attempt by Peter Guthrie Tait.

1890   Percy Heawood showed Kempe's proof to be false.

1891   Julius Peterson showed Tait's proof to be incorrect.

Corollaries of the Proof

- A proof to the Five Color Theorem

- The discovery of Kempe Chains

- Generalization of the Four Color Theorem to other types of surfaces

- Discovery (by Tait) that the Four Color Theorem is equivalent to the statement that a specific type of graph (called a snark) must be non-planar, opening a whole new field of research within graph theory.

Efforts at Proof in the Second Half of the 20th Century

1960s and 1970s German mathematician Heinrich Heesch developed a method called *discharging* to be used in conjunction with computer programs. Heesch also extended the concept of reducibility (that a given configuration can be replaced with something smaller without affecting its chromatic number) and developed computer based methods for testing it.

June 21, 1976 Kenneth Appel and Wolfgang Haken of the University of Illinois announced that they had finally solved the query that had stumped the mathematical world for over a century. The method used was based on the idea that if there existed a planar graph that required more than 4 colors, a minimal counterexample containing the fewest possible regions had to exist, and some impossibility would then have to be true. Computers were then used to conduct this proof by contradiction.

Verified Proofs

1989   Appel and Haken published a 741 page magnum opus that rigorously clarified the proof and defended it against the numerous claims of its imperfection. The proof developed an "unavoidable set" of 1476 configurations, and proceeded (with the use of computers) to show that all of them were reducible. Therefore, all planar graphs are four colorable. Over 1000 computing hours were required to carry out the calculations.

1996   Neil Robertson, Daniel Sanders, Paul Seymour, and Robin Thomas, of Georgia Tech and the University of Ohio, developed a proof similar to Appel and Haken's, yet simplified to feature an unavoidable set of only 633 configurations that were proven to be reducible.

2001   Robertson, Sanders, Seymour, and Thomas came out with an alternative proof in 2001 by proving the Snark Theorem, which, as mentioned before, is equivalent to the Four Color Theorem.

2005   Benjamin Werner and Georges Gonthier (Microsoft Research, Cambridge) used a computerized proof assistant called Coq to actually verify both the unavoidable set and the reducibility sections of the existing proofs.

14.5 SAMPLE OF CODE FROM THE PROOF

To give the reader a brief glimpse into the complexity and intricacy of the computer program written by Robertson, Sanders, Seymour, and Thomas, we have included the function prototypes for the "Reducibility" segment of the proof [11]:

```
/* function prototypes */

#ifdef PROTOTYPE_MAX

void testmatch(long, char *, long[], char *, long);

void augment(long, long[], long, long **, long[16][16][4], char *,
char *, long *, long, long, long, char *, long *, long);

void checkreality(long, long **, char *, char *, long *, long, long,
long, char *, long *, long);

long stillreal(long, long[], long, char *, long);

long updatelive(char *, long, long *);

void strip(tp_confmat, tp_edgeno);
```

```
long ininterval(long[], long[]);
void findangles(tp_confmat, tp_angle, tp_angle, tp_angle, long[]);
long findlive(char *, long, tp_angle, long[], long);
void checkcontract(char *, long, tp_angle, tp_angle, long[], long[]);
void printstatus(long, long, long, long);
void record(long[], long[], long, long[][5], char *, long *, long);
long inlive(long[], long[], long, char *, long);
long ReadConf(tp_confmat, FILE *, long *);
void ReadErr(int, char[]);
#else
void testmatch();
void augment();
void checkreality();
long stillreal();
long updatelive();
void strip();
long ininterval();
void findangles();
long findlive();
void checkcontract();
void printstatus();
void record();
long inlive();
long ReadConf();
void ReadErr();
#endif
```

14.6 REFERENCES

1. Rouse Ball, W.W. (1905). *The Four Color Theorem, in Mathematical Recreations and Essays.* Macmillan, New York, pp 222-232

2. Wilson, R. (2002), *Four Colors Suffice*, London: Penguin Books, ISBN 0-691-11533-8 pg. 2.

3. Thomas, R. (1998). *An Update on the Four-Color Theorem.* Available at *http://www.ams.org/notices/199807/thomas.pdf.* Accessed on February 7, 2016.

4. Wilson, R. (2002). *Four Colors Suffice*, London: Penguin Books, ISBN 0-691-11533-8, pg.18

5. McKay, B.D. (2012). *A Note on the History of the Four-Colour Conjecture.* Available at *http://arxiv.org/pdf/1201.2852v2.pdf.* Accessed on February 7, 2016.

6. Wilson, R. (2002). *Four Colors Suffice.* London: Penguin Books. pg. 24.

7. Martin, J.L. (2013). *The Notorious Four Color Problem.* Available at *http://www.math.ku.edu/~jmartin/MiniCollege2013/slides.pdf.* Accessed on February 7, 2016.

8. Robertson, N., Sanders, D., Seymour, P., Thomas, R. (1995). *The Four Color Theorem.* Available at *http://people.math.gatech.edu/~thomas/FC/fourcolor.html.* Accessed on February 7, 2016.

9. Pegg, E. Jr. (2002), *Book Review: The Colossal Book of Mathematics.* Available at *http://www.ams.org/notices/200209/rev-pegg.pdf.* Accessed on February 7, 2016.

10. Gonthier, G. (2005). *A computer-checked proof of the Four Colour Theorem.* Available at *http://research.microsoft.com/en-US/people/gonthier/4colproof.pdf.* Accessed on February 7, 2016.

11. Robertson, N., Sanders, D. P., Seymour, P. D., and Thomas, R. (1995). *reduce.c.* Available at *http://people.math.gatech.edu/~thomas/OLDFTP/four/reduce.c.* Accessed on February 7, 2016.

CHAPTER 15

CRYPTOGRAPHY

FIGURE 193 Cryptography

A chapter whose topic is computer solutions to Artificial Intelligence problems would not be complete without a discussion of cryptography. Cryptography is the enciphering and deciphering of messages in secret code or cipher; the modern version refers to the computerized encoding and decoding of information [1]. This practice has existed in one form or another for millennia, predominantly used for royal or military communications. In recent times, however, it has become something utilized by most ordinary citizens of the world, albeit behind the scenes, in everyday computer-based activities such as sending e-mails and online transactions.

15.1 BACKGROUND

The earliest known example of encrypted information was discovered in Egypt, dating from approximately 2000 BC. These were hieroglyphics decorating the tombs of kings and rulers, telling stories of their subjects in a coded manner to seem more regal and important [2]. Another example of ancient cryptology is found in the Hebrew writings of Jeremiah, dating from around 700 BC, and also used throughout early biblical Kabbalistic works. This method is known as "Atbash," and works as follows: the first letter of the alphabet is swapped for the last, the second for the next to last, and so on, until the last letter which corresponds to the first. Although originating with the Hebrew language, this is a simple and effective swapping technique that can be applied to almost any other language as well [3].

The first known usage of cryptography for the secretive transmission of important information, such as in wartime, was as early as the 5th Century BC at the hands of the Spartans. They developed a device called a "skytale," a wooden rod around which they tightly wrapped a thin strip of material in a spiral. The message was then written on the material lengthwise down the staff, so that it could only be deciphered when rewrapped on a rod of identical width; otherwise it appeared as gibberish. Another Greek encryption method is known as a Polypius square, or a "checkerboard," in which letters are placed in a grid and are represented by their row and column numbers [2].

The first historical instance of cryptology employed for political affairs was by Julius Caesar in Rome in the first century BC. His method used an offset of three, and every letter was swapped for the one three positions later in the alphabet, at the end looping around to the beginning. Any similar technique, even if the offset is not three, is called a Caesar cipher [2].

It was the Arabs at the turn of the first millennium AD who revolutionized the field by taking a scientific approach to cryptography. This included the introduction of cryptanalysis, the process of analyzing coded matter and reproducing the original text. Muslim scholars such as Ahmad al-Qalqashandi wrote extensively on the subject, and developed important techniques that utilized the probable letter frequencies of plaintext characters to match them with their corresponding cipher characters based upon their frequency in the code. Amazingly enough, this powerful method is relevant even today [2].

The next few centuries saw vast qualitative and quantitative leaps in the study of cryptography. Methods such as the *polyalphabetic cipher* added exponential complexity to coded text. Advances in technology provided machines able to convert plaintext through multiple layers of encryption to yield heavily enshrouded code. On the other hand, communication via telegraph and radio made messages much more susceptible to interception. High profile and far reaching political and military episodes revolved around encrypted messages and their "cracking." Some of the more famous incidents include the Babington plot leading to the execution of Mary Queen of Scots, and the Zimmerman telegraph which brought America into WWI, and the cracking by the Allies of the German Enigma encryption machine as well as the Japanese so-called "Purple" cipher system, which contributed immeasurably to the Allied victory in WWII [2]. These examples serve to underscore the power and importance of an encrypted message, as well as the ever-present reality that vulnerabilities can and will be exploited. As such, it is vital that utmost care must be taken with sensitive data. The focus of this chapter will be modern cryptography as a solution to the complex and global issue concerning almost every individual, which arises when they wish to safely and regularly transmit sensitive information over very public mediums such as the World Wide Web.

15.2 SYMMETRIC KEY ENCRYPTION

The Internet has revolutionized the world as we know it. In the span of just a few decades, our vast Earth has shrunk to the point where almost anything is merely a few mouse-clicks away. Heaps of data are thrown around public domains at a frantic pace.

This is very dangerous, as this data includes personal information that can be private and sensitive. In fact, security experts believe that the greatest security threats to exchanges such as e-commerce transactions, occur at the level of internet communication. The most basic tool to combat this threat is the use of encryption [4].

The simplest encryption strategy is known as "Symmetric Key Encryption." The idea is straightforward and proceeds as follows: say Alice and Bob would like to communicate a secure message. They agree in advance on a key, which they keep a secret. Bob applies the key to the message using a certain pre-arranged algorithm, and the result is the cipher text. When Alice receives this, she uses the same key to recover the message. This can be clearly stated mathematically. Let m represent the original message, k the key, c the cipher text, E the encryption algorithm, and D the decryption algorithm. We can now say that Bob performs $c = E(k,m)$ and Alice retrieves the original message using $m = D(k,c)$ [5]. An image can further illustrate the process:

FIGURE 194 Symmetric Key Encryption

Modern systems for encryption use strings of binary digits as keys. As an example, take a message containing the letter "A" represented by its binary ASCII value of 01000001. One way of encoding it would be to multiply this by an 8 bit binary key, say 01010101. If every byte were transformed in the same way, the recipient of the resultant cipher text could easily decode the message with the same 8 bit key [4].

The complexity and therefore robustness of a symmetric key system is directly proportional to the length of the binary key. In the previous example, the key could be easily discovered using a brute force method, since only 2^8 or 256 possibilities exist. As a result of this, most systems use keys of at least 56 bits. Some use up to 512 binary digits, resulting in 2512 possibilities to check. It is estimated that all the computers in the world combined would need 10 years to chance upon the real key [4].

The original standard for a symmetric key encryption scheme was developed in the early 1970s at IBM, in close collaboration with the National Security Agency (NSA). Known as the Data Encryption Standard, or DES, it was published as a federally approved standard for secure transfer of sensitive data in 1977. DES made use of a 56 digit key, applied to the original data in 64 bit blocks using a complex encryption algorithm. The algorithm involved 16 rounds of processing, in addition to an initial and final permutation, all after splitting the block into two 32 bit halves, to enable alternating processing known as a "Feistal Scheme." The limelight attained by the publication of an NSA approved encryption standard was responsible for catapulting cryptography from an obscure field confined mostly to the government, to become an intriguing and well-researched academic topic [6].

From the get go, there was controversy regarding the security of DES, stemming mainly from the relatively small key size. In the 1990s, one project demonstrated the ability to recover a DES key in 22 hours and 15 minutes [5]. In 1999, the Federal Institute of Standards and Technology (FIST) reaffirmed DES as secure, albeit with a recommendation to use the improved "Triple DES" [6]. At the same time however, FIST was conducting an open selection process for a new and improved symmetric encryption, to be called the AES, or Advanced Encryption Standard. The entry that won is known as the "Rijndael Cipher," created by Joan Daemen and Vincent Rijmen. A comprehensive treatment of the mathematical workings of this algorithm spans 46 pages in the publication by the FIST, and is beyond the depth and breadth of this book. Suffice it to say that it works very well, and in 2001 it was affirmed as the new federal standard for all secure messages [7].

The glaring flaw inherent in symmetric key encryption is the problem of sharing the key to begin with. In the example with Bob and Alice that we started with, it would theoretically be possible for them to have shared the key face to face, before any communications. Practically, however, in almost all real world applications of encryptions, the two parties would not and could not do this. How, then, could the key be safely communicated? This was indeed not possible until the advent of "Public Key Encryption" [5].

15.3 PUBLIC KEY ENCRYPTION

Public key encryption provides the concept for the safe transition of data without the need to securely transfer a shared key. Let us return to the example of Bob and Alice. Bob still wants to relay a message to Alice. This time, however, Alice has two keys. One is accessible to the public and is called the *public key*, and the second she keeps to herself, called the *secret key*. The keys are related in the sense that if a message is encoded with some encryption algorithm using the public key, the original information can be reproduced using a decryption algorithm with the secret key. In this method, it is absolutely required that the secret key cannot be derived just from knowledge of the public key alone, and the cipher text cannot be decoded using just the public key. If these conditions are met, Bob can encrypt his message using Alice's publicized public key, confident that she alone will be able to decipher the message with her secret key. Mathematically, we will again let m represent the original message, c the cipher text, E the encryption algorithm, and D the decryption algorithm. Now, however, Alice has a public key pk and a private (secret) key sk. We now say that Bob performs $c = E(pk,m)$ and Alice retrieves the original message using $m = D(sk,c)$ [5]. To further clarify with an image:

FIGURE 195 Public Key Encryption

This brings us to the matter of the keys themselves. We require a family of encryption functions such that the encryption itself can be easily computed using the public key. It must be practically infeasible to reverse the process and obtain the original message from the cipher text using that same key. Such functions are called *one way functions*. We also require for there to be some additional information, our secret key, which does allow for efficient inverse computation to obtain the original data. This is called *trapdoor information*. A one-way function that contains trapdoor information is known as a *trapdoor function* [5].

In November of 1976, Whitfield Diffie and Martin Hellman of Stanford University published a groundbreaking paper called "New Directions in Cryptography" introducing the concept of public key encryption. In it, they present a working public key system that takes advantage of the difficulty in extracting discrete logarithms. In fact, this is a mathematical problem that currently has no solution. Diffie and Hellman also introduced the idea of a *digital signature* using the public and secret keys. The motivation is clear --- just as it is important to securely transfer data, the recipient might want to confirm that this data is indeed being sent by the purported sender. A digital signature would use the same public and secret keys as would be used for encryption, albeit in reverse. For the signature, Bob would use his private key to "decrypt" a signature message into gibberish. Now anyone can use Bob's public key to "encrypt" the gibberish and recreate the original signature message, proving that Bob was really the one who sent it. This is much like a manual signature, in which the signer alone has the means to do so, and everybody else can easily attest to its authenticity. For the public and secret keys to be capable of performing digital signatures as well as encryption, the functions employed need to work both ways. That is to say, the public and secret keys must both be capable of transforming the data in such a way that only the other key can reverse. The method Diffie and Hellman introduced for encryption does not work as an effective digital signature. In fact, they proposed the search for such a function as an open question [8].

15.4 RSA ENCRYPTION

In 1978, a mere 2 years after Diffie and Hellman challenged the scholarly world to find a public key system capable of both encrypting and digitally signing, a solution was announced. Ron Rivest, Adi Shamir, and Leonard Adleman of MIT electrified the scholarly community and beyond with an elegant public key cryptosystem that used the multiplication of two large prime numbers as the basis for formulating the keys. Their method became known as RSA, an acronym for their three last names. The single direction of the functions is a result of the great difficulty involved in prime factorization of very large numbers. For those interested in a more detailed mathematical description, I quote part of the clear and concise introduction to the solution from the pioneers themselves (taken from "A Method for Obtaining Digital Signatures and Public-Key Cryptosystems"):

> "To encrypt a message M with our method, using a public encryption key (e, n), proceed as follows. (Here e and n are a pair of positive integers.) First, represent the message as an integer between 0 and $n - 1$ (. . ..) Then, encrypt the message by raising it to the eth power modulo n. That is, the result (the

ciphertext C) is the remainder when *Me* is divided by *n*. To decrypt the ciphertext, raise it to another power *d*, again modulo *n* (. . ..) The encryption key is thus the pair of positive integers *(e, n)*. Similarly, the decryption key is the pair of positive integers *(d, n)*. Each user makes his encryption key public, and keeps the corresponding decryption key private. How should you choose your encryption and decryption keys, if you want to use our method? You first compute *n* as the product of two primes *p* and *q*: $n = p \cdot q$. These primes are very large, "random" primes. Although you will make *n* public, the factors *p* and *q* will be effectively hidden from everyone else due to the enormous difficulty of factoring *n*. This also hides the way *d* can be derived from *e*. You then pick the integer *d* to be a large, random integer which is relatively prime to $(p - 1) \cdot (q - 1)$. That is, check that *d* satisfies: $\gcd(d,(p - 1) \cdot (q - 1)) = 1$ ("gcd" means "greatest common divisor"). The integer *e* is finally computed from *p*, *q*, and *d* to be the "multiplicative inverse" of *d*, modulo $(p - 1) \cdot (q - 1)$. Thus we have $e \cdot d = 1 \pmod{(p - 1) \cdot (q - 1)}$." [9]

Public key encryption using RSA works very well and solves the issue encountered with symmetric key encryption. However, public key encryption is much less efficient than the more streamlined symmetric key, and as such, by itself it is not optimal for large transfers of data. The solution to this is a hybrid system called a *Digital Envelope*. Public key encryption is employed to communicate the shared key for use in a symmetric key decryption of the cipher text, thus combining both methods to provide a complete, secure, and practical cryptosystem [10].

Almost four decades have elapsed since the introduction of public key encryption and RSA. From the outset, the authors acknowledged that it was impossible to prove that a system is unbreakable, and only once a method has withstood all possible attacks for a considerable amount of time can it be considered secure. RSA relies on the mathematical difficulty in factoring very large numbers into prime multiples -- the larger the number, the harder it is to factor. In their paper published in 1977, Rivest, Shamir, and Adleman estimated that it would take a computer

4.2×10^{25} years to factor a 500 digit number using the fastest known algorithm, and they recommended using a key of at least 200 digits [9]. As the years have passed, however, the capabilities of computers have grown exponentially, enabling faster prime factorization. In the late 1990s, multiple projects showed that it was possible to break a 512 bit key in a matter of a few months. By 2010, the largest RSA number ever broken was 768 bits, and that was done in two steps: one requiring a half year on 80 processors, the other requiring almost two years on many hundreds of machines [11]. Although this is still mighty slow and impractical, it is slightly disconcerting that we are headed on a trajectory toward breaking up larger numbers more quickly than ever before. Indeed, the current recommendation for key size by the RSA Laboratory is 1024 bits for standard uses and 2048 where extra security and longevity is desired [12].

There are other potential weaknesses as well. One example that affects a small number of RSA applications involves the requirement that the prime numbers used to calculate the key be completely random. Researchers found that in about 0.2% of cases, the system for generating random primes failed to do so effectively [13]. Various other mathematical attacks are theoretically possible under specific conditions. These vulnerabilities, however, are not considered significant. Even the first issue regarding the rapid improvement of computing power available to calculate prime factorization, is nowhere close to being a legitimate concern for the foreseeable future, so long as the key is of sufficient length.

Public key encryption using RSA has weathered the test of time and emerged unscathed. It is one of the most popular encryption systems in existence, with over a billion installations worldwide as of the year 2000. It is imbedded in hundreds of popular software products, a notable example being Windows [14]. Even more recent encryption systems that enjoy widespread use on the internet, such as TLS and SSL, actually use RSA as part of their algorithms. These systems are used by major web sites such as Google, YouTube, and Facebook. It turns out that Hellman and Diffie were quite prophetic in the opening line of their paper on the public key method: "We stand today on the brink of a revolution in cryptography."

15.5 ISSUES REGARDING RSA CRYPTOGRAPHIC SYSTEMS **

The perennial issue in designing Cryptographic systems is that as the keys get longer and more complicated, they are more secure but require more work to decipher and handle.

There is a persistent tradeoff between security, ease of use, and economic factors.

The balance between simplicity and ease of handling, versus complexity and more security coupled with greater handling costs is also an ongoing issue. More complex encryption requires more communication which increases costs. Hence there is great motivation for developing an encryption system which is both effective and unbreakable.

The RSA system is one such system which has been the cryptographic standard for more than 30 years.

Attacks on Public Key Encryption are of greatest concern, especially since the encryption transformations are public knowledge. An adversary can therefore initiate a "chosen plaintext attack" and stronger still is a "chosen ciphertext attack." The security of the environment in which the public key encryption scheme is to be used determines how easily a single ciphertext attack may be effected.

Effective public key encryption schemes assume that a message sender will have a means of obtaining an authentic copy (authentication) of the intended recipient's public key. If that is not the case, then the encryption scheme is subject to an impersonation attack (spoofing).

A number of public key encryption schemes assume that the message to be encrypted is at most of some fixed size (bitlength). If a plaintext message is longer than the prescribed maximum bitlength, it is broken into "blocks" of a fixed size. These blocks can then be encrypted independently.

** The main source for this Section is [15] *Handbook of Applied Cryptography*, Chapter 8: Public Key Encryption By A. Menezes, P. van Oorshot and S. Vanstone, CRC Press 1997.

15.5.1 Examples of RSA Implementation

Example 1: Summary of Algorithm Key Generation for RSA Public Key Encryption

Each entity "A" should do the following:

1. Generate two large random (and distinct) primes, p and q, each roughly the same size.

2. Computer n = pq and ø = (p – 1) * (q – 1)

3. Select a random integer e, 1 < e < ø, such that gcd (e, ø) = 1.

4. Use the Euclidean Algorithm to compute the unique integer d, 1 < d < ø, such that ed = 1 (mod ø)

5. A's public key is (n , e); A's private key is d.

RSA Algorithm Example 2 (simple)

- Choose p = 3 and q = 11
- Compute n = p * q = 3 * 11 = 33
- Compute $\varphi(n)$ = (p - 1) * (q - 1) = 2 * 10 = 20
- Choose e such that 1 < e < $\varphi(n)$ and e and n are coprime. Let e = 7
- Compute a value for d such that (d * e) % $\varphi(n)$ = 1. One solution is d = 3 [(3 * 7) % 20 = 1]
- Public key is (e, n) => (7, 33)
- Private key is (d, n) => (3, 33)
- The encryption of m = 2 is c = 27 % 33 = 29
- The decryption of c = 29 is m = 293 % 33 = 2

https://www.cs.utexas.edu/~mitra/honors/soln.html

15.5.2 Security and Attacks on RSA

Since its introduction in 1978, much importance and responsibility has been attributed to the RSA Algorithm and hence there have naturally been a number of attempts to attack it and breech its security. In this section we will briefly describe some of the methods which have been used to attack the RSA Algorithm.

1. **Factors** – The challenge for the attackers is to recover (decipher) the plaintext from the corresponding ciphertext – and there is no known efficient algorithm for accomplishing this. Hence this is known as the RSA Problem (RSAP). Thus "when generating RSA keys is it imperative that the primes p and q be selected in such a way that factoring **n = pq** is computationally infeasible." (ibid., p288)

Small encryption exponents (i.e. e = 3) may be subject to this since there are algorithms which can fairly easily expose the plaintext. A possible remedy to this problem is adding a pseudo-random bitstring prior to encryption. This technique is called "salting" the message.

Other attacks which can occur include:

2. **Choosing a small decryption exponent** (may be fragile, as was a small encryption exponent). A remedy to this is choosing structural constraints on the plaintext message.

3. **Cycling Attacks,** or in essence, attempts to factor n. Since factoring n is presumed to be intractable, such attacks are rendered to not pose a serious threat.

4. **Unconcealed messages** even though some messages will always be unconcealed, their number will generally be negligibly small.

Some efforts to secure RSA and address progress in computational power include:

1. **A modulus size of at least 512 bits**. In fact in 1996, in order to address the powerful prime factorization techniques developed by Carl Pomerance known as the Quadratic Sieve [18], and a module of a size of at least 768 bits was recommended.

2. **The difference, p - q should not be too small**.

3. **P and Q should be "strong primes," namely**

   (a) p −1 has a large prime factor, r

   (b) p + 1 has a large prime factor, and

   (c) r −1 has a large prime factor.

15.6 REFERENCES

1. *Cryptography*. Merriam-Webster. Available at *http://www.merriam-webster.com/dictionary/cryptography*. Accessed on February 7, 2016.

2. Kahn, David (1996), *The Codebreakers*, NY, NY: Scribner, ISBN 0684831309, pgs. 71 – 125

3. Hoskisson, P.Y. (2010). *Jeremiah's Game*. Available at *http://publications.maxwellinstitute.byu.edu/fullscreen /?pub=1367&index=3*. Accessed on February 7, 2016.

4. Laudon, K., and Traver, C. (2007). *E-Commerce*. Upper Saddle River, NJ: Prentice Hall.

5. Delfs, H., and Kneble, H. (2007). *Introduction to Cryptography*. Germany: Springer.

6. Burr, W.E. (2001). *Data Encryption Standard*. (Part of NIST's anthology *A Century of Excellence in Measurements, Standards, and Technology: A Chronicle of Selected NBS/NIST Publications, 1901–2000*). Available at *http://nvlpubs.nist.gov/nistpubs/sp958-lide/250-253.pdf*. Accessed on February 7, 2016.

7. *Announcing the Advanced Encryption Standard (AES)* Federal Information Processing Standards Publication 197. United States National Institute of Standards and Technology (NIST). (2001). Available at *http://csrc.nist.gov/publications/fips/fips197/fips-197.pdf*. Accessed on February 7, 2016.

8. Diffie, W.; Hellman, M.E. (November 1976). "New directions in cryptography". IEEE Transactions on Information Theory, vol.

IT-22, no. 6. Available at *https://www-ee.stanford.edu/~hellman/ publications/24.pdf.* Accessed on February 7, 2016.

9. Rivest, R., Shamir, A., and Adleman, L. (1977). *A Method for Obtaining Digital Signatures and Public-Key Cryptosystems.* Available at *https://people.csail.mit.edu/rivest/Rsapaper.pdf.* Accessed on February 7, 2016.

10. *What is a digital Envelope?* Available at *http://www.emc.com/emc-plus/rsa-labs/standards-initiatives/what-is-a-digital-envelope.htm.* Accessed on February 7, 2016.

11. Kleinjung, T, et al. (2010). *Factorization of a 768-bit RSA modulus.* Available at *https://eprint.iacr.org/2010/006.pdf.* Accessed on February 7, 2016.

12. Silverman, R. (2002). *Has the RSA algorithm been compromised as a result of Bernstein's paper?* Available at *http://www.emc.com/emc-plus/rsa-labs/historical/has-the-rsa-algorithm-been-compromised. htm.* Accessed on February 7, 2016.

13. Markoff, J. (2012). *Flaw Found in an Online Encryption Method.* Available at *http://www.nytimes.com/2012/02/15/technology/re-searchers-find-flaw-in-an-online-encryption-method.html?_r=0.* Accessed on February 7, 2016.

14. Gale, T. (2007). *Data Encryption.* Available at *http://www.ency-clopedia.com/doc/1G2-2687200161.html.* Accessed on February 7, 2016.

15. Menezes, A, van Oorshot, P. and Vanstone, S. (1997) *Handbook of Applied Cryptography,* Chapter 8: Public Key Encryption CRC Press: New York, New York.

16. Sedgewick, R. *Algorithms (2ⁿᵈ edition).* Reading, Ma: Addison Wesley Publishers.

17. Katz, J, and Lindell, Y. (2015) *Introduction to Modern Crytography (2ⁿᵈ edition).* CRC Press, Taylor and Francis, New York, New York.

18. Pomerance, C. (1996). *A Tale of Two Sieves, Notes of the AMS,* pp 1473 – 1485.

16

RANDOM WALKS ON GRAPHS AND MONTE CARLO METHODS

By Jim Cox
Department of Computer and Information Science,
Brooklyn College, New York,
email: cox@sci.brooklyn.cuny.edu

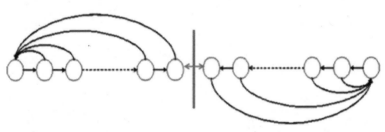

FIGURE 196 Random Walkslem.

16.1. Introduction

This chapter is a revised and popularized version of the paper [6], which is joint work with Paula Whitlock and Wen-Ju Cheng. In this chapter we discuss the relationship among random walks arising from several different applications areas. Principally, we relate the study of random walks on graphs and directed graphs (digraphs) to the random walks arising from certain problems that are solved using Monte Carlo methods. We note that each of these processes, even when they can be carried out efficiently by a computer, are too computationally intensive to be carried out by hand. For example, an efficient random walk (defined below) on a reasonably sized graph may take millions or billions of steps. This might mean only a few seconds on a computer, but years for a human!

First let us define our terminology. A **random walk** on a graph proceeds by choosing uniformly at random which of a vertex's neighbors to visit next. For example, if a vertex has three outgoing edges to three neighbors, the probability of following each edge is $\frac{1}{3}$. In **undirected graphs** (also called **graphs**) the edges connecting vertices are "two-way" (see figure 197 left), while in **directed graphs** (**digraphs**) the edges are "one-way," so that edges at a vertex are either **incoming** or **outgoing** (see figure 197 right.)

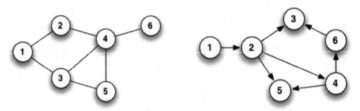

FIGURE 197 An undirected graph on the left and a directed graph on the right.

The degree of a vertex is the number of edges incident upon that node. In a digraph a vertex has both an **indegree** that gives the number of incoming edges, and an **outdegree** that gives the number of outgoing edges. A **vertex** is **balanced** if its indegree equals its outdegree and a **digraph** is **balanced** if each of its vertices is balanced. The **hitting time** of a vertex is the expected (average) time needed for a random walk starting from a distinguished starting node to visit ("hit") that vertex. The **cover time** is the average length of a random walk that visits all vertices. Finally, the **mixing time** is the average time needed for the walk to converge to the **stationary distribution**, that is, the time when the probability of visiting any vertex on the next move stabilizes. For example, a random walk on the digraph in the right of figure 197 left might proceed by visiting vertex 1, then vertex 2, then vertex 4, and finally vertex 5. Since vertex 5 has no outgoing edges, the random walk ends there.

A **Monte Carlo Algorithm** is an algorithm that is typically used to simulate the behavior of other systems. It is not an exact method, but rather a heuristic procedure. It uses randomness and statistics to get a result. In general the computation process uses pseudo random numbers to produce an outcome. It may make one-sided errors, which means it may think there is no solution to a problem (e.g., a Sudoku puzzle) when there is actually one. On the other hand there is no error when a solution is found.

Finally, a **Markov Chain or Process** is a random walk with a set of **states** and a set of **transition probabilities** between states. A random walk on a graph is a Markov Chain. Conversely every discrete Markov Chain corresponds to a random walk on a **weighted graph**, where each vertex represents a state and each edge represents a possible transition, with a weight corresponding to the probability of that transition. In this case the probability of following an edge from a vertex may not be uniform. For example a vertex may have two outgoing edges with probabilities $\frac{1}{3}$ and $\frac{2}{3}$. If transitions are **reversible** we get a weighted graph, and if not we get a weighted digraph. If the resulting digraph is **strongly connected** (you can get from any vertex to any other vertex) the Markov chain is called **ergodic**. The definitions of hitting time, cover time, and mixing time are defined similarly to the definitions for graphs. We have shown how to transform certain "nice" Markov chains into unweighted digraphs.

Let us clarify with a simple example. Say you have a "phone tree" where once you get a call you call everyone on your list (e.g. to say there's no school today.) Suppose instead of calling everyone on your list you roll dice to determine one person on your list to call. This corresponds to a random walk on a graph. The cover time measures how fast the message spreads to the whole town. The hitting time for someone measures how long before they receive a call. The mixing time is how long it takes until the chance that the next person called is a particular individual remains unchanged.

16.2 THEORETICAL APPLICATIONS

A primary theoretical application for the study of random walks on graphs has been to computational complexity theory, the classification of set problems according to the computational resources they use. There is a rich relationship between random walks on graphs and space bounded complexity classes, the sets of problems that can be solved using limited computer memory. The major open and solved problems in the area of log space bounded complexity classes, the sets of problems that can be solved by programs that use only memory proportional the number of bits needed to write the length of the input as a number, can all be restated as problems in graph search and, in particular, random- ized graph search [1, 2, 3, 4, 5, 7]. Random walks can be easily limited to log space memory usage during a graph search, since they only have to remember the number of the current vertex, which takes log n bits. In contrast, a naïve deterministic search would have to remember some history of the visited vertices, using at least linear space in the size of the graph. Practical applications of random walks on graphs have been to percolation problems [8] and to electrical networks [9].

Each of the well-studied log space bounded complexity classes can be transformed into an equivalent class of graph search problems. The model used by complexity theorists is the Turing machine (readers unfamiliar with Turing machines may view these machines as simply a special kind of program running on a very primitive computer.) **L** (computation by a deterministic log space bounded machine) corresponds to undirected graph search, **RL** and **BPL** (computation by a similar machine that uses random bits) correspond to randomized search of certain well-behaved digraphs, and **NL** (computation by a similar machine that uses nondeterminism, similar to NP machines) corresponds to a search of general digraphs. One may ask why one doesn't just use pseudo- random or quasi-random bits for these probabilistic programs? In complexity theory one assumes "truly" random bits. Replacing the truly random bits by a pseudo random number generator that uses a O(log n) sized random seed would show that L = BPL. Perhaps surprisingly, no one has been able to do this. The best result so far is the so-called Nissan-Widgerson generator [1] which can fool random O(log n) space Turing machines (programs) by using a truly random seed of $O(\log^{3/2} n)$ bits. It has also been shown [2] that RL can be simulated deterministically using slightly less space $(O(\log^{4/3} n))$, but it is still more than the original $O(\log^{4/3} n)$.

Much is known about random walks on undirected graphs and these results predated a discovery by Omer Reingold. Reingold [3] shows that any undirected graph can be searched deterministically using only O(log n) work space. To appreciate how surprising this result is, consider that it takes log n bits just to write down the number of a single vertex! Another way of viewing this result is that certain discrete reversible Markov chains can be simulated deterministically, with no loss of efficiency. In some sense all of the Markov chains used in computer simulations are discrete since they generally use finite precision floating point numbers. While the complexity theoretic motivation for studying random walks on undirected graphs has evaporated, the results obtained are still applicable to Markov chains and [10] gives results that relate random walks on undirected graphs with reversible Markov chains. Following Reingold's proof that undirected graph search is in L, the research focus has shifted to random walks on directed graphs in an attempt to clarify the relation between the complexity classes L, RL, NL, and others.

In the following, we summarize some of the known results on random walks on undirected and directed graphs, and then we present some of our new results [5]. The new results relate the cover and mixing times of the random walks to a structural property of the graphs that measure how unbalanced they are. We extend our definition of digraph imbalance [5] to Markov chains and show how imbalance affects performance. In some discrete cases, for example in simulated annealing as applied to Sudoku puzzles [11, 12], a random walk can may take exponential expected time, depending on the input size, to reach a goal state. One reason for this is because the number of possible states is extremely large compared to the input size. Another imbalance occurs if some of the state transition probabilities are exponentially smaller (in the size of the input) than the others. This is certainly not a desirable property, and most applications seek a Markov chain with probabilities that are neither too small nor too large. In practice, if the acceptance probability of a move is very small, the random walk will not make sufficient progress toward convergence.

Conversely if the acceptance probability of a move is too large, this implies a poor sampling of the state space by the walk. Moreover, rounding is often used to bound the precision of the probabilities' representation. We formally defined these properties [6] and termed the resulting Markov chains nicely bounded. Of course, even in the absence of these two imbalance conditions, Markov chains may still have exponential mixing and cover times.

16.3 Random Walks on Graphs

The relation between random walks on undirected graphs and electrical networks has been well studied. Doyle and Snell [9] stated the basic results showing the correspondence between random walks on connected undirected graphs and electrical networks. One can transform a graph into an electrical network by replacing each edge with a 1 ohm resistor. Chandra et al. [14, 15] showed that if we inject the right amount of current, the hitting times and cover times of a random walk on a graph G are proportional to the resistance and voltage in the corresponding electrical network. In a very precise sense the flow of electricity (actually electrical potential) through this network mirrors the "flow" of probability through the graph during the random walk.

There are two other important measures that have been used to bound the mixing time of random walks on graphs. One can calculate a number called the "**Cheeger constant**" of the graph [10] that measures any bottleneck to the flow of probability through the graph. This measure has been adapted to digraphs [13] and gives a direct bound on the mixing time of random walks on digraphs. In figure 198 we see a graph with a bottleneck and hence an exponentially slow mixing time.

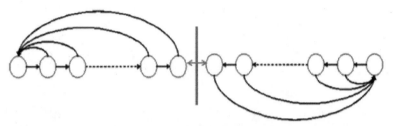

FIGURE 198 A digraph with the bottleneck illustrated by the vertical line segment.

The second measure involves a matrix called the graph **Laplacian**, which is related to the adjacency matrix of the graph. A number can be calculated from this matrix, called the **spectral expansion**, and it determines how fast a random walk "fans out". It also gives a direct bound on the mixing time. Again this measure can be adapted to the directed case [13] and it gives a bound on the mixing time for digraphs. Both of these measures, for the undirected case, have been applied to the mixing times for reversible Markov chains [10].

The problem is that these measures only bound the mixing time and not the cover time. A graph can be rapidly mixing (in polynomial time) but have a terrible (exponential) cover time. The cover time is important when one is employing random methods to search for a solution to a problem. One must ensure that you visit all vertices with high probability to minimize the possibility that you missed a solution. For example, consider a complete binary tree of depth n. This is rapidly mixing (in linear time) since there is no bottleneck to the flow of probability, but the cover time is exponential. If the solution is contained in a single leaf node, then one has to run the random walk for an exponential number of steps to insure finding it with high probability. It is also known that balanced digraphs have good cover times. For this reason, and for complexity theoretic considerations, we identified a structural property of digraphs that measure how unbalanced they are and gives a bound on the cover time [5].

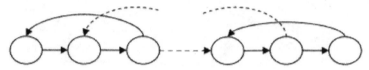

FIGURE 199 A graph that seems close to balanced with a very bad cover time.

In figure 199 we illustrate a family of digraphs with very bad cover times. Each graph consists of a chain of vertices with forward edges, and starting with the second vertex, each vertex has an edge that goes two vertices back. A random walk on this graph has the problem that for every step forward one is just as likely to take two steps back! It turns out that the cover time for this graph, as the number of vertices n increases, grows as the sum of the first n Fibonacci numbers, which is exponential in n. Yet the addition of a single directed edge from the second vertex to the last makes the cover time polynomial in n (fast). Notice also that the graph has only two unbalanced vertices: the second and the second to last vertices in the chain. This suggests that the number of unbalanced vertices is not a good measure of imbalance for cover time.

In [5] we showed that the correct measure of imbalance is the number of asymmetric vertices, defined as follows. We first determine the minimal number of edges that can be removed from the digraph so that it is balanced. This is called the **maximal balanced subgraph**. We then consider the edges from the original graph that are not in this balanced subgraph. Each vertex that at least one of these edges is incident upon it as an outgoing edge is an **asymmetric vertex**. The maximal balanced subgraph may not be unique, but the number of asymmetric vertices is the same no matter which one is chosen. With a little work, one can verify that half of the vertices in our example graph are asymmetric, hence the bad behavior.

The importance of this measure was demonstrated in [5], where we showed that a necessary condition for a strongly connected digraph with bounded outdegree to have a bad cover time is that it has a relatively large number of asymmetric vertices. In particular, if the number of asymmetric vertices is small ($O(\log n)$) then the cover time is polynomial and hence feasible. On the other hand if this number grows asymptotically faster than log n (say $\sqrt{n}$)

then the cover time may be superpolynomial and hence a random walk on a large instance graph may be infeasible for even the fastest computers. In fact one can show that there exist digraphs with $\sqrt{n}$ asymmetric vertices that have exponential cover times.

16.4 MARKOV CHAINS AND MONTE CARLO METHODS

A Markov Chain is nicely bounded if the number of states is bounded by a polynomial in the input size and the transition probabilities are neither too small nor too large. We show in [6] that we can transform every nicely bounded ergodic n state Markov chain M into an equivalent (unweighted) strongly connected digraph GM, so that a random walk on GM corresponds exactly to the Markov Chain. We then identify the Cheeger constant and spectral expansion of M with these numbers for GM. This immediately gives us bounds for the mixing times of these Markov chains. For example, these numbers can be used to prove that a Markov Chain is rapidly mixing, that is, that it converges to the stationary distribution in polynomial time.

We similarly define the notion of asymmetric states for a Markov Chain. We prove in [6] that if a nicely bounded ergodic n state Markov chain M has a small number of asymmetric states (O(log n)) then it has a polynomial cover time. This says that a Monte Carlo method to solve an optimization problem, based on M, will be feasible. Also since mixing time is always less than cover time, this also shows that M is rapidly mixing.

Mixing time is paramount in what are termed Markov Chain Monte Carlo methods (MCMC). For example, when simulating a physical system one often desires to use random samples from some probability distribution, instead of merely employing random numbers which are uniformly distributed. In an MCMC one accomplishes this by constructing a Markov chain M that has the desired probability distribution as its stationary or "equilibrium" distribution. One takes a sample from the distribution by taking a sufficiently long random walk using M. The sample is just the state that the walk ends at. So the pertinent question becomes "How long should the walk be to get a good sample?" This is just a question about the mixing time of the Markov chain M. Our results again show that if the number of asymmetric states of M is not too large then M will have polynomial cover time. This implies that M is rapidly mixing and hence a MCMM method based on M is feasible. Otherwise, one had better pick another Markov Chain for the MCMM!

So, to conclude, while we began our investigation into random walks on graphs motivated by the applications to complexity theory [5], we found that our results extended into the more practical area of Monte Carlo methods [6]. These methods find wide applicability in science but they require powerful computers and are thus not human based.

16.5 REFERENCES

1. R. Armoni, A. Ta-Shma, A. Wigderson, S. Zhou, An o.log4=3 n/ space algorithm for .s; t/ connectivity in undirected graphs, J. ACM 47 (2000) 294–311.

2. D.K. Arrowsmith, J.W. Essam, Percolation theory on directed graphs, J. Math. Phys. 18 (2) (1977) 235–239.

3. A.K. Chandra, P. Raghavan, W.L. Ruzzo, R. Smolensky, The electrical resistance of a graph captures its commute and cover times, in: Proceedings of the Twenty-first Annual ACM Symposium on Theory of Computing, STOC '89, ACM, New York, NY, USA, 1989, pp. 574–586.

4. A.K. Chandra, P. Raghavan, W.L. Ruzzo, R. Smolensky, P. Tiwari, The electrical resistance of a graph captures its commute and cover times, Comput. Complexity 6 (1996) 312–340.

5. W.-J. Cheng, J. Cox, S. Zachos, Random walks on some basic classes of digraphs, in: Proceedings of the 10th International Colloquium on Theoretical Aspects of Computing, ICTAC 2013, in: Lect. Notes in Comput. Sci., vol. 8049, 2014.

6. W.-J. Cheng, J. Cox, P. Whitlock, Random walks on graphs and Monte Carlo methods, Mathematics and Computers in Simulation DOI:10.1016/j.matcom.2015.12.006, 2016

7. F. Chung, Laplacians and the cheeger inequality for directed graphs, Ann. Comb. 9 (1) (2005) 1–19.

8. K.-M. Chung, O. Reingold, S. Vadhan, S-t connectivity on digraphs with a known stationary distribution, ACM Trans. Algorithms 7 (2011) 30:1–30:21.

9. P. Doyle, J. Snell, Random walks and electrical networks, Carus Math. Monogr. 22 (1984) 1–159.

10. U. Feige, A tight upper bound on the cover time for random walks on graphs, Random Structures Algorithms 6 (1) (1995) 51–54.

11. J. Fill, Eigenvalue bounds on convergence to stationarity for nonreversible Markov chains, with an application to the exclusion process, Ann. Appl. Probab.1 (1) (1991) 62–87.

12. T.A. Lambert, P.A. Whitlock, Generalizing sudoku to three dimensions, Monte Carlo Methods Appl. 16 (3–4) (2010) 251–263.

13. R. Lewis, Metaheuristics can solve sudoku puzzles, J. Heuristics 13 (4) (2007) 387–401.

14. N. Nisan, A. Wigderson, Hardness vs randomness, J. Comput. System Sci. 49 (2) (1994) 149–167.

15. O. Reingold, Undirected st-connectivity in log-space, in: H.N. Gabow, R. Fagin (Eds.), Proceedings of the 37th Annual ACM Symposium on Theory of Computing, Baltimore, MD, USA, May 22–24, 2005, STOC 2005, ACM, New York, NY, USA, 2005, pp. 376–385.

PART

MISCELLANEOUS SMALLER PROBLEMS AND TOWARDS A THEORY

17

MISCELLANEOUS PROBLEMS

T his chapter contains five smaller problems from different areas, such as probability, logic, and mathematics. We believe they are sufficiently intriguing to be of interest and value to any dedicated problem solver.

FIGURE 200 Cards Laid Out on a Table

17.1 CARDS/COINS IN THE DARK

Cards/Coins in the Dark is a math puzzle and has two variants: one with a deck of cards and one with a set of 100 coins (Figure 200).

17.1.1 Cards in the Dark

The problem is as follows: You are in a dark room and are given a deck of 52 cards. You are told that 13 of the 52 cards are faceup and are distributed throughout the deck. You are asked to divide the deck into two piles consisting of the same number of faceup cards. You cannot distinguish between the faceup and facedown cards by feeling them, and also, since the room is dark, you cannot see the cards. How can you accomplish this task?

Solution

There are 13 faceup cards. If we randomly divide the whole deck of cards into two piles, the 13 faceup cards will be divided between the two piles. Say if the first pile has n faceup cards, then the second pile will have $13 - n$ faceup cards. So if the first pile had $13 - n$ faceup cards instead of n faceup cards, the two piles will have an equal number of faceup cards.

Thus, if the first pile has a total of 13 cards, then it would have $13 - n$ facedown cards, and if we flip all the cards in the first pile, we would have $13 - n$ faceup cards. So the solution is to divide the cards into two piles, one with 13 cards and one with 39 cards and then flip all the cards in the first pile. Figures 201 to 203 show this solution.

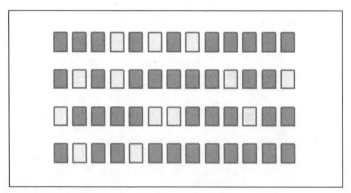

FIGURE 201 The deck of Cards laid out on a table

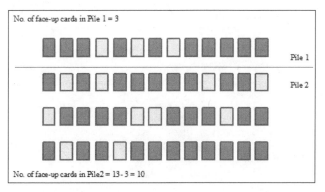

FIGURE 202 The Two Piles of Cards

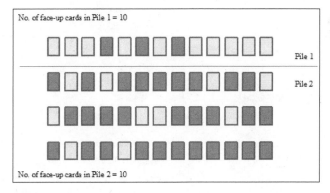

FIGURE 203 After Flipping All the Cards in Pile 1

17.1.2 Coins Version of the Problem

The coins version of this problem has 100 coins on a table in a dark room. Of the 100 coins, 10 coins have heads-up, and the goal is to divide the coins into two piles with an equal number of coins heads-up.

The solution is similar to that of the cards version of the problem. We choose any 10 coins to form the first pile and flip all of them over. The remaining 90 coins form the second pile.

If the first pile originally had n coins with heads-up, the second pile will have $10 - n$ coins heads-up. After all the coins in the first pile are flipped over, the first pile will also have $10 - n$ coins.

17.1.3 References

1. *http://www.calpoly.edu/~mcarlton/riddles.html* (July 10, 2013)

2. *http://wordplay.blogs.nytimes.com/2013/05/20/dark-2/* (July 10, 2013)

FIGURE 204 Pirate and Gold

17.2 TEN PIRATES AND THEIR GOLD

The Ten Pirates and Their Gold Problem has been posed for over 20 years (Figure 204), but it gained attention when some serious mathematicians (Ian Stewart) and computer scientists (Stephen M. Omohumdro) tackled it with some variations in the late 1990s. The problem is as follows: Ten pirates find a buried treasure of 100 pieces of gold (Figure 205). The challenge is to divide the gold in some desirable way according to some constraints (rules). The first constraint is that Pirate 1 is the lead pirate; Pirate 2 is the second in charge; Pirate 3 is the third most powerful; and so on. The pirates have a scheme for dividing the money. They agree that the first pirate (P1) will make a proposal for how the money is to be divided. If 50% or more of the pirates agree with the P1 system, it will be put into effect. If not, then P1 will be killed, and the next most powerful pirate becomes the lead pirate. Now, again with one fewer pirate, the process repeats. The new lead pirate, P2, now suggests a new process for divvying up the gold. It will be voted on, with a 50% vote needed for the leader's suggestion to pass; less than 50% results in the death of the lead pirate.

All the pirates are very greedy and savvy, so they will vote against a proposal if it means they will get more gold if the proposal fails, and thus a lead pirate is killed. They will never vote for a proposal that will give them less gold or no gold.

When you first hear this problem and consider possible solutions, you might think the following: Let's say the lead pirate (P1) wants to be pretty fair and takes 19 pieces of gold, offering 81 pieces of gold to the remaining 9 pirates (9 each). The problem is that he needs 4 pirates to agree with him. And if the 4 pirates see a way to get more gold, they will not vote to go with him.

The lead pirate taking 19 and the rest taking 11 seems pretty fair, but the 4 voting pirates will see a better way for them. If P1 is eliminated (no vote in favor), then a nice scenario might seem to be P2 gets 12 and the others get 8 × 11 (= 88). This seems very reasonable and equitable, but pirates are not known for being equitable. So the pirates might eliminate P2, seeing a scenario like P3 = 16, and the others get 7 × 12 (= 84). Still, there will be pirates who see a way for them to get more gold for themselves who would exercise their veto vote to possibly achieve this.

FIGURE 205 Ten Pirates and their Gold

Using this approach, we can see the following logic could lead to some real results: Imagine if there were only two pirates, P1 and

P2 (Figure 206). P1 would want to take all the gold (100 pieces), leaving P2 with no gold and no say about it (the 50% rule).

FIGURE 206 Two Pirates

Now let us consider the situation with three pirates: P1, P2, and P3 (Figure 207). Pirates are not stupid. They would realize that if they vote against you, P2 gets all the gold and P3 gets no gold after you are gone. Knowing this, P3 will accept your offer of 1 piece of gold, with no gold to P2.1 P2 will not be happy, but your proposal will pass. With four pirates, the same proposal (P3 gets 1 coin) will pass, with P3 giving you the one vote you need to pass (50%) (Figure 208).

FIGURE 207 Three Pirates

FIGURE 208 Four Pirates

The same logic applies to up to 10 pirates, whereby you would give one piece of gold to P3, P5, P7, and P9 and keep the other 99 pieces for yourself. Those four pirates would support your proposal, since otherwise they would receive no gold if your proposal fails.

About the time of Stewart's article in 1999, Steven Omohundro took the problem to another level by asking what happens if there are not only 10 pirates but as many as 200 or 500? He concluded that with 200 pirates, P200 will continue by offering nothing to odd-numbered pirates from P1 to P199 and one gold coin to even-numbered pirates P2 through P198.

However, the situation gets complicated if we go beyond 200 pirates, as P201 and P202 will find themselves lacking sufficient "bribing power" to get support. Matters get even more complicated as we consider 203, 204, . . . , 207 pirates. Omohundro's conclusion, which Ian Stewart shares in the article below, is that as we approach 500 pirates, a pattern that continues indefinitely emerges.

Pirates who can make winning proposals (always to give themselves nothing and to bribe 100 fellow pirates) are separated from one another by ever-longer sequences of pirates who will be thrown overboard no matter what proposal they make—and whose vote is therefore ensured for any fiercer pirate's proposal. The pirates who avoid this fate are P201, P202, P204, P208, P216, P232, P264, P328, P456, and so on—pirates whose number equals 200 plus a power of 2.

Reference

Stewart, I. (1999). "A Puzzle for Pirates." *Scientific American*, 280 (5): May 1999, 98–99. Available at *http://omohundro.files.wordpress. com/2009/03/stewart99_a_puzzle_for_pirates.pdf /*. Accessed on January 10, 2014.

FIGURE 209 Halmos's Handshake Problem

17.3 HALMOS'S HANDSHAKE PROBLEM

Paul Halmos was a famous Hungarian mathematician. He wrote a charming biography of the great Jon von Neumann, who is generally credited with developing the architecture of the serial computer still used today. He also developed the following logic problem, called **Halmos's Handshake Problem** (Figure 209).

As is common, academics will occasionally attend dinner parties. Halmos and his wife attended such a party with four other couples. During the cocktail hour, some of those present shook hands but in an unsystematic way, with no attempt to shake all the guests' hand. Of course, no one shook his or her own hand, no one shook hands with his or her spouse, and no one shook hands with the same person more than once. During dinner, Halmos asked each of the nine other people present (including his own wife) how many hands that person had shaken. Under the given conditions, the possible answers ranged from 0 to 8 hands shaken. Halmos noticed that each person gave a different answer. One person claimed not to have shaken anyone else's hand, one person had shaken exactly one other person's hand, one person had shaken exactly two hands, and so on up to one person who claimed to have shaken hands with all the others present, except his or her spouse—so 8 handshakes in total. So, in summary, of the 10 people present, people gave answers from 0 to 8 hands shaken (Figure 210).

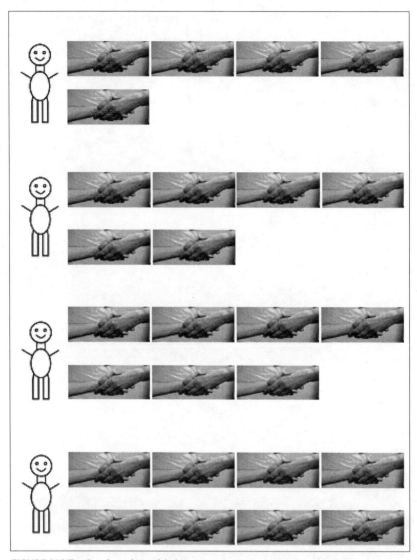

FIGURE 210 Ten People and Handshakes

Now, here is the question: *How many hands did Halmos's wife shake?*

FIGURE 211 How Many Shook His Wife's Hand?

Let's see what we already know (Figure 211). We'll start by considering the person who claims to have shaken 8 hands and call this person A. Whose hands did A shake? Necessarily, A shook hands with everyone else present, apart from his or her spouse (whom we call A(w)). So everyone besides A's spouse {A(w)} shook at least one hand—namely, A's hand (Figure 212).

FIGURE 212 Person A—8 Shakes

So who is the person who shook 0 hands? Since everyone except A's spouse shook at least one hand, the person who shook 0 hands must be A's spouse, A(w) (Figure 212).

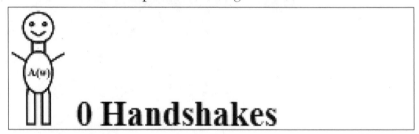

FIGURE 213 Person A's Wife—0 Shakes

Now consider the person who shook 7 hands, whom we'll call B. B didn't shake hands with himself or herself or with his or her spouse {B(w)} or with A(w) (because A(w) shook no hands). That leaves only 7 other people, so B shook hands with everyone else except B and his or her own spouse {B(w)} (Figure 214). And each of these people also shook hands with A, meaning that all of these people shook at least two hands: A's and B's. So the only person left who could have shaken just 1 hand is B's spouse, B(w) (Figure 215). So just as the person who shook 8 hands is married to the person who shook 0 hands, the person who shook 7 hands is married to the person who shook only 1 hand. We can now see a pattern evolving in the solution.

FIGURE 214 Person B—7 Shakes

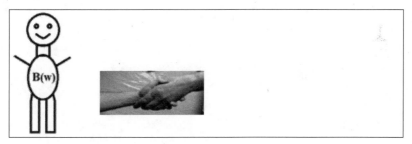

FIGURE 215 Person B's Wife—1 Shake

Similar analysis can be applied to the person who shook 6 hands, C, who could not have shaken hands with himself or herself or his or her spouse, A(w) (who shook 0 hands), or B(w) (who shook only A's hand) (Figure 216). So C shook hands with everyone else, and since C also shook hands with A and B, the only person left who could have shaken just 2 hands is C's spouse, {C(w)} (Figure 217).

FIGURE 216 Person C—6 Shakes

FIGURE 217 Person C's Wife—2 Shakes

Applying the same logic one more time shows that the person who shook 5 hands, D, is married to the person who shook 3 hands, {D(w)} (Figures 218 and 219).

FIGURE 218 Person D—5 Shakes

FIGURE 219 Person D's Wife—3 Shakes

What does this leave us? We know that all the possible people who gave the answers 0, 1, 2, 3, 5, 6, 7, and 8 are all married to other people who answered Halmos's question. The only person who is not married to one of the people who answered the question is the one who answered 4—and that must be Halmos's wife {H(w)}. So Halmos's wife (H(w)) shook 4 hands, and it follows that Halmos (H) did, too (Figures 220 and 221).

FIGURE 220 Halmos—4 Shakes

FIGURE 221 Halmos's Wife—4 Shakes

This problem illustrates that by using *logical inferences* and given the small number of permutations for the problem, it is possible to *exhaustively enumerate* what the number of handshakes was for each person who attended the party. Also, given the small number of possible permutations, it is possible to use a simple notational system and/or graphs to represent solutions.

Reference

Halmos, P. (1973). "The Legend of John von Neumann." *The American Mathematical Monthly* 80 (4). Available at *http:// www.jstor.org/stable/ 2319080 May 5*. Accessed on January 10, 2014.

FIGURE 222 Airline Seats

17.4 RANDOM AIRLINE SEATS PROBLEM

The Random Airline Seats Problem is a type of probability and logic problem whose results are surprising and unexpected (Figure 222). Here is one phrasing of the problem: One hundred people line up in the waiting area to board a plane that has 100 seats available. The first person in this line has lost her boarding pass. Without knowing what her assigned seat is, she randomly chooses a seat. As a result, for each person entering the plane, there are only two possibilities: either his assigned seat is available or it's not. If his seat is not available, he chooses an unoccupied seat randomly. Based on this information, when the 100th person finally enters the plane, what is the probability that he will find his assigned seat unoccupied [1]?

This problem requires a fair amount of logic to determine the solution. Even with the solution revealed, it is still not quite obvious as to how it is obtained. However, those who understand the laws of probability may have a better understanding of how to approach this problem and why the solution is correct.

Solution

There is a 50% chance that the 100th passenger will get to sit in his or her assigned seat. With such a large number of people entering the plane, and the 100th passenger entering last, this answer seems implausible! However, with an analytical approach and some logic, the solution can be easily understood.

A common way to solve this riddle is to mathematically deter-mine the chance that each person sits in his or her assigned seat, but the math gets complicated quickly. However, we can easily come to our answer by analyzing the possibilities that can occur and the effects caused by those possibilities.

For this solution, we'll call a passenger Pn, where n represents that person's place in line. For example, the person who is fifth in line is P5.

We begin by making two observations:

1. *If any of the first 99 people sit in P100s assigned seat, P100 WILL NOT get to sit in his seat.* This observation should be obvious, since somebody else sitting in her seat means he cannot sit in it.

2. *If any of the first 99 people sit in P1's seat, P100WILL get to sit in his seat.* This observation is not as obvious. To make things clear, let's say, for example, that P1 sits in P2's seat. This means that P2 cannot sit in his assigned seat, so he must sit in another. Potentially, P2 will sit in any other seat he chooses. Let's say P2 sits in P3's seat. Then P3 will be in the same predicament that P2 was in and, without an assigned seat, will randomly sit anywhere he wants. Let's then say that P3 sits in Pn's seat. All of the passengers between P3 and Pn will get to sit in their assigned seats, but Pn will find his seat occupied and therefore will randomly sit in any other passenger's unoccupied seat. This will continue until a passenger—say, P50—happens to sit in P1's seat. Once this happens, the remaining passengers will not find their seats occupied and will now be able to freely sit in their assigned seats. P51 will sit in his assigned seat, P52 will sit in her assigned seat, and so forth. Therefore, P100 will get to sit in his or her own seat.

So to summarize these two observations, if P100's seat becomes occupied, P100 will not get her seat. If P1's seat becomes occupied, P100 will get her seat. Therefore, only these two factors determine whether or not P100 will get his or her seat. As for the rest of the seats, we can see from our observations that they make absolutely no difference in determining P100's last seat. When the other passengers choose seats that do not belong to P1 or P100, they are just prolonging the final determination.

It is important, however, to understand that the probability of a passenger randomly choosing a specific seat is exactly the same for every seat. For example, when P1 enters the plane, he has 100 seats to choose from and therefore has a 1/100 chance that he will sit in his own seat and 1/100 chance that he will sit in P100's seat. If he happened to sit in P2's seat, then P2 will have 99 seats to choose from. Therefore, there will be a 1/99 chance that he will sit in P1's seat and a 1/99 chance that he will sit in P100's seat. Generally, if there are n remaining seats available on the plane, the passenger that is next in line will have a 1/n chance he will sit in P1's seat and a 1/n chance he will sit in P100's seat. Therefore, the chance of any passenger sitting in either P1's seat or P100's seat will always be equally likely.

To summarize this solution:

1. P100 will get her assigned seat if any other passenger sits in P1's seat.

2. P100 will not get her assigned seat if any other passenger sits in P100's seat.

3. 1 and 2 are the only two choices that determine P100's seating, and they are always both equally likely to happen.

Therefore, P100 will have a 50% chance that she will be seated in her assigned seat if P1 randomly sits anywhere.

Reference

Galvin, D. (2013). "Probability Puzzler 3—The TSA Wouldn't Like This." Available at *http://www3.nd.edu/~dgalvin1/Probpuz/probpuz3.html*. Accessed on January 9, 2014.

FIGURE 223 The Birthday Problem

17.6 THE BIRTHDAY PROBLEM

The Birthday Problem (or The Birthday Paradox) (Figure 223) is another probability problem whose solution contains rather unexpected results. The original problem is as follows: Suppose you have a random group of people in a room. How many people do you need in this group so there is more than a 50% chance that two of these people have the same birthday (month and day)? Unlike The Random Airline Seats Problem, this problem requires a better understanding of the laws of probability.

Solution

The answer is 23. In a group of 23 random people, there is a 50.76% chance that two or more of them have the same birthday! Although this does not seem to make sense at first, it should become clearer when we present some probability theory.

The question is asking about the probability with regard to two random people in a group of people. A common misconception is that the problem asks for the odds that two specific people will have the same birthday. A direct computation to solve the problem is relatively complex. However, to simplify the problem, we will first calculate the probability that no two people have the same birthday [1].

Let's assume that February 29 does not exist and that there are only 365 days in every year, meaning there are a total of 365 possible birth dates. Say we have only 1 person, whom we will call Person A. Because Person A is only one individual, her birthday could be any one of 365 days, and there is no chance that her birthday will be the same as anyone else's. Therefore, there is a **365/365 = 1 = 100%** probability that Person A will not have the same birthday as someone else.

Let's now add a second person to our group, named Person B. Since Person A already exists in the group, there is one fewer possible birthday that Person B could have whereby B does not match any other birthdays in the group, which is basically Person A's birthday. Therefore, the probability that Person B does not have the same birthday as A is 364/365. Now we need to find the probability that the group does not have matching birthdays. It is important to take note that a person having a certain birthday does not depend on another person having that same birthday. Therefore:

P(None) = (365/365) × (364/365) = .9973 = 99.73%

This means there is a 99.73% probability that no matching birthdays exist in the group. If we continue to add a Person C, that person will have a 363/365 chance that she has the same birthday as the other two people and therefore:

P(None) = (365/365) × (364/365) × (363/365) = .9918 = 99.18%

From these three cases, we can see a pattern emerging. It can be concluded that in a group with n persons the probability that no people will share a birthday is:

P(None) = [(365 × 364 × . . .. × (365 − (n − 1)))] / (365^n)

Simplifying this, we get:

P(None) = [365! / (365 − n)!] / (365^n)

Now that we have developed a general formula, it is simple to calculate the probability that two or more people WILL have the same birthday in the group. All that needs to be done is to subtract 1 from the result of the above formula. Therefore:

P(~None) = P(2 or more) = 1 − [365! / (365 − n)!] / (365^n)

Using our previous example where Person C is added to the group, the probability that two or more people will have the same birthday is:

P(2 or more) = 1 − .9918 = .0082 = .82%

This means there is less than a 1% chance that two or more people will have the same birthday. This seems very small, but by using our formula and substituting n for 23:

P(2 or more) = 1 − [365! / (365 − 23)!] / (36523) = 1 − 0.4927 = .5073 = 50.73%

Thus, we can conclude that in a group of 23 people there is approximately a 50% chance that at least two people will have the same birthday.

Reference

Strogatz, S. (2012). "It's My Birthday Too, Yeah." *New York Times*, October 1. Available at *http://opinionator.blogs.nytimes.com/2012/10/01/ its-my-birthday-too-yeah/?_r=0*. Accessed on January 9, 2014.

17.7 NEWER ARTIFICIAL INTELLIGENCE PROBLEM SOLVING TECHNIQUES

17.7.1 Deep Learning

In an intriguing interview with Charlie Rose, Sebastian Thrun,[2]*** a leading figure in the development of Robotic Systems, reveals some amazing progress in AI systems which are within our grasp in the near future. He points out that the features and power of what is already on the cell phones of millions of people, can be exploited to do research that can and will be of aid to mankind in major ways. For example, he discusses about how the cameras on these phones can already be used to identify images suggesting the presence of skin cancer. This process can be very efficient simply because of the number of images which anyone could quickly generate using no more sophisticated technology than can be found on cell phones today. And the analysis of findings will be more efficient than the work done by an oncologist looking at fewer, specific images. What Thrun is suggesting is given the technologies that are already available and cheap today, much progress can be expected in the near future in a number of arenas including computer vision, medical diagnosis, robotics, etc.

During the past 25 years or so, numerous areas where AI has had success stories have been accomplished by applying big data analytics applying neural networks and other machine learning techniques include face detection, document analysis, driverless cars, face detection, etc.

---

2   The interview (30 minutes) aired on December 28th and can be seen at: *http:// www.charlierose.com/watch/60666797*

We have already seen tremendous progress in Natural Language Processing when language corpora are combined with statistical approaches (see Lucci and Kopec, 2016, Chapter 13, Natural Language Processing). This trend of success combining either machine learning or knowledge-intensive approaches with statistical approaches for positive outcomes, continues. The main problem with machine learning approaches is that they have no "explain facility." Hence they achieve great performance, but have no way of transferring the secrets to their success back to humans who may be able to use them in other successful ways.

During the past 10 years or so, a new approach to using neural nets for successful performance, called "Deep Learning" has been developed as described by Prof. Thrun above. The main idea, in a global sense, is pattern recognition, and by effective pattern extraction using a classification engine. Recent findings in the neurosciences have suggested that the neocortex does not explicitly pre-process sensory signals [2], [3], [4] but rather "allows them to propagate through a complex hierarchy of modules that over time learn to represent observations based on the regularities they exhibit." [5] This discovery is the main motivation behind the subfield of deep machine learning, with the goal of focusing on "computational models for information representation that exhibit characteristics similar to that of the neocortex. [1]

17.7.2 Convolutional Neural Networks (CNN's)

The general notion about neural networks (which goes back more than 60 years) is that somehow they are a model of how the human brain works and when certain values exceed "activation thresholds" neurons are stimulated and activated. Dwelling on this biological model, how it works, and the mathematical analogy between neural networks and the human brain is beyond our purpose or capability here. Nonetheless, it may be accepted that neural networks have layers and values which are propagated through the layers. The more layers that values pass through the more "mature" and "meaningful" they tend to be, rather than of an arbitrary nature.

Perhaps there is a useful analogy here to search techniques (considered a very important domain of AI) and how they have been developed over many decades. The general belief has always been that if a search can be deeper and the values propagated by that search are accurate, then the search is more useful – hence it is predicting the future. The same notion, by analogy can be attributed to the layers of neural networks. Perhaps the more layers that values in a neural network can be propagated through, the more "true" and meaningful those values are!?

So a neural network with more layers provides more meaningful information than one with fewer layers. In the early history of neural networks a big stumbling block was believed to be the absence of a back propagation layer, but with greater computing power during the past 30 years or so, this problem has been resolved. Furthermore, the more layers that can be processed to reach activation thresholds the more effective a neural network is believed to be. Convolutional neural networks with multiple layers, particularly for processing two-dimensional image and video data, have proven effective, especially when combined with earlier work in time-delay neural networks (TDNN) [6], [7]. They reduce learning computation requirements by sharing weights in a temporal dimension, especially when applied to their intended purpose of speech and time series processing ([1], [8]). As stated by [1] "they are the first truly successful deep learning approach where by many layers of a hierarchy are successfully trained in a robust manner. A technique called "digital filtering" helps to obtain and highlight salient features which are invariant to shift, scale, and rotation, by enabling access to elementary features such as orientation of edges or corners [1].

The paper by Lecun et al [9] on MNIST classifying handwritten digits lent much insight to this process either by creating one map per layer or multiple maps.

Outputs form a new feature map that is passed through another sequence of convolutions, sub-sampling, and function flow. This process may be repeated a number of times.

Subsequent layers can combine one or more of the previous layers.

CNN's create their invariances to object translation by combining values from one or more previous layers. This is called "feature pooling" and this is hand-crafted by the network organizer. Pooling is tuned, not trained or learned.

Researchers have applied CNN's to various machine learning problems including face detection [10], [11], document analysis [12] and speech detection [13], [2]. Recently they have been trained with a temporal coherence objective to leverage the frame to frame coherence found in videos.

17.7.3 Deep Belief Networks

The concept of deep learning neural networks is rounded out with Deep Belief Network (DBNs), another deep learning technique also introduced some 10 years ago. These are probabilistic generative models, introduced by Geoffrey Hinton, which are in contrast to the discriminative nature of neural networks [14].

The advantage of generative models is that they provide a joint probability distribution over observable data and labels, hence facilitating estimation of values in both the circumstances which may occur – that is, P(Observation | Label) as well as the reverse, P(Label | Observation). Traditional discriminative neural networks are limited to the latter approach – namely P(Label | Observation). Such networks address problems which occur when backpropagation is applied to deeply layered Neural Networks:

(1) The necessity for a substantial labeled data set for training

(2) Slow learning (with slow convergence times, and

(3) Inadequate parameter selection techniques which tend to lead to poor local optima [1].

DBNs are comprised by several layers of Restricted Boltzmann Machines (RBM), a certain type of neural network (See Figure 224)

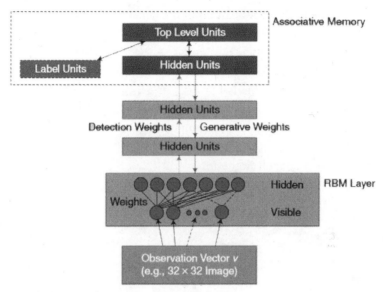

FIGURE 224 Convolutional Neural Networks [1]

They are called "restricted" because they are limited to one single visible layer and one single hidden layer of a neural network. The hidden units are trained to capture high-order data correlations observed in the visible units. Hence the top two layers in essence form an associative memory, with the layers of the DBN connected only by top-down generative weights [1]. The ease by which these connection weights between layers can be obtained makes RBMs an attractive and efficient choice. The generative weights (the initial pre-training) occurs in an unsupervised greedy, layer by layer, manner, facilitated by what Hinton calls *contrasting divergence* [1, 15]. During this training phase vectors are presented to visible units and forwarded to hidden units. Consequently, visible unit inputs are stochastically found in attempts to reconstruct the original input. These back and forth steps with the goal of identifying one step reconstruction, are known as Gibbs Sampling. The difference in the correlation of the hidden activations and visible inputs form the basis for a weight update [1]. Since a single step is needed to approximate the maximum likelihood learning, training time is significantly reduced. Each layer added to the network improves the log-probability of the training data. Hence, that data gains in true representational power. The success of any deep learning process is contingent upon meaningful expansion coupled with utilization of unlabeled data.

Weights are tied together at the top two layers such that the output of the lower layers provides a reference clue for the top layer to associate with its memory contents. Labeled data is used after pre-training in conjunction with back-propagation to improve the discriminative performance of DBNs. The network's "learning" of these weights results in better performance than with back-propagation alone [16].

Arel, Rose, and Karnowski [1] summarize:

"Performance results obtained when applying DBNs to the MNIST handwritten character recognition task have demonstrated significant improvement over feedforward networks. Shortly after DBNs were introduced, a more thorough analysis presented in [17] solidified their use with unsupervised tasks as well as continuous valued inputs. Further tests in [18] [19] illustrated the resilience of DBNs (as well as other deep architectures) on problems with increasing variation. "

An excellent further reference source on DBNs is [20], by their founder, Geoffrey Hinton.

17.7.4 References

1. Itamar Arel, Derek C. Rose, and Thomas P. Karnowski The University of Tennessee, USA.

    Deep Machine Learning – A new frontier in Artificial Intelligence Research.

    IEEE COMPUTATIONAL INTELLIGENCE MAGAZINE, NOVEMBER 2010.

2. R. Bellman, Dynamic Programming. Princeton, NJ: Princeton Univ. Press, 1957. [2] R. Duda, P. Hart, and D. Stork, Pattern Recognition, 2nd ed. New York: Wiley-Interscience, 2000.

3. T. Lee and D. Mumford, "Hierarchical Bayesian inference in the visual cortex," J. Opt. Soc. Amer., vol. 20, pt. 7, pp. 1434–1448, 2003.

4. T. Lee, D. Mumford, R. Romero, and V. Lamme, "The role of the primary visual cortex in higher level vision," Vision Res., vol. 38, pp. 2429–2454, 1998.

5. F. H. C. Tivive and A. Bouzerdoum, "A new class of convolutional neural networks (SICoNNets) and their application of face detection," in Proc. Int. Joint Conf. Neural Networks, 2003, vol. 3, pp. 2157–2162.

6. Y.-N. Chen, C.-C. Han, C.-T. Wang, B.-S. Jeng, and K.-C. Fan, "The application of a convolution neural network on face and license plate detection," in Proc. 18th Int. Conf. Pattern Recognition (ICPR'06), 2006, pp. 552–555.

7. P. Y. Simard, D. Steinkraus, and J. C. Platt, "Best practices for convolutional neural networks applied to visual document analysis," in Proc. 7th Int. Conf. Document Analysis and Recognition, 2003, pp. 958–963.

8. K. Lang, A. Waibel, and G. Hinton, "A time-delay neural-network architecture for isolated word recognition," Neural Netw., vol. 3, no. 1, pp. 23–44, 1990.

9. Y. LeCun, L. Bottou, Y. Bengio, and P. Haffner, "Gradient-based learning applied to document recognition," Proc. IEEE, vol. 86, no. 11, pp. 2278–2324, 1998.

10. F.-J. Huang and Y. LeCun, "Large-scale learning with SVM and convolutional nets for generic object categorization," in Proc. Computer Vision and Pattern Recognition Conf. (CVPR'06), 2006.

11. S. Sukittanon, A. C. Surendran, J. C. Platt, and C. J. C. Burges, "Convolutional networks for speech detection," Interspeech, pp. 1077–1080, 2004.

12. J. Hawkins and S. Blakeslee, On Intelligence. Times Books, Oct. 2004. [40] K. Fukushima, "Neocognitron for handwritten digit recognition," Neurocomputing, vol. 51, pp. 161–180, 2003.

13. S. Sukittanon, A. C. Surendran, J. C. Platt, and C. J. C. Burges, "Convolutional networks for speech detection," Interspeech, pp. 1077–1080, 2004. [13]

14. G. E. Hinton, S. Osindero, and Y. Teh, "A fast learning algorithm for deep belief nets," Neural Comput., vol. 18, pp. 1527–1554, 2006.

15. G. E. Hinton, "Training products of experts by minimizing contrastive divergence," Neural Comput., vol. 14, pp. 1771–1800, 2002.

16. G. E. Hinton and R. R. Salakhutdinov, "Reducing the dimensionality of data with neural networks," Science, vol. 313, no. 5786, pp. 504–507, 2006.

17. Y. Bengio, P. Lamblin, D. Popovici, and H. Larochelle, "Greedy layer-wise training of deep networks," in Advances in Neural Information Processing Systems 19 (NIPS'06). 2007, pp. 153–160.

18. M. Ranzato, F. J. Huang, Y. Boureau, and Y. LeCun, "Unsupervised learning of invariant feature hierarchies with applications to object recognition," in Proc. Computer Vision and Pattern Recognition Conf., 2007.

19. H. Larochelle, D. Erhan, A. Courville, J. Bergstra, and Y. Bengio, "An empirical evaluation of deep architectures on problems with many factors of variation," in Proc. 24th Int. Conf. Machine Learning (ICML'07), 2007, pp. 473–480.

20. *http://scholarpedia.org/article/Deep_belief_networks*

18

CONCLUSION: TOWARD A THEORY FOR PROBLEM SOLVING

18.1 HUMAN WINDOW STUDY

Thus, the study of comparison of Human Window solutions reveals some important properties that good solutions possess, with the key being *extensionality* and a *good choice of representation*. The more visual or graphical a representation is, the more effective it will be as an aid to most problem solvers. Animations or playable games comprise some of the most extensional representations that people can enjoy. These two factors also affect the *comprehensibility* of the solution—another important aspect of the solutions ranked highest in our study of the Human Window. (See Appendix C on the CD.) A theory about the importance of the Human Window may well serve as a bridge between the information age (with its overabundance of data) and the knowledge aid, whereby knowledge can be used for effective learning and decision making.

These results are consistent with a paradigm for science education and problem solving known as the "constructivist epistemology." The basic premise of this school of learning is that knowing is doing. If you can do something, then you know it. The best teachers are those who know how to do something and most effectively explain to others what they know with words, graphics, and methods.

18.2 LESSONS LEARNED

In this section, we discuss some of the lessons learned from studying and analyzing the seven problems in this book as a possible starting point for developing a theory for problem solving. Table 18 summarizes what we have learned about problem solving by examining 10 problems in this book.

No.	Problem	Knowledge Representation	Problem Type	Problem-Solving Strategies
1	The Missionaries and Cannibals Problem	Search tree, state transition diagram, problem state space matrix	Logic, constraint satisfaction problem	Solving subgoals, backtracking, symmetry, search
2	The 12 Coins Problem	Search tree, table	Logic, mathematical	Problem reduction, recursion
3	Cryptarithms	Knowledge table, constraint hypergraph	Mathematical, constraint satisfaction problem	Generate and test, deduction, arithmetic, backtracking, forward checking, heuristics
4	The Red Donkey Puzzle	Pictorial	Sliding block puzzle	Solving subgoals, bidirectional search
5	The 15 Puzzle	Graphical, row by row	Sliding block puzzle	Solving subproblems; numerous methods, including disjoint patterns, database heuristics

No.	Problem	Knowledge Representation	Problem Type	Problem-Solving Strategies
6	The Knight's Tour Problem	Graphical; Tessellations ;	Graph— Hamiltonian Cycle Problem	Patterns and heuristics
7	Mastermind	Characters or Graphic	Logic, combinatorics	Deduction, Five-Guess Algorithm
8	The Monty Hall Problem	Pictorial	Logic, probability	Pictorial, logic, probability
9	Rubik's Cube	Pictorial	3 blocks; patterns	Subgoals, steps, algorithms
10	The Prisoner's Dilemma	Table	Logic, constraint-satisfaction problem	Deduction, iterative, strategical thinking

TABLE 19 Problem-Solving Strategies

18.2.1 The Missionaries and Cannibals Problem

This problem is simpler when compared to the other three problems and can be solved by brute force or by trial and error. However, the most important lesson is that the choice of representation greatly affects the problem-solving process. Therefore, it is advised that before attempting to solve a problem, students take time to get familiar with the problem, understand its nature, and **choose a representation of the problem that most closely resembles the learner's or problem solver's internal representation and understanding of the problem space**. For example, this problem always makes us create a mental image (graphic) of the scene in a real-world setting; hence, a pictorial representation makes sense. The more realistic the pictorial representation, the more suitable it seems in the problem-solving process.

An interesting aspect of this problem is that the goal state is very clear. It is the same as the initial state but on the other side of the riverbank. This indicates a sort of symmetry in terms of time and space. Thus, **solving a problem backward from the goal state is a useful strategy when the problem possesses the** *property of symmetry*.

Usually, a problem where an initial state is to be transformed to a goal state, identifying and **formulating subgoals** can be helpful. However, this can be also be dangerous because people can tend to move only toward the subgoal without considering the possibility of moving to a perceived bad state—that is, one that moves away from the goal and might be the only way to move toward the goal. Sometimes you have to take a step back to move forward. This is evident from the state transition diagram that demonstrated that **moving away from a goal temporarily** is sometimes necessary. However, the ability to recognize when it is necessary to move away (and hence step "backward" from a solution path) may be particular to expert problem solvers or those who are especially familiar (involved) with a problem domain. Finally, one of the preliminary testing subject's strategies of **using trial and error to test various moves to improve learning and planning** for the next move is also an important tool.

18.2.2 The 12 Coins Problem

This problem illustrates the importance of employing problem reduction when feasible. The problem itself is very difficult if one tries to solve it right away without looking into its smaller versions. As discussed in Chapter 4, we started from the most elementary form of this problem to understand the constraints of the problem and the best way of dividing the coins. The pitfalls of dividing the coins into two equal groups were evident from the four coins version of the problem. **Solving the reduced versions of the problem helped us get familiar with the nuances of the problem and differentiate between good and bad weighings.**

Furthermore, one of the important techniques used was to **maximize the amount of knowledge gained from earlier weighings**. Due to the constraint of trying to minimize the number of weighings, sometimes we had to find the odd coin and its relative weight in a single weighing.

Recursion was another important techniques used as we had solved the smaller and elementary versions of The 12 Coins Problem. Recursion helped reduce the problem continually until it was converted to its most elementary form and solved directly.

Furthermore, the use of recursion facilitates the conversion of extensional solutions for subproblems (e.g., 3, 4, 5, 6 coins) to a compact intensional formula that can be generalized for all numbers of coins [17].

18.2.3 Cryptarithms

Due to the nature of arithmetic operations, there are some clues inherent in cryptarithms that can be spotted easily, such as the occurrence of 0, 1, and 9. These clues serve as a starting point for solving the problem. Graphs representing the constraints of the problem help in uncovering the relationships and dependencies between the variables of the problem. Problems like cryptarithms call for the use of a variety of techniques in various stages of the problem-solving process. This is also true for real-life problems where one technique may not offer a complete solution.

Initially, clues and carryovers can help make some progress. After that, the problem solvers veer toward narrowing down the domains of the variables, eliminating some values that will ultimately lead to dead ends. This saves time and avoids unnecessary calculations. When the domain of some variables is low enough to allow an exhaustive search, the generate-and-test technique can be used to facilitate some assumptions, proceed, and backtrack if further search is impossible. Such values are eliminated, and the remaining values are tested.

In addition, columns in the problem were considered one by one as a result of the strategy of **solving subproblems**. Furthermore, a structure like the **Knowledge Table** can be very useful in keeping track of solved variables that can further help in deducing the remaining variables. Experience has shown that many student problem solvers hamper their progress by not being sufficiently organized about what they have ascertained at a given stage in the problem-solving process.

18.2.4 The Red Donkey Puzzle

This puzzle involves the transformation of the initial state to a goal state and thus can be formulated as a series of **subgoals**. The subgoals also serve as milestones that can be **backtracked to** in case one gets lost in the puzzle. As previously mentioned about The Missionaries and Cannibals Problem, there are times when we have to move away from the goal temporarily to be able to move forward.

If the exact goal state of the solution is known, then a **backward search or a bidirectional search** could prove a useful technique. This is akin to chess endgames known as Queen and Pawn Endings. Many chess players unnecessarily tend to avert such endings because they wrongly assume a large branching factor and great complexity, when in fact the number of possibilities is often actually limited, leading to a long, narrow tree.

Additionally, as evident from all four problems, having a playable (either physical or virtual) model of the problem may greatly reduce the learning time, keeping the problem solver's interest alive and helping to test various theories and techniques. Furthermore, the problem solver is relieved of cumbersome complex calculations and memory-intensive tasks and can concentrate on decision making.

In the context of problem solving, the strategies discussed above are the basis of the human decision-making process, but at the same time, humans are restricted by limitations on their computation speed and memory capacities (see Lucci and Kopec, Table 6.3). These limitations can be overcome with the use of computers to aid or complement the human problem-solving process. Furthermore, computers can be used to test different decisions, hypotheses, or ideas quickly to validate their fitness for solving the problem in question, thus eliminating invalid moves and reducing search time.

18.2.5 The 15 Puzzle

The 15 Puzzle has been around for nearly 150 years and has probably been subjected to more applications of AI search techniques than any other problem in this book. Heuristics such as "the number of tiles out of place" or "The Manhattan Distance," coupled with algorithms such as depth-first search, breadth-first search, A° algorithm, and, most recently the disjoint pattern database method, have routinely used The 15 Puzzle as a test bed. We have learned from the MHWC solution that systematic approaches developing the solution row by row are most welcome and easy to comprehend.

18.2.6 The Knight's Tour Problem

The Knight's Tour is also a very old problem that has been the subject of study for thousands of years. The remarkable fact is that solutions must be identified from 4×10^{51} possible sequences. A number of techniques have been used to identify solutions, including subproblems, exhaustive enumeration, heuristics, patterns, and others. There is also some reminder of the 90 – 10 rule in AI. That is, a few heuristics take care of most of the problem space (90%), and then a number of new heuristics (or rules) must be developed to handle 10% of the problem space. In this case, the heuristic that always suggests choosing edge squares is effective most of the time—until it isn't. The problem solver must learn those special cases.

18.2.7 Mastermind

Mastermind is one of the more familiar logic problems subjected to algorithms and computer methods for many years. It is a very logical and intuitive problem that people (even children) can easily comprehend. Understanding the problem is much easier than deciding on the logical methods (or choices) that can be used to make the fewest guesses.

Donald Knuth, perhaps the greatest computer scientist of all time in the United States, decided to address the problem in the mid-1970s. He produced the "Five-Guess Algorithm," which seems to be accepted as the final word on the subject. We believe that one of our contributions here is not only an analysis of the various possible solutions but also a study of these solutions from a Human Window perspective, as well as the study of human subjects' problem-solving activity for Mastermind. (See Appendix A on the accompanying CD.)

18.2.8 The Monty Hall Problem

James Surowiecki's book *Wisdom of the Crowds* discusses how when a heterogeneous crowd (audience) is asked about its opinion, that opinion is more intelligent (informed, correct) than the most intelligent (by IQ) person in the room. In this problem, as described by Yanofsky in his recent book *The Outer Limits of Reason*, the opinion of some 10,000 Mensa members differs from that of Marilyn vos Savant—and they were wrong! Sometimes the ability to abstract and represent (draw) images of a solution bears more significance than anything else.

18.2.9 Rubik's Cube

This too has been a familiar problem for many years. It seems like Rubik's Cube, akin to cell phones, texting, apps, and so forth, is a problem more suitable for young people than adults. We believe that the presentation and discussion of solutions to "The Cube" in Chapter 11 can provide insights for those heretofore stupefied by it. Of course, no learning can come without some attention and work. It is a classic example of illustrating the importance of being able to tackle problems by identifying and solving subgoals.

18.2.10 The Prisoner's Dilemma

The ability to apply problems, ideas, and solution methods from Game Theory to practical and real social problems is of great interest to all. The Prisoner's Dilemma is one such problem from Game Theory that can be applied in many ways to sociopolitical problems, economic situations, and so on.

18.2.11 Miscellaneous Problems

The five miscellaneous problems in Chapter 13 demonstrate that problem solving is in many cases a matter of perspective and experience. Problems need not be long or intricate to be interesting and instructive. The Ten Pirates and Their Gold, for example, sets the stage for thinking about and representing solutions to The Prisoner's Dilemma.

18.3 RETROSPECTIVE, CONCLUSIONS, AND FUTURE WORK

Donald Michie and Danny Kopec first proposed the concept of the Human Window.[3] It states that the solutions to difficult, AI-type problems must meet certain criteria to fall within the bounds of the Human Window. As originally presented in Shweta's thesis, they need to be correct, comprehensible, executable, and of a moderate grain size. It was to her great joy that some 30 years later, Chris Pileggi performed the study of Human Window solutions on The Missionaries and Cannibals Problem, cryptarithmetics, The 12 Coins Problem, The Knights Tour Problem, The 15 Puzzle, and The Red Donkey Puzzle) for his senior thesis project. Pileggi's work was extremely impressive and provided the first application of Michie's ideas to real, mainstream problems and their solutions.

Shweta Shetty assembled and studied the solutions to the problems in this book. As we can see from the Human Window analysis of these solutions, humans are comfortable with solutions that are graphical, not too short or too long, easy to comprehend and execute, testable, and applicable to every problem state.

Furthermore, we now understand that even though we believe we have identified the best solutions to a well-known set of AI problems, this is not enough. Future work needs to focus on how Human Window solutions can best be presented to human subjects. Clearly, with the current and likely future generations, even graphical approaches with rules (on paper) will not suffice. Notions of active participation in learning (patterns) and execution (performing) are necessary. Video (possibly interactive) or animated presentation of our solutions would seem like the best next step in pursuing this research.

Further research is needed to continue this work by delving deeper into the subject of studying human problem-solving

---

[3] Michie liked to credit Michael Clarke for the notion, but it was Michie who indeed wrote more about it and developed the concept via Dr. Kopec's Ph.D. thesis.

processes by using computers as a tool for experimentation. In addition, the thought processes of human subjects should be recorded and analyzed for all such problems, as Luger did for cryptarithm problems. A comparative study of the human learning process, with analysis of how well solutions are actually understood (both before and after solutions are found) seems to be a necessary and important step toward gaining a better understanding of the problem-solving process and how it can be successful.

18.4 SUPPLEMENTAL REFERENCES

1. Amarel, S. (1968). On Representations of Problems of Reasoning about Actions. Donald Michie, editor, *Machine Intelligence* 3, pages 131–171. American Elsevier Publishers, New York, NY.

2. Anderson J.R., Reder L. M., and Simon, H. (2000). "Applications and Misapplications of Cognitive Psychology to Mathematics Education," *Texas Education Review* (1) 2: 29–49.

3. Anzai, Y., and Simon, H.A. (1979). *The Theory of Learning by Doing.*

4. Bryan, J. (2012). *The 12 Coin Problem. http://www.jerrybryan.net/math/12coins.html.* Accessed on April 22, 2013.

5. Bogomolny, A. (2013). *Odd Coin Problems: the 120 Marble Problem—Five Weighings from Interactive Mathematics Miscellany and Puzzles. http://www.cut-the-knot.org/blue/OddCoinProblems.shtml.* Accessed on April 22, 2013.

6. Burton, L., and Burton, M. (1980). *"Problems and Puzzles."* For the Learning of Mathematics (1) 2: 20–23. Published by: FLM Publishing Association. Stable *http://www.jstor.org/stable/40247710.* Accessed on December 23, 2012.

7. Cerveny R.P., Garrity, E.J., and Sanders, G.L. (1990). "A Problem-Solving Perspective on Systems Development." *Journal of Management Information Systems* (6) 4: 103–122. Published by: M.E. Sharpe, Inc. Stable *http://www.jstor.org/stable/40398777.* Accessed on December 23, 2012. *For the Learning of Mathematics* (1) 2: 35–42. Published by: FLM Publishing Association. Stable *http://www.jstor.org/stable/40247714.* Accessed on December 23, 2012.

8. Coleman, P.T. (2011). *The Five Percent: Finding Solutions to Seemingly Impossible Conflicts*. New York: **Public Affairs**, Perseus Books.

9. Elitmus, G. (2012). *Guide to Solve Cryptic Multiplication Question.* Available at *http://elitmusguide.blogspot.in/2012/07/guide-to-solve-cryptic-multiplication.html*. Accessed on January 10, 2014.

10. Eysenck, M.W. (2002). *Simply Psychology,* 2nd ed. New York, NY, Psychology Press Ltd. / Taylor Francis

11. Gunzelmann, G., and Anderson, J.R. (2002). Problem Solving: Increased Planning with Practice .*Cognitive Systems Research* 4(1): 57-76.

12. Logicville. (2012). *http://www.logicville.com/cryptarithm.htm*. Accessed on April 22, 2013.

13. Lucci, S., and Kopec, D. (2013). *Artificial Intelligence in the 21st century*. Dulles, Virginia: Mercury Learning, Inc.

14. Luger, G.F. (2008). *Artificial Intelligence: Structures and Strategies for Complex Problem Solving,* 6th ed. Reading, MA: Addison-Wesley.

15. Manvel, B. (1977). "Counterfeit Coin Problems." *Mathematics Magazine* 50: 90–92.

16. Minsky, M. (1960). *Steps Toward Artificial Intelligence.* In Computers and Thought, (Eds. E. Feigenbaum and J. Feldman), McGraw-Hill, New York, pp. 406-450.

17. Newell, A., and Simon, H.A. (1972). *Human Problem Solving.* Englewood Cliffs, NJ: Prentice-Hall.

18. O'Connor, J.J., and Robertson, E.F. (2012). *Propositiones ad acuendos iuvenes by Alcuin. http://jnsilva.ludicum.org/HMR12_13/AlcuinStA.pdf*. Accessed on December 4, 2013.

19. Polk, T.A., and Newell, A. (1995). "Deduction as Verbal Reasoning." *American Psychological Association* (102) 3: 533–536.

20. Polya, G. (1957). *How to Solve It,* 2nd ed. Princeton, NJ: Princeton University Press.

21. Ruggiero, V.R. (1998). *The Art of Thinking*. Reading, MA: Addison-Wesley. Burton, L., and Burton, M. (1980). "Problems and Puzzles." *For the Learning of Mathematics* (1) 2: 20–23. Published by: FLM Publishing Association. Stable *http://www.jstor.org/stable/40247710*. Accessed on December 23, 2012.

22. Soares, J. (2003). *Will Cryptarithmetic Survive Innovation?* *http://cryptarithms.awardspace.us/survival.htm*. Accessed on April 22, 2013.

23. Unterrainer, J.M., and Owen, A.M. (2006). "Planning and Problem Solving: From Neuropsychology to Functional Neuroimaging." *Journal of Physiology—Paris* 99: 308–317.

24. Brandeis. (2013). *Red Donkey*. *http://www.cs.brandeis.edu/~storer/JimPuzzles/ZPAGES/zzzRedDonkey.html*. Accessed on April 22, 2013.

25. Bsswebsite. (2013). *Red Donkey Puzzle*. *http://www.bsswebsite.me.uk/Puzzlewebsite/Reddonkeypuzzle/Reddonkeypuzzle.htm*.

26. Sweller, J. (1988). "Cognitive Load During Problem Solving: Effects on Learning." *Cognitive Science* 12: 257–285.

27. Kose, E. (2012). Comparing AI Search Algorithms and Their Efficiency When Applied to Path Finding Problems. *Ph.D. Thesis*, New York, NY: CUNY, Graduate Center.

28. Bryan, J. (2012). *The 12 Coin Problem*. *http://www.jerrybryan.net/math/12coins.html*. Accessed on April 22, 2013.

18.5 COMPOSITE PROBLEM PLAYABILITY SITES

The Missionaries and Cannibals Problem – *http://www.smartest-games.com/game/missionaries-and-cannibals/*

The 12 Coins Problem – *http://www.mathplayground.com/coin-weighing.html*

Cryptarithmetic – *http://www.letsgetwordy.com/#am_app*

The Red Donkey Puzzle – *http://www.bsswebsite.me.uk/Puzzlewebsite/Reddonkeypuzzle/Reddonkeypuzzle.htm*

The 15-Puzzle – *http://migo.sixbit.org/puzzles/fifteen/*

The Knight's Tour Problem – *http://www.kongregate.com/games/evgenykarataev/knights-tour*

Mastermind – *http://www.grayman.de/mastermind/index_en.php4*

Rubik's Cube – *http://activeden.net/item/cube-assembler/full_screen_preview/3131480*

ON THE COMPANION DISC

Appendix A - Solutions for Missionaries and Cannibals Problem referred to in Chapter 3.

Appendix B - An Algorithm for The Twelve Coins Problem

Appendix C - A Study Comparing Human Solutions

Appendix D – Programmed Solutions to Problems

- Appendix D.1 - A Program for the "Missionaries and Cannibals Problem" Solution in Picat

- Appendix D.2 - Programs for Cryptarithmetic

  1) Appendix D.2.1 - A Program for a General Alphametic (cryptarithmetic) Solver in Picat

  2) Appendix D.2.2: A Program for the Cryptarithm SEND+ MORE = MONEY written in Prolog

  3) Appendix D.2.3: Another Program for the Cryptarithm SEND+MORE = MONEY written in Prolog

- Appendix D.3 - A Program for The 15 Puzzle written in Picat

- Appendix D.4 - A Program for The Knight's Tour written in Pascal

- Appendix D.5 - Programs for the Red Donkey Puzzle

1) Appendix D.5.1: A Program for the Red Donkey Puzzle written in Java

2) Appendix D.5.2: A Program for the Red Donkey Puzzle written in Picat

- Appendix D.6 - A Program for Rubik's Cube written in Python
- Appendix D.7: A Program for Sudoku written in C++
- Appendix D.8 – Extra: Program for the Towers of Hanoi Problem written in Picat
- Appendix D.8: A Program for The Four-Coloring Problem written in C

Appendix D presents several programs for some of the problems presented in the book. They are written in a variety of languages:

Picat – to compile and run a program written in Picat, go to the main website *http://www.picat-lang.org/* to install Picat and its compiler. A user's guide can be found on this website with instructions on how to compile

Java – to compile and run a Java program, you must download the Java Runtime Environment. To download this and other necessary software for running java programs, visit *http://www.oracle.com/technetwork/java/javase/downloads/index.html*

Prolog – to compile and run a program written in Prolog, visit *http://www.probp.com/download.html* for the download and a user's guide.

Python - to compile and run a program written in Python, you must download the Python interpreter. The download can be found at *http://www.python.org/getit/* with an option to choose from a number of operating systems.

INDEX